Smart Skills: Mastering the Numbers

Smart Skills: Mastering the Numbers

Anne Hawkins

Legend 🔖 Business

Independent Book Publisher

Legend Business Ltd, 107-111 Fleet Street,
London, EC4A 2AB
info@legend-paperbooks.co.uk
www.legendpress.co.uk

British Library Cataloguing in Publication Data available.

ISBN 978-17871982-0-3

Set in Times.

Cover designed by:
Linnet Mattey | www.linnetmattey.com

Legend Business

Independent Book Publisher

CONTENTS

Foreword

Myriads of management handbooks in print purport to provide guidance on the key skills for success and business training manuals also abound. Generally, they suffer from one or both of two defects.

Sometimes, the scope of the book is too broad. Attempting to provide comprehensive advice on all the basic business activities, there is no clear message. Nobody can gain proficiency in every field of marketing and sales, administration, purchasing, book-keeping and financial management in a short period of time, although those who start their own businesses do need to acquire a working knowledge of most. Other titles fail to distinguish between technical capability and personal skills.

There are similar problems with books offering comprehensive advice on the "numbers" management of business which are the essential skills that entrepreneurs and managers of any size of business, as well as management consultants, need to acquire in order to be successful. Although the subject matter is more specialised, there is a difficult balance to be achieved between over-simplification and burdening readers with too much technical accounting detail. In *Mastering the Numbers* Anne Hawkins has trod the tightrope safely; her book is written with great clarity and provides a mixture of good common sense and detail of the accounting and financial topics with which readers will want to be fully conversant.

Like the other subjects in the Smart Skills series all readers can focus to their advantage as mastery of the skills will surely enhance both job satisfaction and their careers.

Jonathan Reuvid

Introduction

This is not a book for accountants.

Neither is it a book for those wanting to learn about the technicalities of book-keeping or the intricacies of published financial accounts.

It is however the book you've been looking for if any of the following strike a chord:

- you're an entrepreneur with a great business idea but are not sure how to explain your plans to the bank or potential investors; or
- you've been promoted up through an organisation to a point at which it's embarrassing to admit you don't understand the financials; or
- you're fed up with going to ask the accountant a question and coming away more confused than you were to begin with; or
- you'd like to understand the meaning of accounting jargon in simple, straight-forward, commonsense terms.

'The numbers' are not created by accountants. They are the culmination of the myriad of choices made by the decision-makers in the business. If you want to master the numbers you'll need to understand how the numbers are compiled, what they are telling you and then use that knowledge to bring them under your control.

This is what this book will help you do.

Note: words in *italics* are included in the Dictionary of Accounting Jargon on p.114.

1. THE OVERVIEW

The 'money-go-round'

Businesses use money to make money.

- Money is brought into the business;
- to buy the things the business needs;
- to create products or services to sell to customers;
- on which the business can earn a profit;
- so there is additional money available to invest;
- so the business can buy more of the things it needs;
- so it can make more products or deliver more services to customers;
- so it can make even more profit;
- so that there is yet more money available to invest ...

It's a profit-generating 'money-go-round'.

Before looking at 'the numbers' it's helpful to look at the above process in a little more detail starting with the different types of long-term finance the business might use.

WHERE DO BUSINESSES GET THEIR MONEY FROM?
Every business has to have some form of long-term finance to provide them with the capital to buy the things they need. This finance usually consists of a combination of Share Capital, Loans and Retained Profits.

| Share Capital | Loans | Retained Profit |

Share Capital

The shareholders own the business but will appoint a board of directors to run the business on their behalf. They buy shares in the hope of earning an income on their investment (dividends) and growth in the value of their investment as a result of increasing share prices. As owners, they are the risk-takers and therefore last in the 'pecking order' when it comes to getting a share of the profits. [For more on the implications to the business of having shareholders to satisfy see Appendix 1, Share Capital.]

Loans

When money is borrowed, a contract is signed committing the business to pay interest and repay the capital as and when it falls due. To ensure contractual obligations are met, the lender will look for some form of security or collateral.

If the business is unable to use the borrowed money profitably to generate the profits and cash to make the agreed payments the bank may move in, sell off some of the business assets to recover the debt and there may be no business left. Hence borrowing money brings financial risk into the business so this risk needs to be managed. [For more information on the financial implications of taking on loans see Appendix 2, Loans.]

Retained Profit

If the business can make sufficient profit to cover all their costs, there will be money left over for reinvestment. This is the most cost-effective way to grow the business as it results in additional funding being made available without having to attract additional share capital (with resulting pressures from shareholders for higher dividends and more growth) or having to increase the financial risk and interest costs to the business by taking on more loans. So profit is not a dirty word. Far from it. The more long-term finance that can be generated internally the better.

The total amount of long-term finance is known as Net Capital Employed.

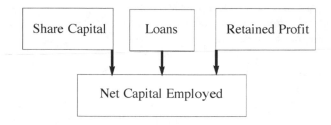

The relative proportions supplied by shareholders as opposed to lenders is referred to as *gearing* and will influence the business' financial risk.

WHAT DO THEY USE THE MONEY FOR?

The management team will determine the way in which the funds raised are invested. These decisions will reflect the design of the products or services and the way the business is being run. Some of the items purchased, for example equipment, will be 'one-off' items intended to be of use to the business over a number of years (i.e. *Fixed Assets*), whereas others such as materials and labour will be of a 'repeat purchase' nature (i.e. *Working Capital*).

The total amount invested in Fixed Assets and Working Capital is known as Net Assets Employed.

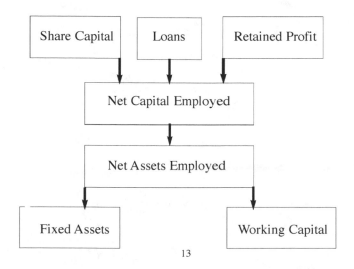

Fixed Assets (also known as Non-current Assets)

The selection of these items is a strategic decision as it sets out the way the business intends to make products or deliver services for potentially many years into the future. As a result, the authorisation process for such *capital expenditure* is challenging (see Chapter 8, Capital Investment Appraisal).

Fixed assets are purchased with the intention of keeping them and using them over a number of years to provide the business with a chosen capability for making and delivering products or services. Therefore it makes sense that rather than putting the total cost of these items into the calculation of profit in the year of purchase, the cost is 'spread' over the useful life to the business to produce an annual charge against profit. This charge is known as *depreciation* or *amortisation*. [For more information on the importance of choosing the right capability and the accounting treatment for these Fixed Assets, see Appendix 3.]

Working Capital

Revenue expenditure provides the business with the materials, labour, bought-in services and expenses it needs to produce its products or deliver its services. Although the aim is to 'pull' these costs through the business as quickly as possible by turning them into products or services customers pay for, at any point in time some will be 'trapped' in the *Working Capital Cycle*.

This cycle follows the flow of cash through the business and back into cash again.

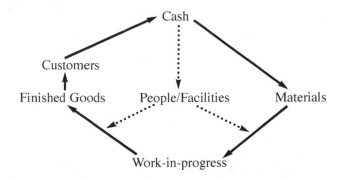

Cash is used to buy materials and pay for the cost of converting them into the products or services the market wants. Goods or services are then sold and cash comes back into the business.

The cycle is usually more complex as materials may be purchased on credit (delaying the outflow of cash) and customers may have negotiated credit with the business (delaying the inflow of cash).

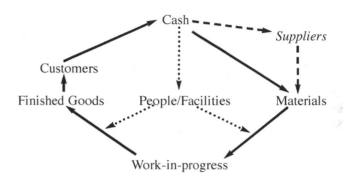

The amount of money tied up in the cycle at any point in time is therefore determined by taking the amount of cash being held; plus the value of inventory (materials plus work-in-progress plus finished goods); plus the value of goods or services that have been delivered to customers but not yet paid for; less the amount of credit from suppliers (i.e. the invoice value of materials that have been received and are therefore in inventory but for which the business has not yet paid.)

A detailed explanation of the cycle and Working Capital terminology is given in Appendix 4, Working Capital.

ARE THEY MAKING MONEY?

The fixed assets and working capital are then put to use to make products or services that can be sold. The total value of sales, or invoices raised in a period, may be referred to as *turnover* or *revenue*.

The next step is to compare the value of sales with the costs incurred in making those products or delivering those services to determine whether the business has made a profit. Included in these costs is not just the cost of materials, labour, expenses etc. but also depreciation, that 'fair and reasonable allocation' of the amount of money invested in providing the business with its capability, as explained above. If the business has got it right, the market will reward it for choosing to organise itself appropriately with selling prices exceeding costs. [Different approaches to calculating product or service costs are explained in Chapter 7 , Costing.]

The profit figure at this stage is often referred to as Operating Profit as the financing costs have yet to come.

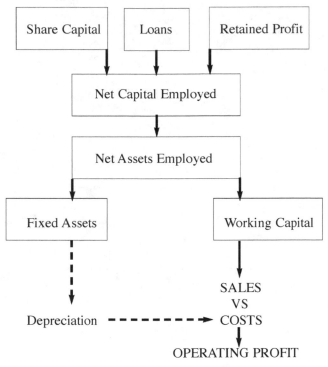

Deducted from the Operating Profit are firstly the costs of interest payments on the loans and then the tax that has to be paid on any profits. The profit measure at this stage is referred to as Earnings and belongs to the shareholders. Some of this they will want to take as dividends, with the rest available to reinvest back into the business as Retained Profit.

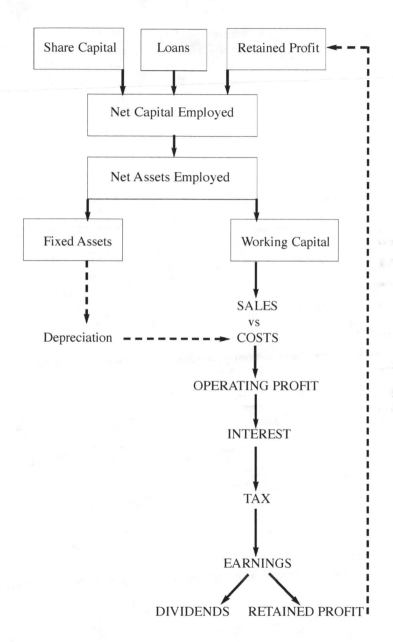

So now you have a more detailed version of the 'money-go-round'.

Businesses raise capital to invest in providing themselves with both the capability (Fixed Assets) and materials, labour and other costs (Working Capital) to make products or provide services.

They work this investment to make products or organise services which they can sell to customers at a profit.

Sufficient profit to cover all their business and financial costs and have something left over to reinvest back into the business to, for example, buy a new machine.

So that next year they can make and sell more products or services so that they can make more profit so that they have even more left over to reinvest back into the business ...

This is a powerful 'money-making machine' and needs mastering.

- The Balance Sheet reports on 'the numbers' in the first part of the model by setting out where the business has got its finance from (Net Capital Employed) and how that money is currently invested (Net Assets Employed).
- The Profit & Loss Account covers the second section, setting out how well the management team have used that investment to generate sales and profit.

[*A word of warning:* The focus so far has been on making a profit – i.e. selling products for more than they cost. However, businesses do not go into receivership because they make a loss but because they run out of cash. As profit and cash flow are not the same thing (and can even move in opposite directions), mastering the profit numbers is not enough.

If you're going to run your business in such a way that you don't just make a profit but you also generate cash you'll also need to master the'levers' to be found in the Cash Flow Statement (see p.53).]

2. THE BALANCE SHEET

or Statement of Financial Position

INTRODUCTION

The Balance Sheet does not tell you what the business is worth. It is a statement at a point in time of where the money came from to finance the business and where that money is currently tied up and reports on the first part of the 'money-making machine' modelled in the previous chapter. (See diagram on p.13.)

The Balance Sheet is called a Balance Sheet because it balances. You can't have money that's come in (from shareholders, lenders or through retaining profits) but then disappears, neither can you have spent money you never had.

READING THE BALANCE SHEET

All balance sheets (or Statements of Financial Position) are snapshots at a point in time showing where the money came from and where it is currently invested.

One of the challenges to those trying to read and interpret them is that not all statements are presented in the same format. This can, at first sight, be confusing. But the 'building blocks' remain the same. Therefore this section will focus on the key items that go into the Balance Sheet and how they are valued rather than deliberating too much on matters of presentation.

Here is a 'skeleton' Balance Sheet in a commonly used format:

	£
Fixed Assets	290,000
Working Capital	210,000
Net Assets Employed	£500,000
	£
Share Capital	48,000
Retained Profits	252,000
Loans	200,000
Net Capital Employed	£500,000

The first thing to notice is that the two halves have been reversed from the extract of the model shown on p.13. 'Where the money came from' is now on the bottom and 'Where the money is now' is on the top.

The Balance Sheet must balance. If it doesn't, someone has made a clerical error. Heard accountants talk about "double-entry book-keeping"? That's because for every financial transaction there will always be two entries in the accountant's books:

Either matching increases to both the top and bottom halves:
e.g. selling additional shares

Share Capital ↑   Cash (included in Working Capital) ↑

or matching decreases to both the top and bottom halves:
e.g. repaying a loan

Loans ↓   Cash   ↓

or equal and opposite entries within the same halves;
e.g. buying new equipment

Fixed Assets ↑   Cash   ↓

Here's that Balance Sheet in a little more detail.

	£	£
Fixed Assets:		
Land and buildings	165,000	
Equipment	125,000	
		290,000
Current Assets:		
Inventory	100,000	
Receivables	180,000	
Cash	5,000	
	285,000	
Current Liabilities:		
Payables	75,000	
Working Capital		210,000
Net Assets Employed		£500,000
Share Capital	48,000	
Retained Profits	252,000	
Net Worth		300,000
Loans		200,000
Net Capital Employed		£500,000

Start with the totals.

A Balance Sheet will have two balancing equal entries so start by identifying those. In this case there is £500,000 of Net Assets Employed ('Where the money is now') and £500,000 of Net Capital Employed ('Where the money came from to buy those things').

Now move into the analysis of these figures starting with the totals in the right-hand column.

The top half of the statement shows where the money is currently invested and here the total of £500,000 comprises £290,000 Fixed

21

Assets and £210,000 Working Capital.

The £290,000 Fixed Assets comprises £165,000 Land and Buildings and £125,000 Equipment.

Working Capital is the net of Current Assets and Current Liabilities (see Appendix 4, Working Capital). In this case £210,000 Working Capital is the net result of £285,000 Current Assets minus £75,000 Current Liabilities.

The Current Assets total of £285,000 comprises £100,000 Inventory (or Stock) £180,000 Receivables (or Debtors) and £5,000 Cash.

As for the Current Liabilities, here there is just one figure of £75,000 for Payables (or Creditors).

Turning to the bottom half of this Balance Sheet format, the statement shows where the money came from to buy the things in the top half. It is important to understand that there is no money to be 'found' in the items shown in this part of the statement – the statement just sets out where the money originally came from.

You can't walk around the business and find the share capital. There's a register of shareholders' names and the number of shares they own but no actual money.

Neither can you find the loans. There are statements from lenders giving values for the loans outstanding but no bundle of £ notes.

Nor can you find the retained profits. You can check back through the Profit and Loss Account over the years to see how much has been reinvested over the life of the business but you're not going to find a pot of money marked "profit", because that money has already been and gone. Look at the top half of the statement again. The profits are up there in the form of new equipment, inventory... and some may (but not necessarily – see p.48) be there as cash.

A warning note: The figure in the Balance Sheet for Retained Profit is cumulative over the life of the business to date. If the business has been successful this value could be very large. Confusingly, this sum of cumulative retained profit is often referred to as Reserves.

[To be pedantic, Reserves is actually a collective term that covers a number of different items but by far the most important to you is that of cumulative retained profits.]

To the layman this use of the word Reserves might imply that there is a large sum of money put by for emergencies.

Not the case at all. There is no cash in Reserves.

The rationale, accountants would argue, behind the use of the word is that, as shown in the diagram on p.17, Retained Profits represent the profits left over for shareholders that, rather than being taken out as dividends, have been 'reserved' for reinvestment back within the business.

So you need to be careful that this unfortunate choice of jargon doesn't result in your having a very false impression of a business' financial security.

Looking back at the statement it can be seen that £48,000 Share Capital and £252,000 Retained Profits are added together to give a sub-total called Net Worth (also known as Shareholders' Funds) of £300,000.

The reason for doing this is to differentiate between the finance that has come from shareholders (either by buying shares or allowing their profits to be reinvested) and the amount that has come from loans.

Once the Loans of £200,000 are added to Net Worth the total, Net Capital Employed, explains where the capital came from to buy those Fixed Assets and Working Capital shown on the top half of the statement.

[If you're still uneasy about the different formats the Balance Sheet can be presented in, take a look at Appendix 5 to see that whilst the layout and sub-totals and terminology may change, 'the numbers' remain the same.]

INTERPRETING THE NUMBERS

"A snapshot at a point in time" ... and therein lies one of the limitations of the Balance Sheet. Those running the business know when the snapshot is to be taken (sometimes monthly, maybe quarterly and certainly twice a year for the shareholders) and although the camera never lies – and the auditors come in to check that's the case – neither does it necessarily give a realistic portrayal of what the business looks like on a 'typical' day. Just as you prepare for a photograph (by looking as professional as you can for a business photograph, or maybe as relaxed as possible for that 'happy family' shot) so too does the business prepare for the event by making itself look as attractive as possible.

The phrase "Get it out the door!" can be heard reverberating throughout the business as everyone scrambles to get the sales (and hence the profits) into the accounts. Inventory levels are reduced, payments are chased up from customers and payments to suppliers are strung out as long as possible. Be aware of these 'window-dressing' tactics when interpreting the numbers.

Before going any further it is important to emphasise again that the Balance Sheet does not give you the 'value' of the business.

What is something worth? Your house, your car?
It's worth what someone would pay to buy it.

It's just the same with a business. If you own the shares you own the business. Therefore a business is 'worth' the number of shares multiplied by the market price for the shares as that is the price you would have to pay to buy it (see Appendix 1, Share Capital).

Just as with any statistical analysis, before using 'the numbers' to interpret what is happening in the business, you need to understand the basis on which they're compiled. In this case it's important to know how the assets and liabilities are valued.

Valuation of Net Assets Employed
Valuation of Fixed Assets
[For an in-depth explanation of the terminology and accounting treatment of Fixed Assets see Appendix 3.]

In the example on the next page, a business buys a piece of equipment for £50,000 intending to use it in the business for 5 years resulting in a *depreciation* charge of £10,000 p.a. to be made against profit. The valuation of the equipment on the Balance Sheet (where it is shown at NBV – see below) falls over time as a result of the depreciation charge as follows:

	Year 1 £	Year 2 £	Year 3 £	Year 4 £	Year 5 £
Cost	50,000	50,000	50,000	50,000	50,000
Cumulative Depreciation	10,000	20,000	30,000	40,000	50,000
NBV	40,000	30,000	20,000	10,000	0

This is important. Look at how the NBV (Net Book Value) is just the result of taking the cost of the equipment less the cumulative depreciation charge to date. It is effectively the 'stock' of fixed asset cost that has yet to be charged against profit. This will not be the same as the saleable value of the asset and therefore should not be viewed as the amount of money the business could realise if they sold it off.

What if the equipment referred to in the example above was a purpose-built press to make a product that nobody else in the world produces in that way? The equipment cost £50,000 and is being depreciated over 5 years so it would be valued in the books at the end of the first year at £40,000. Yet the resale value is probably zero – and indeed the business may have to pay someone to take it away!

It can be difficult to predict useful life accurately. If the equipment above were to be depreciated over 10 years rather than 5, the annual charge would be £5,000 rather than £10,000. As depreciation is a cost that is charged against profit, the number of years chosen will not just affect the Balance Sheet value but also how much profit is declared. The aim is to make the predicted useful life realistic so that the profit figure will provide a fair assessment of whether customers are willing to pay a price that rewards the business not just for the costs incurred for materials, people etc. but also for the investment made in providing the capability to make and deliver those products or services.

If useful life is overestimated then there will be an asset left on your books that is no longer of any use and when that residual cost is written off it will reduce profits. On the other hand, if the useful life is underestimated, then products or services will be over-costed in the early years and under-costed in later years resulting in a distorted picture of where you are making money and therefore the potential for poor decisions concerning your product or service portfolio.

Valuation of Working Capital
[For an in-depth explanation of the investment in Working Capital and the Working Capital cycle see Appendix 4.]

One of the fundamental accounting principles is that of prudency or conservatism. (This is what is responsible for giving accountants the rather unattractive image of being negative, pessimistic, miserable individuals who are always on the look-out for bad news.)

Charged with producing statements to guide others on the financial position of the business, they are required, where there is some uncertainty, to understate rather than overstate how well the business is doing. If there is potentially bad news (e.g. a possible claim against the business) they are required to immediately account for it appropriately – whereas if there is good news (e.g. a large profitable order) they cannot take the benefit until it has actually happened.

Inventory
Here is a clear example of 'prudency' at work. Inventory must be valued at the lower of cost and net realisable value (i.e how much you can sell it for).

So if you are holding inventory that you will be unable to sell for at least what it cost you, you will have to 'write it down' to its saleable value. (Note that this write-off is a cost that will reduce profit.) This means that in many businesses the figure shown on the Balance Sheet is referred to as Net Inventory – i.e. Gross Inventory (the cost of all the inventory you have) less any provisions for scrap, obsolescence etc.

If on the other hand you are holding inventory that you know you will be able to sell at a profit, you must continue to hold it on your Balance Sheet at cost until it is actually sold.

Receivables
This is the amount of money you are waiting to receive for goods or services that have been invoiced to your customers but for which you have not yet been paid.

Once again accountants must be prudent in the value they attribute to this asset by combing through these invoices to identify those where there is uncertainty that the customer will eventually pay. They then create a bad debt provision reducing the value of the receivables asset on the Balance Sheet and matching it by reducing profit.

Cash
The amount of cash you hold – including that in the bank account.

Payables
This is the amount of money you owe other people that has to be paid in the short-term (i.e. within 12 months).

Those amounts you owe your suppliers for buying in the materials and services you then ultimately sell on to the customer are referred to as Trade Creditors. Other creditors may include any bank overdraft and amounts owed (but hopefully not yet due) for tax and dividend payments.

Valuation of Net Capital Employed
Share Capital
Share Capital is valued on the Balance Sheet at its Nominal Value – i.e. at the unit of value given on the share certificate. So if a business has 100,000 shares with a nominal share price of £1, unless additional shares are issued (or shares that are surplus to requirements 'bought back') the share capital will remain on the Balance Sheet at a value of £100,000 regardless of the current market price of the share. [For an explanation of why the ups and downs of the stock market do not have an impact on the Balance Sheet value of the business, see Appendix 1, Share Capital.]

Retained Profit
This is the cumulative figure, over the life of the business to date, of the profits that have been available, after all the costs have been met, to reinvest back within the business. (See Chapter 3, Profit & Loss Account.)

Loans
This represents the total value of long-term loans the business currently has.

***

Balancing the books

Do note that there is no 'balancing entry'. When assets increase or decrease in value there is always an equal and opposite impact on another item on the statement, keeping the Balance Sheet balanced.

Here are some examples of this reflecting the way assets are valued:

- If £10 inventory has gone past its use-by date, under the prudency principle (see above) it has to be written-off. The value of inventory is reduced by £10, obsolescence costs increase by £10 and hence profit falls by £10.
- When fixed assets are depreciated, the assets decrease in value and the charge for depreciation, being a cost of running the business, reduces profit.
- If inventory is purchased for £80 and then sold to a customer on credit for £100, the assets go up by £20 (as £80 inventory is replaced by £100 receivables) and the profit goes up by £20 as shown by the extracts from the Balance Sheet below:

		Step 1 Buy item for £80	Step 2 Sell item for £100
Inventory	–	£80	–
Receivables	–	–	£100
Cash	£80	–	–
Total	**£80**	**£80**	**£100**
Share Capital	£80	£80	£80
Profit	–	–	£20
Total	**£80**	**£80**	**£100**

When the customer pays, the assets just reconfigure with no impact on profit:

Step 3
Customer pays

Inventory	–		–
Receivables	£100		–
Cash	–		£100
Total	**£100**		**£100**
Share Capital	£80		£80
Profit	£20		£20
Total	**£100**		**£100**

Note that the profit is declared when the goods or services are invoiced, not when the customer pays. Perhaps accountants are not being as prudent as they think!

This timing issue is very important when it comes to looking at the difference between profit and cash flow (see p.48)

MASTERING THE BALANCE SHEET INVESTMENT

The Balance Sheet is just one piece of the jigsaw that pictures the financial health of the business. In the absence of some of the other pieces (and importantly an understanding of what the business does), it is hard to judge how well a business is performing.

For example, without a profit figure it is difficult to comment on whether the scale of the investment is appropriate in relation to the profits it has been used to generate. Without a sales figure it is difficult to judge whether the business is holding an appropriate level of stock and successfully managing the amount of credit it allows its customers.

As explained on p.24 , the total value shown on the Balance Sheet, the figure on which the statement balances, is not what the business is worth.

So far from wanting the 'biggest' balance sheet you can manage, you actually want as little as possible. Every £1 invested in the business had to come from somewhere (e.g. a shareholder or a bank) and therefore comes at a financial cost so you want to run your business with as little investment as possible whilst keeping your customers happy.

Keep watching the marketplace and aligning your business accordingly. The market may set the price for your products or services but you determine the cost and hence it's up to you whether you make a profit or not. The customer pays a price that rewards suppliers for doing things efficiently and effectively. They do not pay a premium just because, for example, their supplier uses inappropriate equipment or surrounds himself with a load of unnecessary slow-moving inventory.

Your choice of processes (Fixed Assets) and the way you organise making and delivering your products or services (Working Capital) determine how much investment you need. This is the Goldilocks approach: Not too much. Not too little. Just right. Too much investment (over-capitalisation) and your assets work sluggishly so you end up carrying unnecessary financial burdens that your customer will not pay for in his price. Too little investment (under-capitalisation) and you're forever scrabbling around on a financial knife-edge perpetually hitting your overdraft limit.

To master these Balance Sheet numbers you need to keep challenging your investment to find better ways of doing more with less.

Fixed Assets

As you've seen, on the balance sheet, Fixed Assets are valued at cost less the cumulative depreciation charged to date. For an individual item, this sum represents the share of the original cost that has yet to deliver value to the business through providing a capability to make and deliver the company's products or services.

This NBV of the asset isn't what you're really interested in here as this future depreciation charge is a "sunk cost" – i.e. one that you can't do anything about unless you choose to dispose of the asset and accept the resultant write-off of the NBV against profit.

Instead take a look at the Fixed Asset register that lists each individual item the business owns:

- Have you got the right capability?
- Are you using this investment efficiently and effectively?
- Are there items in the register that you no longer need?

Remember that even if unwanted items have a value on the books yet little or no resale value, the 'profit hit' may be worth taking if it means you can free up space and reduce clutter. What could you do with this space? Take on new business? Rationalise the site? Save on other storage costs?

If you want to master the investment in Fixed Assets you also need to make sure that anything new you buy will pull its weight. Take a look at some of the techniques available to help you do this in Chapter 8, Capital Expenditure Appraisal.

Working Capital

Inventory

If inventory is an asset why do you want as little as possible? Firstly, because every £1 invested in inventory had to come from somewhere and therefore has a financial cost attached. Secondly, because it will result in additional running costs as you have to control it, store it, safeguard it and make sure it doesn't deteriorate.

But, more importantly, because inventory represents risk. By exchanging cash for inventory you increase the risk to the business. What happens if the market changes and those items are no longer required to meet customer demands? What if you change your design or the way you deliver your services and that inventory becomes obsolete?

A word of warning. Before you slash the level of inventory you hold, remember that there is only one person who brings cash into your business. Your customer. Therefore you want to hold the minimum amount of inventory you can consistent with being able to make on-time deliveries to keep your customer happy.

A further word of warning. The amount of inventory you are holding is the consequence of the way you have organised the timing and volume of the flow of goods and services through your business. It's relatively easy to cut inventory levels in the short-term by holding back purchase orders for a while but a few months later you'll probably find your inventory levels are back where they started. To take inventory out of the business – and keep it out – you need to make changes to the way you organise that flow.

Receivables

Almost there – but not quite. When you invoice your goods or services to your customers the invoice value goes into your sales figure and you calculate and declare the profit you have made.

But have you achieved any real financial benefit yet? All you have done is move some of your assets into your customer's warehouse. It's your money that's still tied up. Until the customer pays for what you've sold him you have not finished the job! If you can sell for cash that's great. If you can't then look to negotiate the shortest terms you can. Customers don't take credit – you agree it by negotiation. If necessary evaluate the trade-off between price and credit-terms. It may pay you to shave a little off the price to collect the cash that bit faster. If you have long-term contracts then go for stage-payments wherever possible.

And, once you've agreed terms, make sure customers stick to them. Don't give them excuses not to pay. Deliver a quality product or service on time with the correct paperwork – and don't forget to invoice them!

Be professional about the way you manage customer credit. Build relationships not just with the buyers in your customers' businesses but also with those involved in the payment process so that you can 'nurse' your invoices through their system to make sure you get paid on time.

Cash

Much as accountants love cash (see p48) you don't want too much of it. After all, what's the point of raising money to invest in a business just for that investment to sit around as cash? Your investors may as well have just put their money in the bank – and you become a target for takeover as others see the opportunity to put this cash to better use. But neither do you want too little of it as that will result in you lurching from one cash flow crisis to another and hefty overdraft charges as well.

Payables

Working Capital is the net of Current Assets and Current Liabilities. So taking credit from your suppliers means you can finance some of your inventory (and if you're lucky even your receivables) with someone else's money. That's got to be a good thing.

But don't overdo it. Firstly there's probably a trade-off here between price and payment terms so make sure you get it right from your point of view. Secondly make sure you take credit through negotiated terms. Just not paying suppliers tends to backfire as it not only puts you in a poor negotiating position for price reviews and if for any reason supply is constrained but it also causes you wasted time, energy and capacity when they put you on "stop" (i.e. suspend deliveries until you have paid). Your defence against such sanctions? You'll end up having to lay in additional inventory to act as a buffer – which brings in additional cost and risk to the business (see above).

Whilst making sure all those assets are working hard and pulling their weight it's also important to master the way they are being financed. It's time to turn your attention to the section of the Balance Sheet that reports on where the money came from.

Take a look at your *gearing,* the relative proportions of finance supplied by lenders as opposed to shareholders. A business with high gearing has lots of borrowing with relatively little shareholder investment; a business with low gearing has relatively little borrowing with a high proportion of its assets being financed by shareholder money.

Loans represent 'third party cold-blooded contractual' money coming from those who have a right to a return on their investment (interest payments) whether the company has a good year or not. Shareholders on the other hand, because they own the business, are the risk-takers. With no contractual right to a return they are last in the 'pecking order' for a share of the profits. So the higher the gearing in your business the greater the financial risk as even in difficult times interest payments will have to be met or your business risks the lender exercising their rights to seize any collateral they have secured on the loan.

Conversely, if your business has low gearing (and is coping with its existing interest payments easily – see p.40, Interest Cover) it is said to have leverage – the ability to take on additional borrowing. This is a good position to be in as borrowing money is a quick way to bring in additional capital to, for example, seize an opportunity to grow the business either through taking on additional orders or through acquisition.

3. THE PROFIT AND LOSS ACCOUNT

or Income Statement

INTRODUCTION

Whereas the Balance Sheet reports how your business is financed and how you've chosen to invest that money, the Profit and Loss Account tells you how well you've used that investment in Fixed Assets and Working Capital to create profits by making and delivering products or services to your customers. Whilst the Balance Sheet is a snapshot at a point in time, the Profit and Loss Account covers a specific period of time (usually a month, quarter, half-year, financial year or financial year-to-date).

The statement starts at the top with the value of your sales and finishes with the amount of profit left over for the shareholders (usually referred to as Earnings or Profit After Tax). A separate statement then sets out how much of the Earnings has been taken out of the business as dividends and how much has therefore been left over, after all your costs have been met, to reinvest back into the business

The information that goes into the externally published Profit and Loss Account is summarised rather than detailed which, amongst other things, avoids potentially highly sensitive commercial information being made available to competitors. Profit and Loss Accounts produced for internal purposes do not usually cover the full range of costs but focus instead in more detail on the cost of operating the business.

READING THE PROFIT LOSS ACCOUNT
External Format

As with the Balance Sheet, the format and jargon used in the statement will vary between businesses but the essentials, of starting with sales then step-by-step taking account of the business costs, remains the same.

	£
Sales	1,000,000
Cost of Sales	700,000
Gross Profit	300,000
Distribution costs	85,000
Administration expenses	115,000
Operating Profit	100,000
Interest	20,000
Profit Before Tax	80,000
Tax	16,000
Profit After Tax	64,000

The statement starts with the total value of all the invoiced sales during the period that may also be referred to as turnover or revenue. As you proceed down the statement, you 'take the temperature' by measuring profit at different stages as you take account of more and more of the business costs.

The first costs to be deducted from the sales are the Cost of Sales (COS) – those costs directly associated with making the products or services that have been sold (e.g. labour, materials and running costs). Gross Profit is the result of deducting this Cost of Sales figure from the Sales. Notes to the accounts may provide more detail of the costs that have gone into the value for COS. Amongst these costs are *depreciation* and *amortisation* – the charges that result from the accountant, for the purposes of the Profit and Loss Account, spreading the purchase price of fixed assets (e.g. equipment and buildings) over their useful life to the business rather than putting all the costs into the year of purchase.

After Gross Profit come costs such as distribution (including sales and marketing costs) and administration expenses that are part of the operating costs of running the business, but are not seen as activities that are directly associated with making products or delivering services. The profit level at this stage is known as Operating Profit or Earnings Before Interest and Tax (EBIT).

From Operating Profit, the cost of interest on any borrowed money is deducted arriving at Profit Before Tax (PBT).

Once the tax is deducted you are left with Profit After Tax (PAT) or Earnings, which is the amount of money left over for the shareholders who, as the risk-takers in the business, get whatever's left over after everyone else has had their costs met.

The final step (which will usually be shown in a separate statement) sets out how much of the shareholders' profits (i.e. Earnings) has been paid out to them as dividends and hence how much they have agreed to reinvest back within the business.

Internal format

Take a look again at the summarised nature of the above statement. You couldn't run your business without much more detailed information on how you're performing. Therefore statements published for internal use will go into a great deal more detail and will focus on that part of the statement over which the local management team are deemed to be accountable – usually just as far as Operating Profit.

That's why Operating Profit is commonly referred to as "the bottom line".

As you have seen, it's not in reality the bottom line. There are more deductions to come. However, these deductions (interest, tax and ultimately dividends) are usually considered to be the result of decisions outside the remit of the local management team and therefore not something over which they should be judged.

The 'customer' for the internal statement is not the shareholder or the government but local managers. The format and level of detail into which the internal statement goes should be driven by the needs of managers for information they can use in their decision-making. There is no 'rule book' for how these internal reports must be prepared – just a requirement that they should 'mirror the reality' of the comparison between the price the market has been prepared to pay for the goods or services that have been delivered to them and the cost of the resources the business has consumed in achieving those sales.

Every business is different. No two companies bring in the same materials, then use identical equipment and skills to turn them into identical products or services for identical customers. Therefore each business should have a way of costing its products or services that is 'tailor-made' rather than 'off-the-peg'. There are however some common approaches to the way this is done.

Some businesses start by deducting the variable costs (those that vary with the volume of sales – e.g. materials) from the value of sales to determine what is known as the contribution. The contribution has to cover the fixed costs of the business (those that do not vary with the volume of sales – e.g. rent) with any surplus being profit.

Others might use a traditional overhead absorption costing system where overhead costs such as depreciation, rent, utilities and supervisory and managerial salaries are loaded on to the back of labour and/or material costs through an absorption (or burden) rate.

Perhaps the business uses a standard costing system where expected costs for labour, materials and overheads (known as standards) are established at the start of the year with differences reported throughout the year as variances.

[For a more detailed explanation of some of the alternative methodologies used in calculating and reporting on product or service cost see Chapter 7, Costing.]

Note: EBITDA (Earnings Before Interest, Tax, Depreciation and Amortisation). Whilst this figure does not appear as such in the Profit and Loss Account it is an important component of the Cash Flow Statement and may be calculated and shown as a note or appendix to the Profit and Loss Account.

As explained above, EBIT is another term for Operating Profit.

	£
EBIT	100,000
Depreciation and Amortisation	25,000
EBITDA	125,000

As depreciation and amortisation have already been included in the costs charged against sales in calculating EBIT, they are 'added back' to EBIT to arrive at EBITDA. This is explained in detail on p.51.

INTERPRETING THE NUMBERS

So what does the Profit and Loss Account tell you?

Less than you might think – although it does represent an important aspect of long-term survival; has the market been willing to pay a price for your goods or services that exceeds the cost you've incurred in satisfying those needs?

When you look at a Profit and Loss Account you must remember that Operating Profit is compiled on 'the matching principle' with the sales value being compared to the costs associated with making those sales.

It is neither a comparison of sales against total costs incurred nor is it a statement comparing cash receipts with cash payments.

The value of sales is the total of all the invoices raised during the period – unless you sell everything for cash, this will not be the same as the cash you have received.

Cost is the price of the resources you've consumed in making the products or services that have been sold – the 'attributable' cost. Unless you pay for everything in cash and don't keep any stock this will not be the same as the value of the cheques you've written.

In other words when the accountant is preparing the Profit and Loss Account they are simply looking down the road at what has been sold during the period the statement covers and limiting their questioning to:

- What is the invoiced value of the goods or services that have left the business?
- What costs are tied up in those goods or services that have been sold?
- Hence how much profit has been made?

With their back to the business the statement takes no account of either costs that have been incurred but haven't yet 'gone out on the back of the lorry' (i.e. inventory); neither do they concern themselves with what has been happening to cash.

But the Profit and Loss Account still attempts to provide important information by comparing market prices with the cost to the business of achieving these sales.

By using the matching principle the accountant tries to ensure that by using attributable costs they are comparing 'like with like'.

Take the example of a business that buys in three items and then sells two. If the Profit and Loss Account measured the sales value of the two against the cost of the three the resultant figure would be meaningless. If instead it compares the sales value of the two with the cost of two (the other one sits in the Balance Sheet as inventory), the statement can guide users as to whether the business has organised itself in such a way that the price it can command in the market for its products or services exceeds their cost.

[It is this matching principle that also drives the need for the accountant to prepare "accruals" and "prepayments". Not all bills are received on a monthly basis so when the accountant is preparing the Profit and Loss Account they need to make appropriate adjustments. If utility bills for example are received quarterly in arrears and 'lumps' of utility cost are included in the statement just once a quarter this would distort the picture of what costs the business is really incurring (and hence how much profit they are making) each month. Instead the accountant will include an "accrued" charge each month based on an estimate of the cost of the resources consumed with a small correction made each quarter when the bill comes in and the actual cost is known. Other costs, such as subscriptions, may be payable annually in advance.

In this instance rather than take all the cost in the first month the accountant feeds the cost into the Profit and Loss Account on a monthly basis through a prepayment adjustment.]

The extent to which selling prices have exceeded costs are usually commented on in the context of their "margins". Margins are calculated by measuring profit as a % of sales:

Example: $\frac{(\text{Selling price} - \text{Cost})}{\text{Selling price}} \times 100\%$

This may be done by individual product or service or for the business as a whole. Reported margins will depend on where you 'draw the line' on which costs to include in your costing system, and margin comparisons between different product or service lines will be distorted by the extent to which there is cross-subsidisation taking place within the costing system. There are those who would argue therefore that there is little information other than of a very generalised nature on cost, and hence profit, to be gained from the Profit and Loss Account (see Chapter 7, Costing).

If you're looking at a Profit and Loss Account that goes beyond Operating Profit you'll find the cost of interest payments to those who have lent the business money. Borrowing money brings financial risk into the business as interest payments must be made (see p.12) so it is important to look at how easily the business is servicing this cost.

This can be assessed by calculating the Interest Cover – i.e. calculating how many times the interest cost could have been paid out of Operating Profit.

Example: $\frac{\text{Operating Profit}}{\text{Interest Costs}} = \frac{£100,000}{£20,000}$

Interest Cover = 5

The higher the interest cover the lower the risk. If a business has low *gearing* and high interest cover it is said to have leverage – the potential to borrow more money, if required, at a reasonable rate of interest.

As far as the next step, taxation, is concerned, whilst most businesses (and individuals) try and organise themselves in such a way that they can legitimately minimise their tax liabilities, the amount charged is predominantly driven by government fiscal policy.

The final number to interpret is that of Earnings. One of the key measures businesses use to assess how well they are meeting their shareholders' needs is *Earnings Per Share* (EPS). This measure is calculated by taking the Earnings figure and dividing it by the number of shares in issue and provides a measure (and importantly, over time, a trend) of the 'profit' per share for the owners.

Armed with a Profit and Loss Account and a Balance Sheet you are now able to assess a key part of the management task – how effectively the investment available (as set out in the Balance Sheet) has been used to deliver profit (as measured by Operating Profit). This concept of "profitability" is explained in detail on p.62.

MASTERING PROFIT

All too often when looking for ways to improve the Profit and Loss Account numbers, attention turns to slashing costs.

Don't forget to look for opportunities to improve the top line as well.

Pricing for Profit

It's always very tempting to shave a little off the price to guarantee winning an order – but do your sales team really understand that any discounts come straight off the bottom line?

Look at the impact giving a 1% sales discount has on profit for this business:

	Before:	After:
	£	£
Sales	100,000	99,000
Costs	95,000	95,000
Profit	5,000	4,000

Profit falls by 20%!

Whereas look at the benefit a small increase in selling prices can have:

	Before: £	After: £
Sales	100,000	102,000
Costs	95,000	95,000
Profit	5,000	7,000

In this instance a 2% increase in selling prices increases profit by 40%.

And raising your prices might not be as hard as you think.

Check the terms of any sales contracts for escalation clauses and make sure you trigger them when appropriate. It's up to you to do this – your customer is unlikely to remind you!

Make sure that those responsible for agreeing contracts with customers are commercially astute and understand exactly what is included in the price and what should be invoiced as 'extras'. The building industry has a reputation for being good at this. When you're negotiating the contract make sure you also agree the basis for charging any extras then consider invoicing them separately so that if they are challenged, payment for the 'core' work is not delayed.

And while you've got the sales team in your sights, take the opportunity to share with them the benefits to be had of selling additional lines on a customer's order. Look at the costs you incur on activities such as marketing, selling costs, administration and distribution. For many businesses these will not increase if the customer adds an additional item to their basket so the difference between the selling price and the cost of making the product will fall straight to the bottom line. In the service industry, if you've already got someone on-site make sure your team are trained the opportunity to sell that extra service.

In the light of the above, take a look at the way you reward your sales team. Make sure they're motivated to win the 'right' business at the 'right' price.

Managing costs

Now take a look at those costs.

Here's where a few numbers can win people round.

Let's assume times are really tough and your profit margin is perilously tight.

	£
	£
Sales	100,000
Costs	99,000
Profit	1,000

Initially there will inevitably be those who fail to share your enthusiasm to find ways to reduce costs.

"Why bother? If we're only making £1,000 profit and we find ways to reduce costs by 3%, that's an awful lot of angst to go through to increase profit by 3%; that's only an extra £30!"

They're missing the point and you'll miss an opportunity.

Profit quadruples.

	Before:	After:
	£	£
Sales	100,000	100,000
Costs	99,000	96,000
Profit	1,000	4,000

If you want to make even more impact on your audience show them what happens to the business' *profitability* if you can reduce costs and 'shrink' your investment (see p.65).

Even though you've now convinced everyone of the benefits you may still be wondering where on earth you can find yet more cost savings. You have already 'cracked the whip' over those making the product or delivering the service and can't see how you can get them to work harder. You've tussled with your suppliers and just don't know how you can source any cheaper.

Where is there left to go?

Take a good look around you and you'll find people wasting the company's money. Not because they're lazy but because: firstly, you haven't got your processes organised as effectively as they can be; and secondly, because you don't always get everything right first time. Remember your customer pays a price that rewards you for having best practice and for getting it right. If you choose to have convoluted, resource-consuming processes that's a cost to the business that the customer won't want to pay for. If the way you make things, or the way you deliver the service, or your administration systems are complex and prone to error, you will end up frequently having to 'put things right'. That's another cost the customer isn't willing to bear.

The costs you incur are a consequence of the way you've decided to set out and organise your business. Reflect back on those two categories of investment set out in the Balance Sheet as seen on p.20.

Fixed Assets
When you choose these 'facilities' or 'processes' you lay out the way you intend to run your business for many years into the future. The cost to the business is, for the purposes of the Profit and Loss Account, spread over the asset's useful life to calculate an annual depreciation charge against profit (see appendix 3, Fixed Assets). Depreciation is therefore the cost of the investment you have made in providing your chosen capability to meet market needs and you look to recover this cost through the price the market pays for your products or services. The choices you make will also drive the 'running' costs that you incur – e.g. your choice of equipment will affect maintenance and electricity costs; your choice of premises will affect space costs such as rates and heating.

Once fixed assets have reached the end of what was originally deemed to be their useful life to the business (the period over which they were depreciated) there is no further depreciation charge to be made so continuing to use them may seem a great way to improve profits. But there may be downsides to continuing to use fully depreciated equipment (for example increased maintenance costs, decreased reliability, reduced competitiveness through failure to be able to offer up-to-date technology etc.), and it is this weighing up of the advantages to be had in making new investment against the cost it brings to the business that forms the basis of the *CAPEX* decision. (See Chapter 8, Capital Expenditure Appraisal.)

Working Capital
The way you organise the journey from cash through your business and back into cash again will have implications to the costs that end up in your Profit & Loss Account.

Working Capital Cycle

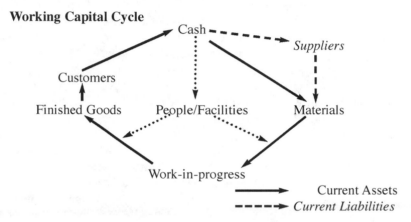

[For a detailed explanation of the cycle see Appendix 4, Working Capital.]

Payables
Your choice of suppliers and the terms and conditions of the purchase orders placed on them will determine not only the price paid but also the costs you incur for carriage inwards, receiving, storage, disposal of packaging etc.

Inventory
The way you organise the speed with which materials come into the business, are transformed into the goods or services the customer wants and are then delivered to them will not only affect the amount of investment you need to keep that working capital cycle turning but will also influence your running costs. Inventory is an asset that you have to look after so you incur handling, storage and security costs. The more inventory you have around, the greater the complexity, so the more you

will spend controlling it (e.g. scheduling, record keeping, stocktaking) and the greater the risk of 'write-offs' (as a result of, for example, inventory losses and obsolescence) – an additional cost to the business that therefore reduces your profit.

Receivables

Whilst you will negotiate as little credit to your customers as you can, unless you've managed to get cash terms (or even better cash upfront), your customer profile will influence the amount of cost you have to incur in collecting payment of your invoices. Do you sell to lots of different customers or just a few? Are your customers local, national or international? How much commercial leverage do you have with them when it comes to making sure they pay on time? Are the necessary checks carried out to make sure your customer is credit-worthy before you take the order? Any bad debts that have to be written off will also reduce your profits.

Remember that costs don't just happen, they are caused by the choices people make. Every time a decision is made there will be cost implications. For effective cost control you therefore need to make sure people understand the financial implications of the choices available to them. Certain decisions may constrain the choices available to the next tier of decision-makers.

Profit by design

Design decisions are a good example of this. Your business is there to serve market needs. Once you've decided which needs you're going to address and the price customers will pay to have them met, you then have to design the product or service that will satisfy those needs. These design decisions are fundamental in determining cost and hence whether you can make a living out of serving that market. For example, the choice of materials you'll use will determine the list of potential suppliers which will then drive not just price and payment terms but the cost you will incur on other aspects such as freight inwards, storage (do you have to buy in bulk?), controlling quality (do they source inspect?), ensuring reliability of supply (do you have to lay in buffer stock?) and administration (can your systems 'speak' to each other?).

As for the costs that will be incurred converting those materials into products, the starting point for determining these will be driven by whether there is in-house capability to do the work required to achieve the design or whether it will need to be sub-contracted out. Then there are the costs of achieving the required level of quality that will stem from the design parameters....

The list of 'knock-on' impacts to cost that originate from the design go on and on. Every line drawn on the designer's easel has £ notes written all over it. Remember that profit is the difference between the selling price and the cost. If the market sets the selling price, your only chance to control your profit is to master those costs. If you treat your designers as 'fluffies', kow-towing to their creative impulses and allowing them to be devoid of any responsibility for cost, you will lose control of your profit.

Margins of Error
You may be surprised that this section hasn't been full of references to "margins" and how to improve them. As explained on p.40, reported margins will depend on where you draw the line in deciding which costs to include in your costing system. In addition, as every costing system has its 'winners and losers', margins may be inappropriate in guiding decisions such as which product or service lines should be expanded and which should be curtailed (see Appendix 9, Product Life-Cycles).

And once you get into the detail of individual product or service margins there's also the danger of the 'cake-cutting farce' wherein instead of trying to reduce the size of the cake (the total costs), energy is wasted on merely trying to cut the slices in different proportions (getting costs reallocated to someone else's product or service).

Just to make matters even worse, reporting on costs is the prime area for using generic terminology in a uniquely 'localised' way!

So, before using any costing information for decision-making purposes it is essential to establish how 'the numbers' have been calculated and therefore their relevance to the matter in hand.

Treat cost 'information' with extreme caution!
Most should come with a business health warning:
> "Under no circumstances should these numbers be used in decision-making." (See Chapter 7, Costing.)

4. THE CASH FLOW STATEMENT

INTRODUCTION

Whilst Balance Sheets and Profit and Loss Accounts have been around for hundreds of years, the Cash Flow Statement, as a published document, is a relatively recent development. As explained below, when businesses become more 'sophisticated', profit and cash flow tend to drift apart, and with only the Balance Sheet and Profit and Loss Account to work with, it is less obvious to those reading the accounts when companies are getting into difficulties.

Cash is the lifeblood of the business. You use cash to pay your workforce, pay your suppliers, pay the bank their interest, pay the taxman their dues and pay the shareholders their dividends. Without cash your business grinds to a halt.

But as long as you're making a profit... surely that's enough?

No. Businesses don't fail because they make a loss but because they run out of cash.

You see, once a business:

- takes credit from its suppliers; and/or
- gives credit to its customers; and/or
- does not buy and sell everything the same day (i.e. has inventory); and/or
- purchases facilities or processes (i.e. Fixed Assets)

then TIME has entered the business, so profit and cash flow drift apart.

And not only are profit and cash flow not the same thing, they may not even move in the same direction.

A business can start with cash, make a profit and yet end up at the end of the period with less cash than it started with.

(Conversely a business can start with no cash, make a loss during the period and still end up with more cash than it started with but this isn't a particularly enjoyable or sustainable process.)

Therefore to master the financials you need to run your business in such a way that you don't just make a profit but that you also generate cash.

READING THE CASH FLOW STATEMENT

Cash flow is the difference between cash that has been received and the cash that has been paid out. The Cash Flow Statement shows whether the amount of cash held by the business has increased or decreased during the period and explains why this has happened.

There are different ways in which this statement is presented but whilst the sequence in which items are dealt with varies, the 'building blocks' remain the same.

The starting point, particularly for statements produced for internal use, is usually the amount of profit made during the period – which is why the statement is sometimes referred to as the "Profit to Cash Reconciliation".

In working through the following explanation it will be useful to refer to the example shown overleaf.

Figures in (brackets) are cash outflows:

Cash Flow Statement

	£
Operating Profit	100,000
Depreciation	25,000
EBITDA	125,000
Increase in Inventory	(22,000)
Increase in Receivables	(29,000)
Increase in Payables	8,000
Cash Flow from Operating Activities	82,000
Interest Paid	(20,000)
Tax Paid	(12,000)
Capital Expenditure	(30,000)
Dividends Paid	(28,000)
Increase in Share Capital	3,000
(Decrease) in Cash	(5,000)

Cash Flow from Operating Activities

This is the term that is used to represent the cash flow that has resulted from running the business as distinct from any financing or investment activities. As can be seen from the example above, it considers both cash flowing as a result of Operating Profit and the impact of changing levels of Working Capital.

Operating Profit and Cash Flow

Making a profit (i.e. selling goods or services for more than they cost) is a great way to help bring cash into the business. You will recall from the section on the Profit and Loss Account that there are many different 'levels' of profit but the one usually used to start off the Cash Flow Statement is Operating Profit, also known as EBIT (Earnings Before

Interest and Tax). This is the profit after all the business costs (materials, payroll, expenses, depreciation and amortisation etc.) have been deducted from the sales value but before financing costs such as interest, tax and dividends have been charged.

There is an adjustment to Operating Profit that needs to be made if the Cash Flow Statement is going to eventually explain what has happened to the cash. Take another look at the business costs referred to above. They include depreciation and amortisation. These charges are the accountant's mechanism for being 'fair' in how they calculate profit by spreading the original purchase price of Fixed Assets over their useful life to the business rather than including all the cost in the year of purchase. (See Appendix 3, Fixed Assets). So the depreciation and amortisation charges for the period will have been included as a cost before arriving at Operating Profit. But these charges have nothing to do with cash moving into or out of the business. Cash flowed in the past when the business originally bought and paid for the asset. Nobody pays or receives cash for depreciation or amortisation. Therefore to look at how the business has performed from a 'cash' perspective the accountant has to 'add back' those depreciation and amortisation charges to EBIT thereby effectively restating the profit to a level 'higher up' the Profit and Loss Account – EBITDA (Earnings Before Interest, Tax, Depreciation and Amortisation).

[Depreciation and amortisation may also be referred to as "Non cash expenses". There may be other such expenses where the cost has been included in the Profit and Loss Account but where there are no cash flow implications (e.g. creating a provision for future warranty claims) and the statement will need to adjust for these as well.]

Working Capital and Cash Flow
Once the adjustment to EBIT has been made to arrive at EBITDA, the next items in the statement address the impact of the constrained perspective the accountant has in calculating profit. Take another look at that picture on p.38. Profit is the difference between the sales value of the goods invoiced during the period and the cost of the resources consumed in enabling the business to make and deliver the goods that have been sold.

It is important to note the following:

- Profit considers just the cost of the goods or services sold – not the costs incurred
- Profit looks at sales invoices – not cash receipts
- Profit looks at costs – not cash payments

To move to a 'cash' perspective, adjustments therefore have to be made for the following.

The increase or decrease in inventory

Carrying out this adjustment converts the "cost of goods and services sold" in the Profit and Loss Account into the "costs incurred" during the period regardless of whether they relate to goods or services that have been sold or are still held in inventory and will be invoiced in a future period.

If the inventory value has increased then you must have incurred more costs than just those that have found their way into the Profit and Loss Account.

Conversely if the inventory value has decreased then the costs you have incurred will be less than the costs included in your Profit and Loss Account.

The increase or decrease in receivables

By allowing for this the "sales" figure included in the Profit and Loss Account is converted to "cash receipts".

The increase or decrease in payables

Adjusting for this increase or decrease converts "costs incurred" into "cash payments".

[If you want to work through an example of these working capital adjustments they are included in the worked example in Appendix 6.]

Interest and Tax

The statement shows the amount of Interest and Tax paid – note this may be different to the figures charged in the Profit and Loss Account due to the timing of payments.

Capital Expenditure

Having adjusted the profit figure for the accountant's depreciation charge to take it out of a statement concerned with inflows and outflows of cash (see above), the next step is to include the cost of any Capital Expenditure (CAPEX) during the period as this is the point at which cash really does flow.

Dividends

The statement shows the dividends paid which may be different to the figures shown in the supplementary statement to the Profit and Loss Account due to the timing of payments.

Financing Activities

The statement also sets out the cash flow resulting from increases or decreases in long-term finance (e.g. share capital and loans).

A worked example of the Cash Flow Statement is provided in Appendix 6.

INTERPRETING THE CASH FLOW STATEMENT

Take another look at that complete statement on p.50.

As few people within an organisation play a key role in decisions on how the business is financed (and as cash flow problems can not be perpetually resolved by just bringing in additional capital), it makes sense to focus on the areas most people can influence.

We are therefore left with what can be referred to as the '5 levers' to generate cash in a business.

$$
\begin{aligned}
&\text{EBITDA} \\
&+ \text{Movement in Working Capital:} \\
&\qquad \Delta \text{Inventory} \\
&\qquad \Delta \text{Receivables} \\
&\qquad \Delta \text{Payables} \\
&+ \underline{\text{Capital Expenditure}} \\
&= \text{Cash Flow}
\end{aligned}
$$

Note: Δ means 'the increase or decrease in'

Remember that this is not the accountant's complete cash flow as it only includes those items that are under the control of local managers and therefore need to be 'mastered'.

EBITDA
This is Operating Profit (or EBIT) adjusted to exclude the impact of any charges for depreciation and amortisation – see p.51. EBITDA is generated by selling goods or services to the market at a price that exceeds their cost.

Movement in Working Capital
Increases or decreases in the elements of working capital will have an effect on cash flow.

- If inventory increases this is 'bad' for cash.
- If receivables increase this is 'bad' for cash.
- If, however, payables increase this is 'good' for cash.

If you're unsure of why this is, look at the Working Capital cycle explained in detail in Appendix 4.

Every time the cycle 'swells' (because the business holds more inventory or allows customers more credit or takes less credit from suppliers), cash is 'sucked into' the cycle. On the other hand when the cycle is 'squeezed' (by holding less inventory or allowing customers less credit or taking more credit from suppliers) cash is released.

Capital Expenditure
This is the amount spent on new facilities or processes in the period.

From the above adjustments you can see why profit and cash flow will not have the same value (unless coincidently all the items in the middle net out to zero); neither will they necessarily even move in the same direction.

If the business makes a profit but the other levers head in the 'wrong' direction then cash flow may be negative.

If the business makes a loss but 'good' things happen elsewhere on the statement then cash flow could still be positive.

Examples:

	£	£
EBITDA	10,000	(10,000)
Movement in Working Capital:		
Δ Inventory	(2,000)	4,000
Δ Receivables	(6,000)	9,000
Δ Payables	1,000	(1,000)
Capital Expenditure	(5,000)	nil
Cash inflow/(outflow)	(2,000)	2,000

So should you always expect to be able to get 100% "cash conversion" (i.e. see all your EBITDA flowing down to the cash flow line)?

It very much depends on what is going on in your business at the time.

Ironically businesses tend to be at their most vulnerable, from a cash perspective, when they're successful as increasing volumes of cash are flowing out before they start to flow in again.

On the other hand, if there is a downturn in activity and the warning signs are spotted and acted on promptly, cash may well flow in as Working Capital is 'ratcheted down' and Capital Expenditure put on hold.

[For more information on the impact of product life-cycles on cash flow, see Appendix 9.]

MASTERING CASH FLOW
To master cash flow you must set about managing and controlling the '5 levers' referred to above.

EBITDA
Forget the jargon and think "profit".

Nobody manages cash flow by thinking about depreciation or amortisation. Focus instead on how you can improve your profits.

Whilst you don't necessarily have to start with a profit to generate cash it makes life much easier and infinitely more pleasant if you do!

If you're making losses then the only way you can keep the cash flowing in is to 'shrink' the business, reducing the investment in working capital and reining back on capital expenditure – or continually bringing in additional finance which will become both increasingly difficult to find and expensive when you do.

You make a profit by selling your goods or services into a market at a price that exceeds the cost. It is important therefore that you've clearly identified the market you are serving and have aligned your business to that market so that you can meet those needs as efficiently and effectively as possible. Customers do not pay a price premium to charitably support inefficient suppliers. Gone (for most businesses) are the days of "cost plus" pricing where the price would be determined by an agreed mark-up on whatever it cost you to provide those goods or services. The market sets the price according to the value it places on the product or service you are providing. You should be doing everything you can to 'position' your offering in the marketplace in such a way that you can command the highest price possible (by the quality and reliability of your products or services, your excellent supportive relationship with your customer etc.) but ultimately you don't set the price; the market does.

But that does not mean you abdicate all financial responsibility as to whether you make a profit or not.

Whilst the market may set the selling price, you determine the cost by the way you go about your business. Take a look at p.41 (Mastering Profit) for some ideas on how to get the EBITDA you deserve.

Movement in Working Capital
Take another look at that Working Capital cycle on p.45.
Remember, you're looking for ways to 'squeeze' rather than 'swell' the investment.

Inventory
If inventory is an asset why do you want to get rid of it?

Not only because for every asset there is an equivalent liability (e.g. the money you had to borrow from the bank to finance it) and because it requires you to incur additional costs (e.g. handling and storage), but also because it's a risky way to tie up your money.

As soon as you embark on your journey around the cycle and move out of cash you bring risk to the business:

- What happens if you buy the wrong inventory?

- What happens if there's a modification to your product or the way you deliver your service so that the inventory is no longer required?
- What if there's a change in the market making the inventory obsolete?

Your aim must be to whiz through the cycle as fast as you can holding as little inventory as possible, consistent with keeping your customer happy. And there's the rub.

There is only one person who brings the cash into your business.
Your customer. So it's vital that you can give him what he wants when he wants it. The only reason for holding inventory is because it's the only way you can work within the order leadtime your customer is willing to accept. So, every time you reduce the leadtime it takes to produce your goods or services the less inventory you will need to hold.

What determines your leadtime?
The market should have determined your product or service specification (after all you should be meeting their needs, no more, no less) but it's down to you how you've decided to produce it – and the design decision is critical here.

The answers to these questions will start you thinking about what is driving your leadtime:

- Which suppliers do you use?
- Can you negotiate consignment stock with them?
- Have you looked carefully at the 'cost' of volume discounts (e.g. additional initial investment, handling, and storage)?
- Do you do all the work yourself or do you use sub-contractors?
- How efficiently does the work flow through the process?
- Are there 'bottlenecks'?
- Are some tasks difficult and prone to result in scrap or rework requiring you to hold buffer stock just-in-case?

But before you empty the shelves be careful. Understand your market. In some markets availability is paramount. If you supply critical components for oil-drilling equipment the customer will send a helicopter to collect the part. Because of the cost of downtime to the customer, the price you charge is secondary to the importance of having that part on the shelf. Therefore, in this case you may align yourself with your market by holding substantial inventory (although even then not more than you need!) – but you will, of course, have made sure that the prices you can charge will reward you for the investment you have had to make and the additional risk you have therefore had to take.

Receivables

- Is your business sales-driven?
- Is there a 'get-it-out-the-door' mentality?
- Do you have a hockey stick*?

[*This is when, instead of a nice steady stream of sales throughout the month, very little happens in the first week or two, things gradually pick up in week 3 and then the vast majority of sales happen in the last few days of the month. Picture the daily sales graph and it has the shape of a hockey stick.]

If you have any (or all) of these, in the chaos that surrounds month end, shipping and invoicing mistakes will happen, making the payment difficult to collect. Think about what happens to your business's finances when you make a sale. All you do is move your money into someone else's warehouse. There's no real financial benefit to your business until the customer pays you and, until he does, your cash is still at risk. Therefore, you want to make sure that everyone in the team understands that the job isn't finished until the customer pays.

If you can make cash sales, that's great (as are progress payments if you can get them). But where customers expect credit, salespeople need to ensure that just like price, this is a matter for negotiation.

Every time salespeople allow your customers credit it means cash is tied up in receivables. Not only is additional investment required to finance this but there is also additional risk.

- What happens if the customer won't pay?
- What happens if the customer goes under before he pays?

- What happens if you've overstretched yourself financially by taking on a large order so that you can't pay your bills in the meantime?

<u>Whose job is it to collect the cash from customers?</u>
Everyone in the business. This critical step in the cash flow journey has to be managed professionally.

You can't collect money where there isn't an invoice.
Check your processes to make sure there are no 'shortcuts' allowing goods or services to be delivered without invoices being raised. If you've negotiated a contract with stage-payments make sure those involved understand what those trigger-points are and that the invoices are raised promptly.

Customers won't pay if they didn't place an order.
It's often said that "everyone works for the customer" – but in that case they need to be paid! Beware of the rush to 'help a customer out' where costs are incurred before the order is received.

You can't collect on an invoice where there isn't a price.
Once again, in the desire to be helpful, businesses expose themselves to grave risks by commencing work on a TBA (to be agreed) basis. This is particularly risky (and you put yourself at a severe commercial disadvantage in subsequent negotiations) in the case of services where, once performed, they cannot be 'returned', and customer-specific products where there is no alternative customer for the goods.

You can't collect if it isn't due...
Credit terms need to be clear and understood. Whilst "Net 30" means payment 30 days after invoice date, "Net monthly" means payment is due on the last day of the month following the one in which the invoice is dated – so that could mean up to an extra month's credit for your customer. If you're involved with shipping goods overseas it's especially important to get advice on the precise meaning of the various terms used.

... but you can 'nurse' it through the system!

It's important to establish good working relationships with your customers – and not just with the buyers. Don't wait for invoices to become overdue. If your customer is strapped for cash and is deciding which suppliers to pay you want to make sure you make the cut. By understanding your customer's payment authorisation processes and the people involved in that flow, you can progress your invoice through the system ensuring it has been 'signed off' and is ready for payment well before the due date.

Payables
You might think the advice is going to be to take as much credit from your suppliers as you can get away with by ignoring any agreed payment terms and stringing them along for as long as possible.

It isn't. If you're going to set up your business in such a way that you can race through the Working Capital cycle as fast as you can and at minimum cost, you're going to need good relationships with carefully selected suppliers. Price matters as do negotiated payment terms (particularly if your customers are looking for long credit periods from you). But so do quality, lead time and reliability of supply. Remember that whilst taking additional credit from your supply chain improves your cash flow, having to lay in buffer stocks to protect yourself against being placed on 'stop' does the opposite. And it doesn't stop there:

- What about the additional costs you incur by playing one supplier off against another?
- Who has to take time out to deal with irate phone calls from unpaid suppliers?
- What if your failure to pay pushes your supplier over the edge and into liquidation? What will it cost you to approve another supplier?
- What is the cost of disrupted production?
- Will you end up paying for overtime and premium transport costs if you're still to fulfil your customer's order on time?

All these costs go against profit, therefore reducing your EBITDA. Another blow to cash flow.

So the message is to take the negotiation of credit terms seriously with your suppliers. Make sure that your buyers understand that the longer the credit period the less cash you have to find to keep your Working Capital cycle turning. But they must be terms your supplier can afford. If not, you may end up paying him earlier anyway just to keep him afloat. Once you've agreed terms, keep your word.

Capital Expenditure

When businesses carry out Capital Expenditure (i.e. the purchase of Fixed Assets) they are investing their money now in assets that they believe will bring value to the business for more than one financial year. That's why, when it comes to calculating profit, the accountant spreads the purchase price over the asset's useful life by charging a 'fair' amount (i.e. depreciation) against profit each year.

But whilst from a profit perspective the costs are spread, it's not what is happening to the cash. The cash flows out of the business in the year of purchase. The challenge is to make sure you buy the 'right' Fixed Assets. If you've aligned yourself correctly with your market and have set yourself up to make the products or services the market needs in the most cost-effective way using the most appropriate processes, the market will reward you for your investment in the price it pays for your goods or services. That's good for EBITDA and hence good for cash.

However, purchasing Fixed Assets is a risky business because you have to spend the cash now in expectation of that stream of profit (and cash) in the future. [For more discussion on the approaches taken to evaluate CAPEX requests see Chapter 8.]

5. FINANCIAL RATIOS AND OTHER MEASURES OF PERFORMANCE

INTRODUCTION

Numbers taken in isolation may mean very little.

Is a monthly sales figure of £200,000 'good' or 'bad'? Without something to compare it with (e.g. a forecast or last month's figure) there is little that can be said.

Sometimes other financial figures are needed to form a view.

Is an inventory value of £50,000 too high or too low? If you knew the average value of goods or services shipped per month, you could get a better picture by restating the information as a "number of days inventory".

Even then, without knowledge of the kind of business you were looking at, it would be hard to comment. 30 days inventory may be a great achievement for certain types of manufacturing businesses but to a volume retailer, who plans to turn their inventory over every few days, it would be a disaster.

Therefore you need to take care when reviewing ratios or performance measures to look at them in the context of the business and also focus more on ratios and trends rather than absolute values.

You can take any two numbers and use them to create a ratio but for it to be meaningful there must be an inter-relationship that you are trying to master. Businesses tend to evolve their own variants but here are some of the most common.

Profitability (Return on Capital Employed)

If you were to be offered the opportunity to invest in a venture that guaranteed you a profit of £1,000 next year would you be interested?

Setting aside questions of legality and trust, the most important question you would want answered is, "How much would I have to invest?"

If it was £10,000, and a 10% return was better than you could make elsewhere, you might be tempted. If on the other hand you were told you would have to invest £1,000,000 you'd walk away.

What matters to you is therefore not profit but profitability, i.e. how much profit you make relative to how much had to be invested to earn that profit.

In businesses profitability is usually measured as Return on Capital Employed (ROCE), which is expressed as a % and calculated as follows:

$$\text{ROCE} = \frac{\text{Operating Profit}}{\text{Net Capital Employed}} \times 100\%$$

Operating Profit (also known as EBIT) is the profit after all business operating costs have been met but before any financing costs. It is also commonly referred to as "the bottom line" because it is often seen to be the lowest point on the Profit and Loss Account over which local management have control and therefore accountability (see p.36).

Net Capital Employed (NCE) is the total of long-term finance invested in the business both from shareholders (*Net Worth*) and from lenders (*Loans*) and is shown on the bottom half of the Balance Sheet as presented on p.21 .

Using the figures from the Profit and Loss Account on p.35 and the Balance Sheet on p.21:

$$\text{ROCE} = \frac{\text{Operating Profit}}{\text{Net Capital Employed}^*} \times 100\% = \frac{£100,000}{£500,000} \times 100\% = 20\%$$

[*Note that as the Balance Sheet balances, Net Capital Employed (how much has been made available to invest) equals *Net Assets Employed* (where that investment has been made – i.e. *Fixed Assets* plus *Working Capital*).]

ROCE therefore sums up a key aspect of management's task. Given the amount of investment at their disposal (NCE), how effectively have they used this to firstly, through their CAPEX decisions, set out what they can offer the market in terms of business capability (Fixed Assets) and secondly organise the way the business will operate (Working Capital), in order to make and deliver products or services on which they can make an Operating Profit?

Encapsulating aspects of both the Balance Sheet and the Profit and Loss Account, this ratio might seem a little difficult to get to grips with. To master the ratio it's helpful to break it down into two parts using 'the multiplier'. Introduce Sales (from the Profit and Loss Account) into the top and bottom of the ratio as follows:

$$\text{ROCE} = \frac{\text{Operating Profit}}{\text{NCE}} \times 100\%$$

$$= \frac{\text{Operating Profit}}{\text{Sales}} \times 100\% \quad \textbf{X} \quad \frac{\text{Sales}}{\text{NCE}}$$

[Remember that when you multiply two ratios together you can 'cancel out' the two Sales figures ending up with the original ratio.]

As the Sales figure in the example was £1,000,000 (see p.35) the ratio becomes:

$$\text{ROCE} = \frac{£100,000}{£1,000,000} \times 100\% \quad \textbf{X} \quad \frac{£1,000,000}{£500,000}$$

$$= 10\% \quad\quad\quad\quad \textbf{X} \quad\quad 2$$

$$= 20\%$$

$\frac{\text{Operating Profit}}{\text{Sales}} \times 100\%$ is the Profit Margin and in this example is 10%

As you have seen on p.63, Net Capital Employed (NCE) equals Net Assets Employed (NAE) so:

$$\frac{Sales}{NCE} = \frac{Sales}{NAE}$$

$\dfrac{Sales}{NAE}$ is known as Asset Turn and in this instance is 2.

Therefore: ROCE = Profit Margin **X** Asset Turn.

So if you can improve either your Profit Margin or your Asset Turn – or, better still, for a 'multiplied' benefit, both – you will improve profitability.

Mastering the Profit Margin
There are two ways to improve your margin.
You can either increase your sales without proportionately increasing your costs and/or you can eliminate unnecessary costs from the business.

Increasing your sales might involve selling more products or services – but it could be a simple matter of making sure you're pricing your sales appropriately and including everything you're entitled to on your invoice.

If you can add an extra 1% to your invoices (noting that this increase also increases your Operating Profit) then profitability, using the above example, increases from 20% to 22% as shown below:

Sales increases from £1,000,000 to £1,010,000
Operating Profit increases from £100,000 to £110,000

$$ROCE = \frac{Operating\ Profit}{Sales} \times 100\% \quad \textbf{X} \quad \frac{Sales}{NAE}$$

$$= \frac{£110,000}{£1,010,000} \times 100\% \quad \textbf{X} \quad \frac{£1,010,000}{£500,000}$$

$$= 11\% \qquad\qquad \textbf{X} \qquad 2$$

$$= 22\%$$

As far as eliminating costs are concerned, motivate waste-reduction activities by demonstrating the substantial impact on profit margins (and therefore ROCE) of a relatively small saving in cost.

Using the figures as before:

Sales are £1,000,000 and as your Operating Profit is £100,000 your costs must be £900,000.

If you can reduce your costs by 3% (£27,000) then Operating Profit increases to £127,000.

Your calculation of ROCE then becomes:

$$\text{ROCE} = \frac{\text{Operating Profit}}{\text{Sales}} \times 100\% \quad \textbf{X} \quad \frac{\text{Sales}}{\text{NAE}}$$

$$= \frac{£127,000}{£1,000,000} \times 100\% \quad \textbf{X} \quad \frac{£1,000,000}{£500,000}$$

$$= 12.7\% \quad\quad\quad\quad \textbf{X} \quad 2$$

$$= 25.4\%$$

Mastering the Asset Turn

This ratio measures how well you are 'working' your assets to generate sales. Once again there are two ways to improve your Asset Turn.

One is to increase Sales without proportionately increasing your investment in Fixed Assets and Working Capital.

The other is to maintain your value of Sales whilst releasing unnecessary investment in the business by rationalising those Fixed Assets and squeezing that *Working Capital cycle*.

The benefits to be derived from increasing your Sales have been referred to above. Now consider how to challenge that investment.

Fixed Assets

Fixed Assets are purchased through the *CAPEX* decision and are frequently justified on the basis of the additional sales they will bring to the business. Therefore the relationship between the 'offering' of capability made to the market through the investment in Fixed Assets and the success that brings in terms of winning orders for the business is tracked through the Fixed Asset Turn.

$$\text{Fixed Asset Turn} = \frac{\text{Sales}}{\text{Fixed Assets}}$$

To master this ratio you need to make sure that your business gets the CAPEX decision right (see Chapter 8) and then markets this capability successfully.

Working Capital
The ratios used to scrutinise Working Capital will vary between businesses but typically you will find:

$$\frac{\text{Working Capital*}}{\text{Sales}} \times 100\%$$

*This will usually exclude Cash

The aim is to reduce this % by mastering its constituent parts of Inventory, Receivables and Payables.

Inventory
Inventory investment is usually expressed as a number of days' inventory or through inventory turns – i.e. the number of times the inventory is 'turned' in a year.

$$\frac{\text{Inventory}}{\text{Average daily Sales}} = \text{No. days inventory}$$

[*Note* that as it is unlikely that your inventory will be held in exactly the right proportions for your sales, this will not be the number of days you could survive if you 'turned the tap off' and stopped all deliveries from suppliers.]

Some businesses will calculate average daily sales looking backwards, whilst others will make the ratio more meaningful by looking forwards using the sales forecast.

Instead of using average daily Sales, some businesses may try to make the absolute figure more realistic by using average daily Cost of Sales which also removes the susceptibility of the ratio to changes in pricing, and alleviates the impact of changes in the sales mix.

Inventory turn, the number of times stock is 'turned over' in a year is:

$$\frac{365*}{\text{No. days inventory}}$$

*Some companies use the number of working days per annum.

If appropriate these ratios may be analysed further into different categories of inventory e.g. raw materials, work-in-progress (WIP) and finished goods.

Inventory ties money up and brings risk to the business.
Check how the inventory ratio is calculated in your business. Remember you want inventory days to be going down or inventory turn going up!
You don't master inventory by focusing on inventory values. The amount of inventory you're holding is a consequence of the way you've designed and organised production of your products or services. The only reason for holding inventory is that without it you are unable to meet your customers' needs in an acceptable timescale.
Therefore, the faster you can move through the process of bringing in materials and then getting them out through the door as finished goods or services to satisfy a customer order the better.

Receivables
Receivables investment is usually measured in "debtor days". Remember that even when your goods and services have been invoiced and sold to your customers, there's no real financial benefit to you until you've collected the cash. The extent to which you are mastering this last step of the cash-generating Working Capital cycle is calculated as follows:

$$\text{Debtor Days} = \frac{\text{Receivables}}{\text{Average Daily Sales}}$$

As the receivables figure relates to sales that have already been made, the appropriate sales figure to use here is one that looks backwards rather than forwards.

Your aim is to have the lowest number of days you can.

Further information is usually provided in the form of an "Aged Receivables Report" which analyses the total receivables figures into the value of invoices that are not yet due and those that are overdue.

Overdues are then analysed according to the extent to which payment is late – e.g. under 30 days, 30-60 days, 60 days+.

To comply with the principle of prudency (see p.26) businesses have to make a provision for "bad debts" covering those invoices over which there is some uncertainty that payment will eventually be made. This may be done by providing for all invoices overdue by, say, 60 days.

Whilst making a provision effectively 'writes off' these debts as far as valuing assets for the Balance Sheet is concerned, this is merely a question of prudency – there should never be any question over your continued determination to be paid!

For further pointers on how to master the collection of debts see p.58.

Payables

Payables allows you to finance some of your inventory (and possibly even your receivables) using your suppliers' money. To monitor the extent to which you are using the credit negotiated with your supply chain, you can calculate your Creditor Days:

$$\text{Creditor Days} = \frac{\text{Payables}}{\text{Average Daily Purchases}}$$

This rather broad brush ratio may be of limited use if credit terms vary between suppliers.

There are many variants of these Working Capital ratios.

To master them, understand how they are calculated and the influence your actions have on them. Make sure the ratios are calculated on a consistent basis and then assess your success by looking at the trend rather than the absolutes.

***

Liquidity Ratios

Liquidity is about having enough cash when you need it. A "liquid" asset is cash or something that can be turned into cash quickly.

Text book ratios include the following:

Current Ratio

$$\frac{\text{Current Assets}}{\text{Current Liabilities}} = \frac{\text{Inventory + Receivables + Cash}}{\text{Trade Creditors* and other short-term debt}}$$

*Amounts owed to suppliers

This calculates the 'cover' provided by the *Current Assets* for the short-term debts as shown in the *Current Liabilities*.

Acid Test Ratio

$$\frac{\text{Current Assets − Inventory}}{\text{Current Liabilities}}$$

This more stringent measure excludes inventory on the grounds that it is not considered to be a liquid asset as it takes time firstly to turn it into a saleable item and secondly for the invoice to progress through receivables and arrive eventually as cash.

For liquidity measures to have any meaning, you have to understand the nature of the business and the 'timescales' attached to each part of the Working Capital flow.

Inventory may be a liquid asset to a retailer with rapid turnover on their shelves and where customers pay in cash but not to a business with lengthy contracts on which there are no stage-payments.

Receivables may be considered to be a liquid asset if typical credit terms to customers are a matter of days but not if they are a matter of months.

When looking at the Current Liabilities the important point to ascertain is when these debts will fall due. Your material suppliers may have negotiated to give you 60 days credit but some of those other debts may have very different terms.

Use your knowledge to answer the key question.

Does your business have, or will it have, sufficient cash to meet its obligations as and when they fall due?

***

Gearing

Gearing provides an assessment of financial risk by measuring the proportion of long-term funding provided by lenders (Loans) against that provided by shareholders. The amount provided by the shareholders, known as Net Worth or Shareholders' Funds, comprises both the Share Capital and the Reserves (i.e. profits left over for shareholders that have been reinvested back into the business rather than taken out as dividends) – see p.23.

Gearing is calculated in a number of ways including:

$$\frac{\text{Loans}}{\text{Net Worth}}$$

or:

$$\frac{\text{Loans}}{\text{Net Capital Employed *}}$$

* i.e. Net Worth plus Loans

In both cases, the higher the gearing the greater the financial risk as loans have to be serviced (i.e. interest paid) regardless of how well the business has performed whereas shareholders, as the owners and hence risk-takers, have no such guarantees (see p.12).

Of course if you can organise your business so that you can continue to keep the customer happy whilst driving excess investment out of your Fixed Assets and Working Capital, you're going to be able to reduce the amount of long-term funding you need.

If you do this by repaying some of your loans you'll not only reduce that gearing but also reduce your interest costs thereby improving your profit.

Take a look again at all those fixed assets and working capital. Are you sure there's nothing else you can 'squeeze'?

**

Earnings per share (EPS)

The shareholders own the business and therefore earn whatever is left over after all the business costs have been met. This figure is referred to as Earnings. (Some of these earnings will be taken out as dividends with the rest being reserved for reinvestment back into the business.)

$$\text{Earnings Per Share} = \frac{\text{Earnings}}{\text{No. of shares}}$$

EPS therefore reflects the 'profit' earned on each share and will be used by shareholders to assess the performance of the business in using their investment effectively.

To improve the earnings you need to maximise your sales, whilst minimising both your operational and, (by minimising the amount of investment you need to finance those fixed assets and working capital,) your financing costs.

To do this you need to:

- make sure you understand your customers' needs and that you design your offering to meet those needs. No more and no less;
- ensure you attract as much revenue as you can from meeting those needs;
- align your business capability with the market so that you produce your goods or services at a minimum cost; (see Appendix 3, Fixed Assets.)
- maximise the speed through which products or services flow through that capability; (see Appendix 4, Working Capital.)
- have a 'right first time' approach that minimises wasted time and materials.

**

Measures of Performance

You might be in business to make money, but that doesn't mean that every performance measure needs to have a £ note attached to it.

Making money is about supplying goods and services to the market at a price that exceeds the business costs.

All the costs, including financing costs.

So it's quite simple. You want to sell as much as you can at minimum cost and with minimum investment, and internal measures of performance need to monitor how you well you are doing this.

What should you measure to become more competitive?

Imagine you've decided to enter a marathon and before embarking on a challenging fitness programme, you go to your doctor for a health-check. You are a mass of complex biological processes. The doctor cannot possibly measure everything so he selects a key group of measures to assess how fit you are now and what areas you can work on to improve your fitness and hence your competitiveness. He might measure blood pressure, cholesterol levels, do a simple blood test, check your BMI ...

It's just the same with companies.

Look at your business. There is a mass of activities going on and it would be crazy to try to measure everything. So you need to find a balanced group of measures that can 'paint the picture' of what is going on, tell you how you are performing, indicate opportunities for improvement and provide an early warning when things start to go awry.

This is where internal measures of performance (MOPS), often referred to as Key Performance Indicators (KPIs) or "metrics", come in. Ever mindful of the need to eliminate unnecessary costs to the business they should use data that is easily captured, be simple to calculate, provide rapid feedback and be readily understood. Visual displays such as graphs can help.

Some of these metrics will be obviously financial, whilst others may not appear to be so. Look again. You should be able to find the link.

Every metric should be capturing an aspect of your business' performance in doing more with less. And that's how you make money.

However, just as you should be careful what you wish for, you should be careful what you measure.

You get what you measure. What gets measured gets managed.

So not only do you need to check that you're measuring the right things, you also need to ensure a holistic approach to improving your performance.

Go back to the example of your preparations for the marathon. If the doctor told you that the only thing preventing you from putting in a world-class performance was that you needed to lose weight, what would happen? You'd just focus on shedding those kilograms to the detriment of other aspects of your training regime and end up less competitive than when you started.

It's just the same with metrics.

If you measure someone just on their ability to say reduce inventory levels they'll achieve them – but you'll probably have some aggrieved customers when, with shortages, you fail to deliver on time.

Measure solely on on-time delivery and you'll need another warehouse to store products on a just-in-case basis.

Push for purchasing savings and you'll end up with stacks of surplus materials bought in bulk at 'bargain prices'.

Select your metrics carefully to achieve that balance.

And once you've chosen those metrics make sure you communicate clearly to everyone how the decisions they take contribute to each of the measures. So if, for example, you're measuring inventory turn you need to make clear that that's not just down to the people in operations; others including designers and the teams in sales and purchasing all have roles to play.

Some businesses follow this up to the extent of having a series of departmental or even personal metrics cascaded down from the 'top-level' business metrics through a process called "policy deployment". In this instance whilst the despatch manager's contribution to improving inventory turn might be assessed by measuring the average time taken to ship finished products, the salesperson's metrics may include a measure of the reliability of their sales forecasts.

6. BUDGETING

INTRODUCTION

What is it about the word "budget" that causes people to panic?

Rather than being delighted on receiving the news that they're now going to be responsible for setting and managing their own budget, many feel overwhelmed and ill-equipped for doing so.

Forget the budget for a moment. Can you plan your activities and those for the people around you and monitor how you're all doing, taking corrective action where required? Then you've already mastered the difficult part of the task. The only bit you're missing is attaching a financial valuation to those plans – and that's the easy part.

All budgeting and budgetary control involves is preparing plans, attaching £ notes to them, using information prepared by your accountant on a regular basis (usually monthly) to check your progress against those plans and taking any appropriate corrective action.

THE BIG PLAN

It's important that the budgeting process starts at the top level with a 'team plan'.

A football club may have the 11 most talented individuals on the pitch but, without agreement on the goalmouth into which the team are intending to shoot, the tactics they're going to use and the position each player is going to play, they will not end up with the best team performance.

It's just the same in your business. You may have the best sales people in the world, an outstanding production team, expert buyers and a design capability second to none. But if there's not a clear understanding of the market opportunity the business is targeting, the products or services that are to be designed to meet those needs and how these are to be produced, there will be chaos.

Salespeople will sell anything and make promises to customers that can't possibly be met.

Designers will come up with fantastic products for which there are no markets (or markets in which the value placed on the product or service is far less than the costs that would be incurred in producing them).

Buyers will bring in large quantities of materials on which they have negotiated fantastic discounts – but that nobody actually needs.

And as for those in production? Caught in the middle with customers screaming for products or services that at best can't be delivered in the timescale promised (and at worst don't exist) they'll just keep making anything (and often on overtime) just to hit those production targets.

There has to be a better way.

It starts at the top. Your business exists to make money. How are you going to do that? Businesses need to understand their markets so that they can identify the opportunities that they're going to exploit. Making money means you need to sell products or services into markets where the value customers place on having their needs met exceeds the cost you're going to incur in making them.

This needs careful planning and there need to be timescales attached to these plans. Most businesses will make detailed plans for the next financial year but these should be an integrated part of a longer-term vision ensuring the seeds are sown for future years where appropriate by, for example, investing in research, developing new markets and investing in new technology.

The next step is to identify the limiting factor. In most companies this is the amount of business you believe you can win – i.e. the sales forecast. In some instances the limiting factor may be something else, for example, the availability of personnel with a particular skill, the ability to source certain raw materials or the capacity of the equipment.

(While this limiting factor might constrain the business' ability to make money in the short-term, it should feature right at the top of the 'to-do' list as it identifies what is holding the business back.

Opportunities should be sought to shift the constraint to the right by, for example, identifying new markets, cross-training, redesigning products or services and *CAPEX*.)

Now the top-level plan is in place it needs to be cascaded down through the business so that everyone can work what out what they will need to do (and therefore how much it will cost) to achieve their part of the plan. As there will only be limited resources available, this needs to be done in a way that tries to ensure that resources are allocated in the best interests of the business.

That's where the budgets come in.

MAKING IT WORK

Once all budget holders have worked out how they are going to achieve their part of the plan and therefore the budgets they will require, these budgets are then added up to see what 'the numbers' would look like if the plan were achieved and therefore whether the plan is acceptable.

To do this a forecast Profit and Loss Account, Balance Sheet and Cash Flow Statement are prepared together with forecast key ratios. Almost inevitably the result will be unacceptable on the first attempt so budgets will need to be re-examined and the process repeated until the plan is acceptable and the budgets can be approved. Even then there may be a further iterative loop to pass through if the final forecast has to be signed off by a higher authority such as head office.

These revisions to budgets can be fraught with difficulty if either due to the pressure of time or a general lack of co-operation from budget-holders, accountants end up slashing budgets to 'fix' the numbers.

Inconsistencies result where, for example, sales forecasts are maintained whilst packaging costs are cut without any rationale as to how such savings are to be made.

A complete lack of ownership then follows making budgetary control difficult to enforce. And next year, budget holders, wary of a repeat of indiscriminate budget-chopping, pad their budgets in anticipation and the process degenerates into a game of poker rather than a rational attempt to allocate scarce resources to where they can be used most effectively.

Once the forecast is agreed the process of budgetary control can begin. Actual expenditure is measured against the budget to check progress against the plan. Where spending is not in line with the plan, there needs to be action. This may be to carry out 'corrective action' to get back in line with the budget or to send a message up the line to say that the plan needs to be revised.

MASTERING YOUR BUDGET
Setting the budget
All too often there is a tendency to work back-to-front with a 'This is what I want, this is what I'm going to do with it, therefore this is what you'll get' mentality. Start at the beginning, not the end.

Step 1: The reason you need a budget is that you have a role to play in achieving the team plan. There is a job for you to do. Understand what that job is, the level of performance required, and the timescale in which it needs to be achieved.
Step 2: Use your expertise to examine the options and then decide what is the most appropriate way of achieving your part of the plan.
Step 3: List down the resources you'll need: people, services, equipment, materials...
Step 4: Attach financial values to that list – and the accountant should be well-equipped to help you with this stage.

It's helpful, once you've prepared your budget, to have a session with someone who will challenge what you've come up with – not to be difficult but to give you the chance to reflect on the process and ensure you can justify the assumptions and choices you have made. A fresh pair of eyes might also spot that glaring omission or inconsistency.

Note that the more thought you've put into the process the better you are able to defend yourself in the face of budget cuts as you can demonstrate the clear link between inputs and outputs and therefore the logical consequence of reducing the resources made available to you.

Here's a list of some other Dos and Don'ts.
Don't pad your budget to give yourself an easy life. Budgeting is about allocating scarce resources in the optimum way to maximise the long-

term financial performance of the business. So don't hog resources that could have been used profitably elsewhere.

Do be clear about the assumptions you have made. This will allow those reviewing your budget to make sure these are consistent throughout the business (e.g. if you've budgeted to invest in new equipment, someone needs to budget for the maintenance costs, additional supplies etc.) and will help you later in explaining your under or overspends.

Don't underestimate the importance of the task. Caught in the hurly burly of day-to-day affairs, looking so far ahead may seem an inappropriate use of your time. It isn't. If the business is to move ahead in a co-ordinated and controlled manner there needs to be a clearly-communicated plan to avoid people working frantically but, because they're unwittingly pulling against each other, getting nowhere.

Do involve those around you. The more people involved in drawing up the plans, the greater the commitment.

Don't make it an annual event. Keep a budget log (see below) and keep looking 12 months ahead. It's easier to keep adjusting the plan rather than starting with a piece of blank paper once a year however …

Don't do a 'last year plus inflation' budget. The budget is about the future not the past. An understanding of the costs you've incurred this year can help you plan for the future but the one thing you know for certain about next year is that it will be different.

Don't leave it to accountants!

And even when that budget has been agreed and signed off…

Don't file it away because you now have the task of …

Controlling the numbers

Your budget sets out the resources that have been agreed you need to fulfil your part of the team plan. Resources are limited so it's important you use the ones made available to you as effectively as possible.

A budget is not a licence to spend! If you can achieve the tasks required of you with fewer resources than you thought you'd need, all the better. That creates the opportunity for the business to go ahead with other proposals that had previously been deferred for want of adequate resources.

The more thought you put into your planning and budgeting, the easier it will be to monitor how you're doing and understand reported savings and overspends. These reports should not throw up any surprises if you're in control of what you're doing and keep an eye on the plan. You should know whether a task is taking more or less time than forecast; you know at the point of authorisation whether an item of expenditure is more expensive or cheaper than planned.

Only costs for which you are responsible and can control should be on your budget. The accountant may apportion costs across the business for other reasons (e.g. costing) but that should not happen for the purpose of budgetary control.

As you go along, keep a diary or budget log in which you note down significant abnormal activities or unexpected 'one-off' costs. This will help you understand your costs and therefore improve the quality of your forecasting.

Inevitably all will not go exactly to plan. So you have to act. There's no point having a plan and monitoring your progress against that plan if it doesn't result in any actions. Firstly check whether the saving or overspend is just a matter of timing. If so, make sure that those co-ordinating the financial results understand this. Where there are deliverable savings flag up the opportunity to use those resources elsewhere. Don't assume you have the 'right' to use them to cross-subsidise an overspend on one of your other budgets or on a 'pet project'. Where there is an irretrievable overspend this needs drawing to the attention of the accountant who will need to make revisions to their forecast.

Budgets are set to optimally allocate scarce resources at a point in time and needs change. It's helpful if you have the type of business culture where budget-holders get together on a regular basis to update each other on how they're doing so that resources can be re-allocated if necessary in the best-interests of the business. If for instance energy prices rise faster than anticipated and the site manager is faced with an unavoidable major overspend, there may be actions others can take to alleviate the situation. The sales manager may decide they could delay the appointment of a new administrator for a month thereby saving salary costs. The maintenance manager may postpone the plan to bring in decorators to re-paint the canteen. And the human resources manager could immediately launch an energy-saving initiative.

7. COSTING

INTRODUCTION

You're in business to make money.

To do this you need to be selling your products or services for more than they cost.

How do you know if you're doing this? You have invoices that tell you how much your customer values what you are doing – but what about your costs?

All businesses do this:

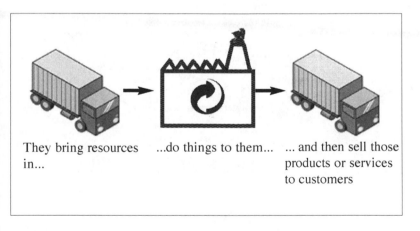

They bring resources in...   ...do things to them...   ... and then sell those products or services to customers

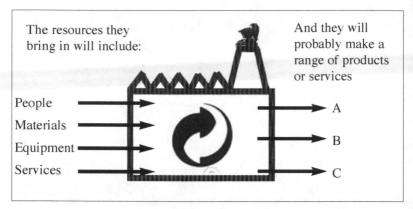

The resources they bring in will include:

And they will probably make a range of products or services

People
Materials
Equipment
Services

A
B
C

But which resources were required to make each product or service?

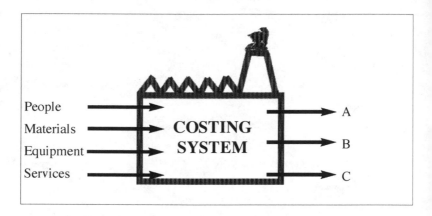

People
Materials
Equipment
Services

COSTING SYSTEM

A
B
C

The logic-link put in place to match resources to outputs is the costing system.

UNDERSTANDING YOUR COSTS IS CRITICAL TO UNDERSTANDING YOUR BUSINESS

You use costing information to determine product margins and therefore whether individual products or services are 'good' or 'bad' for business. This drives marketing decisions such as encouraging your sales team to identify more market opportunities for profitable lines whilst cutting 'loss-makers' from your portfolio

If you're looking for ways to improve your profits by driving down your costs you need to understand where those costs are being incurred and be able to measure whether your actions have had the desired effect.

You also want to be able to weigh-up the costs of operational choices available to you; for example, do you continue to do a task in-house or do you outsource?

Where do you look for the information for these types of decisions? All too often it is assumed that it is readily available and can be lifted directly from the costing system. After all, when you report your product or service costs so accurately (often to several decimal places) they must be correct... mustn't they?

The harsh reality is that cost information is a matter of professional judgement. Give 12 highly qualified accountants the task of costing one of your products or services through the business and they will come up with 12 different correct answers. All of these answers would pass the audit test. Not only would the 12 answers differ, but also it is highly probable that none of them would be relevant in assisting you with the decision you are trying to take.

It is therefore important that you understand the basis of any cost information provided and can adjust it, where appropriate, to suit the purpose for which you intend to use it.

It is worth noting that one of the things you rarely use your costing information for is pricing. Few businesses are able to price their products or services on a 'cost-plus' basis. The market sets the price based on the value it places on your offering. Having therefore made sure that your customers maximise their perception of the value offered (not just of the more obvious product or service attributes but also your excellent quality, reliable on-time delivery etc.) you then price at the highest level you can and still win the business.

But not any business
You do need to have an understanding of your costs to know when to walk away from the table and decline to bid – or, for strategic reasons,

take on unprofitable work while understanding the financial impact it will have on your business.

REPORTING COSTS
External reporting

External reporting requires the compilation of "attributable cost" to measure against the value of sales in determining profit in the Profit & Loss Account (see p.38).

The difference between the total costs the business has incurred and those that have 'left' the business through the Profit and Loss Account will be the value of inventory that is shown on the Balance Sheet.

As external reports require stock to be valued at the total cost incurred in bringing it to its current condition (i.e. as raw material, WIP or finished goods) both the Profit and Loss figure for attributable cost and the Balance Sheet value of inventory are usually calculated using an "overhead absorption costing" system. In such systems product or service costs include material and labour together with overhead costs such as supervisory salaries, electricity, depreciation and rent that are 'loaded' on to those product or service costs through the use of cost rates (see below).

[In businesses with internal costing systems where products or services costs just include the costs of material and labour, rather than having to introduce a second parallel costing system, if the overhead element of the inventory value is relatively small or can be confidently estimated, auditors may be satisfied with a reasoned uplift to be added to the internal cost to allow for the overhead.]

In financial reports, costs should be at 'actual' so if your business uses a standard costing system (see Appendix 8) an adjustment will have to be made to bring those standard, or predicted, costs back to actuals.

Internal Reporting

Whereas there are rules for the compilation of costing information for external reporting, no such rules apply for internal reports. The purpose of internal reporting is to provide colleagues with useful information to help inform them in their decision-making. Some businesses will use the same approach for both external and internal reporting. Others will choose to 'cut and dice' the data in a different way.

The job of the costing system is to mirror the reality of what is going on in the business by reflecting the resources required to make each product or deliver each service. Look back at that diagram on p.82.

There are no two businesses that bring in identical resources and do exactly the same things to them in exactly the same way so as to produce exactly the same products. Therefore no two businesses should have identical costing systems.

But there are common approaches used some of which are explained in the next section.

COSTING TECHNIQUES

Look back at the diagram on p.82 showing the costing system as the logic-link between the resources brought into the business (i.e. the costs incurred) and the products or services that you are in business to make.

The logic-link you choose will determine which of those resources are deemed to have 'gone out of the business on the back of a lorry to the customer' (i.e. have been sold) and the ones that remain in the business as inventory. The technique chosen will also determine the way in which cost information is reported.

Take a look at some of the different kinds of resources coming into the business:

- Direct Materials
- Direct Labour
- Production Overheads
  e.g. production supervisors' and managers' salaries, utilities, depreciation of equipment, rent and rates
- Other Costs (often referred to as SG&A – Sales and General Admin)
  e.g. sales department salaries and expenses, administration salaries and expenses

Direct materials are those that form an integral part of the products or services you are producing. For example, the flour you use in the bread you sell would be a direct material whereas the material you use to clean your ovens would not.

Direct labour are the payroll costs of the people who are seen to work on the product or perform the service rather than those carrying out supervisory or administrative functions.

Production overheads are those payroll and other costs incurred in supporting the manufacture of the product or the delivery of the service other than direct materials and direct labour.

A word of warning. This is an area fraught with localised terminology and the use of generic jargon used in unique ways. Take the wrapper off terms used in your business such as "indirect costs", "overheads" and "expenses"; then look at what's inside and you'll see where they fit in the spectrum.

As you go down the above list you can see that it becomes increasingly difficult to find an accurate way of attributing resources to products or services.

Direct materials are relatively easy to attribute. After all, you can either purchase materials specifically for a product or a contract and collect the costs this way (an approach known as "job costing") or you can have a list of the materials you need for each product or service you supply (often referred to as a "bill of materials" or BOM) and use this to cost the materials used.

Nor is direct labour too hard to deal with. You can either have people booking to a specific product or contract (job costing) or have a list of the tasks that have to be carried out to complete a product or deliver a service (often referred to in manufacturing as a "layout") and use this to cost the labour you have used.

Beyond this it gets difficult:

- How do you determine how much supervisory time was required for contract A rather than contract B?
- What about the relative cost of electricity they required?
- How much depreciation should each contract bear?
- What about rent and rates?
- How do you determine the cost of the administration support they required? What about the selling costs?

If your business wants to include these kinds of costs into the reported costs of products or services they're going to have to use some form of absorption costing whereby products or services absorb these 'non-direct' costs through the application of cost rates.

These rates are also known appropriately as burden rates as costs are 'loaded' on to the back of products or services travelling through the business on their way out to a customer.

Absorption Costing

Advocates of full absorption costing are of the opinion that all business costs (other than financing) should be attributed to the cost of products or services you supply and therefore include them all in the costing system. Those referring to their costing systems as being of the overhead absorption variety usually exclude the resources used outside production activities (i.e. those used in support activities such as selling and administration) from the costing system and write these costs off as and when they are incurred.

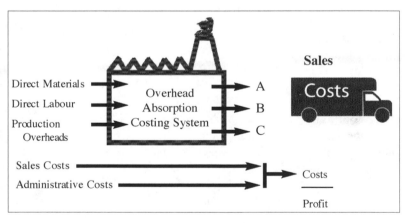

This means they are entered straight into the Profit and Loss Account as a cost of doing business in that period.

If you've ever heard accountants talk about whether a cost is "above the line" or "below the line" they'll be discussing whether it should form part of the product or service cost (i.e. be "above" and go into the costing system) or be simply written off as and when incurred (i.e. be "below" the line).

For the sake of simplicity the term overhead will be used from this point onwards to describe any 'non-direct' cost that is to be included in the costing system. Whatever the range of costs included in these overheads, you'll need some basis for absorbing them into your product or service costs.

The first step is to decide what will be your cost centres (sometimes referred to as cells). These cost centres will provide particular processes (e.g. one might do machining, another assembly) through which your products or services may pass on their way out to the customer. Not all products or services will necessarily travel through the same cost centres, neither will they necessarily place the same demands upon them.

For example, product X might need to pass through a machining, plating and assembly process; product Y just requires machining and assembly; product Z may just require assembly.

Once these cost centres have been decided, the next step is to determine the overhead costs that 'belong' to each cost centre through a process of allocation and apportionment. For example if supervisors work in specific cost centres, their payroll costs can be allocated specifically to that centre.

Not all costs are so easily allocated, however. What about your electricity bill? Unless you resort to having a meter fitted to each cost centre area you're going to have to apportion overheads on some appropriate basis. If most of the electricity costs go on heating, you might want to do this on the basis of floor area. If, however, the key determinant is the power used by machines, you may decide that an apportionment based on the horsepower of machines in each cost centre is more appropriate.

Once you've gone through all your overheads allocating and apportioning you will now have a total overhead cost for each cost centre.

You still have to find some way of passing the cost of running each cost centre on to the back of those products or services that require its capability and this is done through applying a cost rate.

By looking at the forecast you can determine the demand for each cost centre's services. You can then use this as shown below to calculate the cost rate at which overheads should be charged. Some businesses include the direct labour cost in with the overhead therefore coming up with a "labour and overhead" rate.

For example, if the result of allocating and apportioning the overhead costs shows a total overhead cost to run a cost centre of £200,000 and the forecast shows that 2,000 hours of work are scheduled to take place in that centre, the cost rate will be:

$$\frac{£200,000}{2,000 \text{ hours}} = £100 \text{ per hour}$$

For each hour of work a product or service requires in this cost centre, it will 'pick up' £100 of overhead costs.

If all goes according to plan and the overheads actually cost £200,000 and 2,000 hours of work are actually carried out, then the objective will have been met with all the overheads passed out on to the backs of products. Of course, things won't go exactly to plan and inevitably you will "under" or "over" absorb your overheads.

You "under absorb" (bad news) if you spend more than you expected and/or fail to generate 2,000 hours of work – i.e. your actual cost rate is higher than planned.

You "over absorb" (good news) if you spend less than expected and/or generate more than 2,000 hours of work – i.e. your actual cost rate is lower than that set.

In a business where there is a significant cost in managing the supply chain, one of the cost centres may be the cost of sourcing, purchasing and receiving materials. Having reached a total cost for the centre (as part of the allocation and apportionment process referred to above) this cost is usually absorbed on the basis of the value of materials purchased.

For example, if the supply chain cost is £100,000 and £1,000,000 of materials are forecast to be purchased in the year, the cost rate will be:

$$\frac{£100,000}{£1,000,000} = 10\%$$

Every material purchase will be 'marked up' by 10% to cover the overheads. This mark-up is often referred to as a handling rate.

Businesses using an overhead absorption costing system would report in a format along these lines:

	Product X		Product Y		Total
	£		£		£
Sales		800,000		200,000	1,000,000
Direct Mats.	30,000		70,000		100,000
Direct Lab.	180,000		20,000		200,000
Production Overheads	360,000		40,000		400,000
Cost of Sales		570,000		130,000	700,000
Gross Profit		230,000		70,000	300,000
Selling					85,000
Admin.					115,000
Operating Profit					£100,000

Activity Based Costing (ABC)

ABC is another form of absorption costing (usually a "full" one, including all the costs) but it approaches the establishment of cost centres from a different perspective.

Here it is argued that people do not manage costs, they manage activities that cause cost to be incurred e.g. taking orders from customers, purchasing materials, setting-up machines, running machines, packaging and delivering products. Therefore the higher the demand a product or service places on those activities, the higher should be the cost.

The first step is to identify the activities that are going to be used as cost centres.

The next step is to decide on the "key drivers" (the factors responsible for determining the level of demand placed on each activity.)

The "activity cost rates" are then calculated by taking the cost of the activity and dividing it by the number of times that activity is expected to be demanded in a year.

Take the example of a business that decides that one of its main activities is that of sourcing, progressing and receiving parts into the business and that products requiring lots of components should therefore pick up more of these costs than those that don't. If the costs incurred in supporting those activities bringing parts into the business is £150,000 and the number of parts brought in during the year is expected to be 7,500 then products would pick up £20 cost for every part they require.

If, instead, the number of purchase orders placed is seen to be the key driver, and it is expected that 3,000 orders will be raised, products would pick up a cost of £50 for every purchase order issued for them.

Contribution Costing

This approach sorts the costs into "variable" (those that will increase or decrease with the volume of activity) and "fixed" costs (those that will not). Variable costs would include costs such as materials, whereas rent and rates would be treated as fixed. The variable costs would go into the costing system whereas the fixed costs would not.

The difference between the selling price of an item and its variable cost is referred to as its contribution and is the amount that it can contribute to 'the pot'. The money in the pot must firstly cover the fixed costs. At the point at which this happens, the business "breaks even". The contribution from every unit sold beyond this point will therefore form the period's profit.

	Product X £	Product Y £	Total £
Sales	800,000	200,000	1,000,000
Less Variable Costs	243,750	93,750	337,500
Contribution	556,250	106,250	662,500
Fixed Costs			562,500
Operating Profit			£100,000

Lean Accounting

Lean Accounting is not about having an efficient accounting system that produces accounting information in a waste-free timely manner (although that's an aspect of "lean" that should be looked at). It is about producing relevant information to steer the business on its improvement journey – and that includes the way products and services are costed.

Any form of allocation is an anathema to the lean protagonist who would regard virtually everyone in the organisation as direct to one of the "valuestreams" (usually product or product types) running through the business – and, if this were not the case, would want to reorganise the organisational structure so that they were. The same view would be taken for virtually all other costs.

With the exception of materials, costs are seen to be the result of having taken the decision to offer that valuestream's capability to the market and therefore should be written off in the month in which they are incurred. Inventory is therefore valued at material cost only.

	Valuestream A	Valuestream B	Total
	£	£	£
Sales	800,000	200,000	1,000,000
Cost of materials used	30,000	70,000	100,000
Valuestream Costs	580,000	100,000	680,000
Valuestream Profit	190,000	30,000	220,000
Business Costs			120,000
Operating Profit			100,000

MASTERING COSTING INFORMATION
A Cautionary Note
Changing your costing system doesn't change the underlying financial performance of your business.

It may cause a 'blip' in the profit figure and your stock valuation if you rethink which costs are going to be written-off to the Profit and Loss Account and those that you will store away on the Balance Sheet until those products or services to which they've been attributed are eventually sold. But when it comes to the crunch you haven't fundamentally changed a thing. You've bought the same things for the same amount of money and sold the same things at the same prices. If you want to make more money you need to increase sales and/or reduce costs, not just reshuffle them. It's not about how you cut the cake – it is about the size of the cake you're cutting.

To master the numbers you need to critically assess the costing information available to you.

Set aside those external reports. You don't manage your business from them. Turn to the management reports. Look at the cost of your products or services and then drill down to ascertain how those costs have been compiled. Remember that your costing system is the slave not the master. Its job is to reflect what is happening in your business.

Is the information provided useful – or even remotely relevant – to the decisions you are taking?

Costing Systems Compared
Absorption systems
These systems are criticised for being not just useless, but positively misleading for most decision-making. Yet the costing information they provide may look impressively accurate. But look at where those costs came from and the 'professional judgements' that went into their compilation.

- Which costs are to be included in the system and which are to be treated as 'below-the-line'?
- How many cost centres should there be?
- How should the boundaries between cost centres be drawn?
- What data collection systems should be put in place so that costs can be allocated rather than apportioned?
- Where costs are apportioned on what basis should this be done?
- What should be used as the denominator (the item at the bottom) in calculating the cost rate – e.g. labour hours or machine hours?

The choices made determine the costing information provided.
Change the choices and the product costs change.
So don't be deceived by those decimal places. Whatever costing system you use it should 'mirror the reality' of what is going on in the business.

Absorption costing systems were used in manufacturing businesses at the start of the 20th century. Picture the reality of a factory at that time. A building stuffed with people 'turning the handle on machines'. With such a high proportion of direct costs (people and materials) any weakness in the way other costs were absorbed was unlikely to be significant.

Contrast that with businesses today. Take a look at the spectrum of your costs and determine what those proportions are now. The greater the proportion of costs to be absorbed the increased likelihood of a distorted reflection from that mirror.

But the main attack on absorption costing comes from those who cite its irrelevance to decision-making and the way it can encourage 'bad behaviour'. For instance, you want to hold the minimum amount of inventory you can whilst meeting the needs of your customers (see p.31 if you're unsure why this is).

You also get what you measure. An over-fixation on cost rates will motivate people to make sure they get 'the hours' regardless of whether customers want those jobs or not. Whilst this lowers the cost rate and therefore makes the products you do sell look cheaper, all you have really done is to hide costs away in your Balance Sheet under the disguise of unnecessary inventory.

Example:

- Customers have placed orders for 2,000 units of product;
- Each unit requires £90 material and 1 hour of work;
- Labour is paid at £10 per hour;
- Overhead costs are £200,000.

If just the 2,000 hours of work necessary to fulfil the customers' orders are done the overhead rate is:

$$\frac{£200,000}{2,000 \text{ hours}} = £100 \text{ per hour}$$

The unit product cost would therefore be:

	£
Direct Material	90
Direct Labour	10
Production Overhead	100
Product Cost	200

and there would be no inventory.

If the selling price were £250 the profit per unit would be £50.

If, however, the decision were taken to work 2,500 hours and therefore make 2,500 items the overhead rate would be:

$$\frac{£200,000}{2,500 \text{ hours}} = £80 \text{ per hour}$$

The unit product cost would therefore be:

	£
Direct Material	90
Direct Labour	10
Production Overhead	80
Product Cost	180

With a selling price of £250 the profit per unit has jumped to £70.

But is the product really more profitable?
There would now be 500 units in inventory at a value of £90,000; i.e. The business has spent £45,000 on materials (500 units x £90) and paid their workforce £5,000 (500 units x £10) to carry out work they didn't need. Add to this the £40,000 of overhead cost they've already incurred but have 'hidden away' by attaching it to items that have not yet been sold, and you have the £90,000 of inventory. What a farce!

When it comes to using costing information for decision-making get ready to 'strip down' and 'reassemble' those costs. Think about which of the costs going into those rates are relevant to the decision.

Have you ever walked through a factory and seen a state-of-the-art piece of equipment standing idle whilst an antiquated relic is crunching its way through the job? The reason? The cost rate given for using the new machine is very high and it is therefore calculated to be 'cheaper', even though it takes longer, to use the old equipment.

What a nonsense. The rate for the new equipment would include a meaty chunk of depreciation – a 'sunk' cost, one that has 'been and gone' and is therefore irrelevant in deciding which machine to use.

What about the make/buy decision? Setting aside considerations other than the purely financial (such as whether you would be in danger of setting up a future competitor or one who could cut you out and deliver direct to your customer), would it be cheaper to carry out this work at a sub-contractor rather than do it yourself?

Don't use an unadulterated absorption cost-rate for the cost comparison! Go through your costs and identify what incremental savings or additional costs you would incur if you did outsource. Unless in so-doing you can bring in other work you had previously outsourced or relieve a bottleneck in your operation that is constraining the amount you can pull through your business for your customers, you are likely to end up paying your suppliers' overheads as well as your own!

The same problem arises with quantifying the financial benefit from "improvement" activities. Assume your cost rate is £50 per hour. If you save an hour in the time it takes to make a product you won't make a cost-saving of £50 – unless you can fill that hour with productive work you would otherwise have been unable to do. After all, virtually all those costs included in the rate will still be there.

Activity Based Costing

The introduction of the ABC approach was not a panacea for all known illnesses but it did the trick of opening people's minds to the fact that there was not just one way, the traditional absorption method, to cost products. Two of the criticisms of absorption costing were that it usually failed to encompass all the business costs (therefore giving a usually false impression that somehow all those other below-the-line costs would fall proportionately across the product range) and that the way cost rates were calculated meant they failed to pick up on where one product caused 'more hassle' than another – and where there's hassle there's cost.

By covering all costs and using activities as the basis for cost rates, ABC is an interesting approach. Many criticise it as being expensive to set up and maintain and of little relevance to decision-making.

It does however have its uses. Done as an occasional rough exercise it can provide a 'health-check' on your costing system to see whether the information you're currently being provided with is substantially skewed and therefore at danger of pointing you in the wrong direction (see Appendix 9, Product Life-Cycles).

It can also help to assess the impact on costs of a proposed change in product mix by highlighting activities for which there will be increased or decreased levels of demand.

And it can trigger cost improvement activities. If, for example, the activity rates calculated show a cost of £100 to raise a purchase order, two things should happen. First there will be an attempt to reduce the number of purchase orders placed to 'avoid' the cost (of course there is no real saving to the business until the costs that go into the calculation of the activity rate are reduced as a result of the reduction in demand for the activity) and second there will be an enthusiasm to re-engineer the process to make the activity of raising a purchase order cheaper.

Contribution Costing

The obvious difficulty here is deciding which costs are variable and which are fixed for the timescale under consideration. Direct labour costs are a particularly tricky one. There will be other costs that are semi-variable, e.g. electricity and delivery vehicle costs. Therefore, it is important to know where the line has been drawn so that you can make any necessary adjustments if using this information as a starting-point for your decisions.

It could be argued that this is very useful information for some decision-making. If you know the variable (or "marginal") cost of a product or service, you know that if you can sell it at a price in excess of that cost the difference will make a positive contribution to the business' bottom line.

But that information can also be extremely dangerous in the wrong hands! Just selling products or services at a price above their variable costs isn't sufficient. Making a contribution may be enough for that incremental opportunity whereby pricing competitively (whilst not upsetting your existing customer base) you can fill short-term surplus capacity by winning an order that you might otherwise have lost; but, as a rule, you need to be taking on business that covers your fixed costs and provides sufficient profit to make the business a worthwhile venture.

(Not only that, but don't forget to think through the implications of any additional investment required on the Balance Sheet. The increased investment required in *Working Capital* when taking on additional business is often overlooked. Remember that it's not profit you're after but *profitability* – see p.62.)

If you can't sell at a price that covers all your costs and earns enough profit to make the business sustainable into the future then there's something wrong with how you've aligned your business to the market.

Perhaps full absorption costing, taken with a pinch of salt, has a role to play after all!

Lean Accounting

With all costs other than material being written-off as incurred, the internal Profit and Loss Account gives a clear statement of the financial cost of providing the capability offered to the market as a valuestream and whether the market has taken up that offering.

If the business is correctly aligned it will have been able to pull orders for the customer through the business at a price that has allowed it to recoup those costs.

There is clarity of vision here. To improve profit the business must attract more orders and/or have customers value their offering more highly and/or organise their valuestream more efficiently by eliminating waste. With no cost absorption to lead you down the wrong track, decision-making is guided by looking at the incremental financial costs and benefits to the valuestream.

8. CAPITAL EXPENDITURE APPRAISAL (CAPEX)

INTRODUCTION

Your heart sinks. You want to buy some new equipment and you've just been told that, as it is categorised as Capital Expenditure, you'll have to submit a CAPEX request. The convoluted time-consuming processes these applications go through are legendary – why is it so difficult to get approval for such expenditure?

Of course the amount of money involved is often relatively substantial for the business and therefore a significant financial commitment. But it's more than this.

Capital expenditure (the purchase of *fixed assets*) is a strategic decision. By definition it involves the purchase of an asset that will, it has been argued, bring 'value' to the business for a number of years. Your fixed assets define the capability you offer in the marketplace. When you carry out capital expenditure you lay out the way you're intending to meet market needs for many years into the future. If you get this strategic choice wrong and your competitors get it right it can kill your business.

Who do you want to pay for your capital expenditure? Ultimately, your customers. The selling price for your goods or services is almost always determined by the marketplace, not by how much it has cost you to meet those needs. So if you get the capital expenditure decision right, the market places a value on your products or services that exceeds your costs. All your costs, including the cost of the investment you've made in those fixed assets. Customers however will not pay you a premium to compensate you if you've chosen a process that is not as cost-efficient as your competitors.

Before evaluating the financials there will need to be a discussion about the strategic implications of the proposed investment to make sure it fits with the direction the business is taking. Once that has been agreed then it's time to start work on the numbers.

[*Note:* Before launching into the CAPEX process do check you need to do this. Businesses need to be pragmatic. Whilst in theory any investment that is made that will result in an asset that is of use to the business over a number of years is a fixed asset, and therefore constitutes capital expenditure, businesses will have a threshold beneath which small value purchases are treated as part of the normal running costs – i.e. "revenue" rather than "capital". This threshold will be determined by the size of the business and the emphasis placed on scrutinising proposed expenditure.]

SETTING OUT THE CASE
Don't start with the numbers, start with the story.

Why does the investment seem an attractive proposition?

Make a list of all the impacts (positive and negative) of the proposed project. The financial evaluation will be based on the "incremental" cash inflows and outflows that would result from the investment so, when drawing up this list, keep asking yourself, "What difference would this project make to the business?"

Here are some thoughts to get you started.
If the focus of your proposal is to increase sales:

- Will there be an increase in the volume of existing products or additional lines?
- Perhaps you're proposing to increase prices (or reduce warranty costs) as a result of improved quality?
- What additional equipment would you need?
- Would you need to increase the workforce who make the product or deliver the service?
- Will you need additional materials?
- Would you need to increase your salesforce and/or your marketing activities?

- What impact will it have on your packaging and distribution costs?

If the focus is around cost-saving:

- What would you need to buy?
- Where would you expect savings to be made?
- Will you need as many people, or as much overtime?
- Perhaps you won't have to use as much material or could save on the space the business occupies?

This is why CAPEX submissions should not be left to accountants!

You are the one best-placed to articulate what your proposal would involve and what it would offer. By all means run your list past colleagues to see if they can spot anything you've missed.

The next step is to quantify those incremental impacts
For example:

- "We will sell an additional 100 units of product per month."
- "We will save 20 hours of overtime each week."
  (Note the absence of £ notes at this stage!)

This is the hardest step of all in the CAPEX process.

"You can't make a silk purse out of a sow's ear."
It's a classic case of GIGO – "Garbage In Garbage Out". All the fancy financial evaluation techniques in the world can't make a sensible decision from incorrect information.

Take each item on your list in turn. Talk to those who might be able to help. Given that the nature of the investment is to spend money now to get benefits in the future there will inevitably be some uncertainty.

Allow for the personalities of those involved – some colleagues will be born optimists others cautious pessimists. Especially where the impact is significant to the decision, ask people for their 'best case' and 'worst case' scenarios as this will help you later when you're doing *sensitivity analyses*. It might help you improve the quality of the information you're given if you also remind people that the post-audit phase will provide everyone with the opportunity to re-visit their forecasts and reflect on the accuracy of the predictions they made as part of a feedback and learning process.

The final step is to express those quantified impacts in financial terms – so a helpful accountant at this stage can be invaluable!

Here's a simple example:

The designer has spent the last 6 months (and £90,000) creating a new product for the range.
The sales manager wants to make the case for bringing it to market so collects the following information:

– A pre-launch marketing campaign would be required costing £50,000 with additional advertising costs of £10,000 per annum.
– The market life for this product is expected to be 3 years with sales volumes and prices as follows:

	Units	Price(£/Unit)
Year 1	1,000	200
Year 2	2,000	180
Year 3	1,250	160

– If given approval to proceed, the company would have to buy a dedicated machine which will cost £200,000.
– The company depreciates machines over 5 years.
– The cost/unit for materials and labour is projected to be:

	Cost(£/Unit)
Year 1	110
Year 2	100
Year 3	80

– Overheads are allocated to products at 100% materials and labour

The first step is to produce a table identifying the incremental cash flows with the outflows shown in brackets.

Year	0 (Now)	1	2	3
	£	£	£	£
Design Cost				
Marketing	(50,000)			
Advertising		(10,000)	(10,000)	(10,000)
New Machine	(200,000)			
Sales Revenue		200,000	360,000	200,000
Mat/Lab Costs		(110,000)	(200,000)	(100,000)
Depreciation				
Overheads				
Cash flow	**(250,000)**	**80,000**	**150,000**	**90,000**

Note that some of the information gathered does not result in any incremental cash flows:

- Design cost – this is a "sunk cost". It has already happened; whether the project proceeds or not will make no difference so it is therefore not an 'incremental' cash flow.
- Depreciation – there is no cash flowing when depreciation is charged. The cost of buying the equipment is included as a cash outflow at the time of purchase.
- Overheads – all the incremental costs have already been included elsewhere so the accountant's allocation of existing cost is not relevant.

[*A word of warning.* When carrying out your own project appraisal, remember you are just looking for incremental cash flows. Be extremely wary of how you use any 'cost' information provided to you for this purpose. In all probability, using cost information such as cost rates lifted straight from your costing system will not give you the right answer as they will include costs that will not change regardless of whether you go ahead with your project or not – e.g. rent and rates (see Chapter 7 – Costing)]

It is important to emphasise that the evaluation techniques that follow just use the figures from that bottom line of the table, the total projected cash flows in each year. They evaluate whether it is worth proceeding with a project that would require spending £250,000 now for predicted cash inflows of £80,000 in Year 1; £150,000 in Year 2; and £90,000 in Year 3.

Note what these numbers really are – the summation of 'best estimates'. Remember the numbers generated by these techniques will only be as good as the information that was provided.

THE FINANCIAL EVALUATION

There are a number of evaluation techniques that you (or your accountant) may carry out on your proposal.

Payback

This is the simplest technique and identifies the time it would take for the project to recoup the initial outlay if all goes according to plan.

The cumulative cash inflows are calculated so that the point at which the project is forecast to recover the initial outlay can be determined.

The shorter the payback period, the more attractive the project.

Using the example from p.103:

	Net Cash Flow (NCF) £	Cumulative Net Cash Flow (Cum. NCF) £	
Year 1	80,000	80,000	
Year 2	150,000	230,000	← Payba
Year 3	90,000	320,000	

Initial Investment: £250,000

The initial outlay should be recouped in just over 2 years.

If a greater level of accuracy is required this may be done by interpolation. By the end of year 2 a further £20,000 is needed to payback the £250,000. As £90,000 is expected to flow in during year 3 the payback point would be calculated as:

Payback = 2 yrs + (£20,000/£90,000) yrs = 2.2 yrs (or 2yrs 3mths)

One of the strengths of the technique is that it is straightforward and easy to understand and interpret. Another strength is its focus on the early years. Projects involving CAPEX extend into the future often over many years. Wherever there are forecasts there is uncertainty. It is reasonable to assume the short-term is easier to predict than the long-term; so, in this respect, the shorter the payback period, the lower the risk.

But this focus on the short-term, just to the point of payback, is also the technique's major weakness.

Consider these three projects:

Project	A	B	C
	£	£	£
Initial Outlay	10,000	10,000	10,000
Net Cash Flow:			
Year 1	10,000	2,000	2,000
Year 2	–	8,000	4,000
Year 3	–	2,000	6,000
Year 4	–	1,000	8,000
Year 5	–	1,000	10,000
Payback:	1 year	2 years	2.7 years

If you select on payback period alone, you'll choose A. Aren't you tempted by B or C even if you do have to wait a little longer to recover your initial outlay? It's therefore useful to do payback alongside one of the other methods that takes into consideration all the project cash flows.

[*Note:* Payback periods and depreciation periods are not the same thing. The payback period is the time it takes to recover your initial project outlay and is part of the CAPEX decision. If the project is approved any fixed assets purchased will then be depreciated over their useful life to the business to enable profit figures to be meaningful – see Appendix 3, Fixed Assets.]

Discounted Cash Flows (DCF)
Another of the weaknesses of the simple payback calculation is that it fails to consider the 'time' value of money.

Assume interest rates are 10%. If you were given £1,000 you could invest it in the bank and at the end of a year you would have £1,100.

So if you invest £1,000 in a project that will pay back £1,000 in a year's time is that good enough?

No. You'd want to get back at least £1,100 as that is what you could have earned just putting your money in the bank. Cash received in the future is therefore not as valuable to you as cash received today.

In DCF techniques, discount factors are applied to "discount" future cash inflows to 'today's money terms' allowing a more meaningful comparison of the relative worth of cash flows over a period of time. [For an explanation of the calculation and interpretation of discount factors see Appendix 7, Discounted Cash Flows.]

The DCF techniques most commonly used are explained below.

Net Present Value (NPV)

The NPV of the project is the value to the business, in today's money terms, of proceeding with the project. The higher the NPV the more attractive the project.

The first step is to establish the discount rate the business uses. (This will reflect the average cost of the capital available to them.)

Discount tables are then used to identify the discount factors to be applied to each of the annual cash flows to determine their NPV. The total of these NPVs can then be compared with the initial outlay to determine whether the project is 'worth doing'.

If the overall NPV is positive the project is acceptable on this criterion; if it is negative it is not.

Using the example on p.103 and assuming a discount rate of 10%:

	NCF £	Discount Factor 10%	NPV £
Year 1	80,000	0.909	72,720
Year 2	150,000	0.826	123,900
Year 3	90,000	0.751	67,590
			264,210
		Initial Investment:	250,000
		Project NPV:	14,210

In this case the overall NPV is positive making the project acceptable on this basis – the business will be £14,210 'better off' if it proceeds with the project.

It's interesting that at this point people invariably get twitchy and note that "it's a bit close, isn't it?" Of course, ultimately, whether the business wins or loses from going ahead with the project will depend on the accuracy of the forecast.

The advantages of using NPV are that it allows for the time value of money and considers all the cash flows throughout the lifetime of the project.

The disadvantages are that there will inevitably be some question over the appropriate discount rate to use and that a simplistic approach of 'the highest NPV wins' gives no consideration of the differing scales of competing projects, as shown in the example below.

Project Alpha requires an initial outlay of £3,000 whereas Project Beta requires £30,000. The project cash flows (NCF) for the 4 year life of the projects are included in the table below:

	Discount Factor (10%)	ALPHA		BETA	
		NCF (£)	NPV (£)	NCF (£)	NPV(£)
Year 1	0.909	1,000	909	10,000	9,090
Year 2	0.826	1,000	826	10,000	8,260
Year 3	0.751	1,000	751	10,000	7,510
Year 4	0.683	1,000	683	10,000	6,830
			3,169		31,690
Initial Investment:			3,000		30,000
Project NPV:			169		1,690

Discounted Payback
Some businesses prefer to see the payback calculation (see p.104) carried out on discounted rather than absolute cash flows.

Using the original example and the net present values of the annual flows as shown on p.106:

	NCF £	Discount Factor 10%	NPV £	Cumulative NPV £
Year 1	80,000	0.909	72,720	72,720
Year 2	150,000	0.826	123,900	196,620
Year 3	90,000	0.751	67,590	264,210

Discounted Payback

Initial outlay: £250,000

Discounted Payback (using the interpolation method – see p.104):

2 yrs + (£53,380/£67,590) yrs = 2.8 yrs (or 2yrs 9 mths)

Internal Rate of Return (IRR)
Rather than use a specific discount rate, some businesses ask for the project's IRR. This is, in effect, the discount rate at which the project "breaks even" – i.e. where the project NPV would be zero.

As discount rates increase, future cash flows are more aggressively discounted thereby reducing the project NPV.

IRR would usually be determined by using a simple computerised application but it can also be done manually on an iterative basis or by interpolation as shown below.

Using the original example, the project has already been discounted at 10% but is now also discounted at 14%.

	NCF £	Discount Factor 10%	NPV £	Discount Factor 14%	NPV £
Year 1	80,000	0.909	72,720	0.877	70,160
Year 2	150,000	0.826	123,900	0.769	115,350
Year 3	90,000	0.751	67,590	0.675	60,750
			264,210		246,260
	Initial Investment:		250,000		250,000
	Project NPV:		4,210		(3,740)

The IRR, the rate at which the project NPV would be zero, is somewhere between the two rates and can be interpolated to be approximately 13%.

As the IRR is the break-even discount rate for the project, if the business' discount rate rises above the IRR, the future cash inflows no longer compensate for the initial outlay so the project would no longer be financially viable.The IRR therefore helps assess one of the aspects of risk – the amount by which your 'cost of money' would have to change before you would change your mind about the acceptability of the project.

The advantages of this technique are that it allows for the time value of money, it considers all the cash flows, it does not require agreement on a discount rate and can be used when comparing projects of differing scales.

The disadvantages are that the mechanisms of the technique assume that the cash inflows can be re-invested at the same rate as that generated by the underlying project and that, given that there is no consideration of scale, it could encourage the selection of lots of small projects that become difficult to manage.

Most businesses set 'hurdle rates' that projects must meet if they are to be tabled for serious consideration – e.g. the project must payback within 3 years and have an IRR in excess of 12%.

Even if a project passes these tests and is therefore 'acceptable', there will usually be limited cash available and so there will still have to be a competition to decide which projects should go ahead. Such decisions will rest on the contribution the project will make to the strategic plans, the financial returns and, remembering that there is always a weighing-up of risk against return, the relative risks involved.

MASTERING INVESTMENT APPRAISAL

The main problem with capital investment appraisal is that it's about the future. And there's always uncertainty about that. Investments like these usually require the business to 'speculate to accumulate'; to outlay cash now in the expectation of being rewarded with more than compensating cash inflows in the future.

That's a risky business. Whilst any project will carry an element of risk, some are inherently more risky than others – e.g. requiring the use of a technology that is new to the business rather than an extension of existing technology; or launching new products into new markets rather than existing products to new customers. The riskier the project the better the projected returns are going to have to be to make it an attractive proposition.

And speaking of projected returns, look back at that table of incremental cash flows on p.103.

Do you recall that comment about GIGO? The financial techniques that you've just seen only use those 4 figures at the bottom of the table to answer the question:

> "Does it make financial sense to proceed with a project that requires us to spend £250,000 now in return for a cash inflows of £80,000 in the first year then £150,000 in the second year and £90,000 in the third year?"

But where did those numbers come from?
They are the result of adding together a number of 'best guesses'.

How accurate are they going to be?
Hopefully some should be fairly definite – e.g. the cost of buying the machine as quotes should be available.
But what about the incremental sales? How accurate do your sales forecasts tend to be?
What about those incremental cost projections? Do you invariably make the margins you plan to make even on existing business?

Beware the 'spurious accuracy' that can result from throwing a few numbers into financial algorithms that, by their very nature of being merely equations, can appear to 'predict' the outcome very precisely.

There is a balance to be had between risk and return so it's helpful to understand how sensitive your proposal is to the assumptions made in coming up with those cash flows.

You've seen how relatively simple it is to run the numbers through the financial evaluation techniques so take time to run a few different scenarios (often referred to as "what ifs?") to establish how wrong you'd have to be with those best guesses before you would change your mind about whether a project is acceptable or not.

This is also helpful in establishing what are the critical aspects that are key to the success of the project to ensure they are well-managed if the project goes ahead.

When it comes to choosing the financial evaluation techniques to be used it's worth pointing out that it's a good idea for the business to use more than one method. As mentioned earlier, the techniques have strengths and weaknesses so it is helpful to get a more rounded view. Where there are competing projects, the 'rankings' resulting from the evaluations may vary according to the technique used.

Here is a simple example of three competing projects:

	A	B	C
	£k	£k	£k
Initial Outlay	**100**	**100**	**500**
Incremental Cashflows			
Year 1	70	35	0
Year 2	35	35	0
Year 3	15	35	100
Year 4	15	35	300
Year 5	15	35	300
Year 6	15	35	300
	165	210	1,000

Applying the financial techniques already explained the results are as follows:

	A	B	C
Payback	1.9yrs	2.9yrs	4.3yrs
NPV at 10%	£31,833	£52,409	£135,664
IRR	25.7%	26.4%	15.8%

The rankings are therefore:

	1st	2nd	3rd
Payback	A	B	C
NPV at 10%	C	B	A
IRR	B	A	C

No two rankings are the same!

The advantage of using a number of techniques is that you can look for 'trade-offs' – e.g. is it worth waiting an extra year for B to payback compared with A when it brings significantly more value to the business (as measured by the NPV) and has a slightly higher internal rate of return?

If you've done the financial evaluations and you don't like the answers, work out why your project is unattractive. Look back on those predictions you made that resulted in those annual cash flows on which the financial tests were carried out. Review your options.

To improve the result you'll need to:

- reduce outlays
- and/or improve cash inflows
- and/or delay outlays
- and/or expedite inflows.

If the initial outlay includes the purchase of equipment could you:

- Negotiate a better price?
- Negotiate stage payments? – weigh this up carefully if it results in a higher price.
- Lease rather than buy? – again considering any cost and risk implications.

If the benefits on offer are increased sales :

- Have you got the volumes right?
- What about the prices?

- Could you reduce the credit period to customers to get the cash in faster?
- Have you considered stage payments from customers if applicable?

Look at those other costs:

- Have you just included incrementals?
- Could you rethink design or method to reduce costs?
- Have you got the balance right between what you do yourself and what you buy in from others?
- Could you extend payment terms from your suppliers?

But do be realistic. If you're overly optimistic it will come back to bite you when the project fails to deliver those promised returns. Because if you go ahead, you should take the time at a later date to review whether the project met (or possibly exceeded) the financial expectations.

Whilst it may be difficult to accurately isolate every incremental cash flow that has happened as a result of implementing a project it's worth looking back and having an open discussion about where your predictions were sound and where they were not.

This should not be a finger-pointing exercise. Far from it. It should be an opportunity to learn from the experience to understand how it can be done even better next time.

Dictionary of Accounting Jargon

Accruals are costs that have been 'incurred' but not yet paid for but which, under the *matching principle*, must be included in the calculation of profit.
Amortisation, like *depreciation*, is a way of, for the purpose of calculating profit, spreading the cost of certain *fixed assets* over their useful life to the business.
Attributable costs are those costs associated with the products or services that have been sold – see *matching principle*.
Balance Sheet is a statement at a point in time of where the money to finance the business came from and where it is currently invested – see Chapter 2.
CAPEX is a term that often refers not just to *capital expenditure* but also the approval process – see Chapter 8.
Capital expenditure is the purchase of *fixed assets*.
Carrying amount is an alternative term for NBV.
Cash flow is the increase or decrease in the amount of cash held.
Cash Flow Statement analyses the cash flows arising from operating, financing and investment activities in the business. The statement can be used to reconcile the difference between profit and cash flow – see Chapter 4.
Consignment stock may be supplier's stock, often held on your premises, that can be called off as and when required. The stock only becomes 'yours' (and therefore your investment and your risk) as and when you need it. Conversely, your customers may require you to hold consignment stock for them.
Contribution is the difference between the selling price and the variable cost of a product or service – see p.91.
Cost of Goods Sold (COGS) is an alternative term for *Cost of Sales*.
Cost of Sales are the costs directly associated with making the products

or delivering the services that have been sold (e.g. labour, materials and running costs) - see p.35.

Cost rate is the rate applied to product or service costs to allow for overheads or shared costs – see p.89.

Creditors is an alternative name for *payables*.

Current assets is the sum invested in *inventory*, *receivables* and cash - see p.132.

Current liabilities is the money owed to others (e.g. suppliers) that is due to be paid within 12 months – see p.132.

Debtors is an alternative name for *receivables*.

Depreciation is a charge against profit each year for the cost of providing business capability through the investment in *fixed assets* – see p.128.

Discounted Cash Flow (DCF) adjusts future *cash flows* to their *net present values* by applying the relevant *discount factors* – see p.105.

Discount factors are the opposite of compound interest factors and are used to discount future money flows into their equivalents in 'today's money' – see Appendix 7.

Earnings are the profits left over for shareholders after all other costs have been met – see p.36.

Earnings Before Interest and Tax (EBIT) is another term for *operating profit*.

Earnings Before Interest, Tax, Depreciation and Amortisation (EBITDA) is calculated by adding the *depreciation* and *amortisation* charges back to *EBIT* - see p.37 and p.51.

Earnings Per Share (EPS) is a measure of performance of the shareholders' investment – see p.71.

Fixed assets are items purchased with the intention of keeping them and using them over a number of years to provide a capability to make products or deliver services.

Fixed costs are costs that do not vary with the volume of output – e.g. rent.

Gearing measures the relative proportions of capital supplied by shareholders as distinct from lenders - see p.71.

Gross Profit is the difference between the sales value and the *cost of sales* – see p.35.

Income Statement is an alternative name for the *Profit and Loss Account*.

Incremental cost is the additional or marginal cost.

Internal Rate of Return (IRR) is the discount rate at which an overall project *Net Present Value* is zero – see p.108.

Inventory is the sum of money invested in raw materials, work-in-progress (WIP) and finished goods.

Loans are sources of long-term funding for which there is a contractual obligation to make the agreed interest payments and capital repayments – see Appendix 2.

Marginal cost is the additional cost incurred and is a term often used in relation to the extra cost of producing one more unit of output – see p.97.

Matching principle is used to make the profit figure meaningful by stating that the value of sales must be compared to the costs associated with those sales regardless of whether payments for these resources (such as materials and labour) have or have not yet been made – see p.39.

Net Assets Employed (NAE) is the total investment in *fixed assets* and *working capital* – see p.13.

Net Book Value (NBV) is the value at which *fixed assets* are stated on the *Balance Sheet* being the purchase price less the cumulative *depreciation* charged to date – see p.25.

Net Capital Employed (NCE) is the amount of long-term finance invested in the business comprising share capital, reserves and loans – see p.12.

Net Current Assets is an alternative name for *working capital*.

Net Present Value (NPV) is the value of a *cash flow* in 'today's money'. Projects covering a number of years can be evaluated by applying *discount factors* to future cash flows thereby allowing for the 'time value' of those flows – see p.106.

Net worth is an alternative name for *shareholders' funds*.

Nominal value of a share is the value shown on the face of the share certificate as distinct from the current price at which shares are being bought and sold.

Non-current Assets is an alternative name for *fixed assets*.

Operating Profit is the difference between the sales value and all the business costs but before the financing costs of interest, tax and dividend – see p.35.

Overhead rate is an alternative term for *cost rate*.

Payables is the amount of money owed to suppliers for goods or services that have been received but have not yet been paid for.

Payback is the time taken for a project to recoup the initial outlay – see p.104.

Prepayments are costs that have been paid but, as their 'value' has not yet been 'received', to comply with the *matching principle*, are excluded from the calculation of profit.

Profit & Loss Account details the sales, costs and profit for the business over a specific period of time – see Chapter 3.

Profitability is a measure of the amount of profit made relative to how much had to be invested to earn that profit – see p.62.

Profit After Tax (PAT) is an alternative term for *earnings*.

Profit Before Tax (PBT) is *Operating Profit* less interest costs – see p.35.

Receivables is the amount of money owed by customers for goods or services they have received but have not yet paid for.

Reserves is a collective term for financial gains made by the business that belong to the shareholders and therefore form part of *shareholders' funds*. Included in reserves is the business' cumulative *retained profit* – see p.23.

Retained Earnings is an alternative term for *retained profit*.

Retained Profit is the profit available to reinvest back into the business after all costs have been met – see p.16.

Return On Capital Employed (ROCE) is a measure of *profitability* – see p.63.

Revenue is an alternative term for the value of invoiced sales.

Revenue expenditure is expenditure on running costs (i.e. all operating costs excluding the purchase of *fixed assets*).

Sensitivity analysis helps assess risk by recalculating proposals on a 'what if' basis to ascertain the factors that are critical to success.

Share capital comprises the number of shares in issue valued at their *nominal value*.

Shareholders' funds is the total long-term finance provided by shareholders and comprises *share capital* and *reserves* – see p.23.

Standard costs are usually set at the start of each financial year and normally reflect expected cost levels for material, labour and overhead costs – see Appendix 8.

Statement of Financial Position is an alternative name for a *Balance Sheet*.

Stock is an alternative name for *inventory*.

Total Equity is an alternative name for *shareholders' funds*.

Turnover is an alternative term for the value of invoiced sales.

Variable costs are costs that vary with the volume of output – e.g. materials.

Variance is the difference between a standard and actual cost – see p.147.

Working Capital is the net investment in *current assets* and *current liabilities*.

Working Capital Cycle is the flow of *working capital* from cash back into cash again as the business makes, delivers and sells its products or services – see Appendix 4.

Written-Down Value (WDV) is an alternative term for *NBV*.

Appendix 1

Share Capital

One of the ways to provide the business with long-term capital is to attract investors to buy shares. (With a new business these may initially be friends and relations but could eventually be the general public.)

Why does anyone buy shares?
   To make money.

How do you make money out of owning shares?
   You hope (note this important 4-letter word) to make an income from your investment when the company pays a dividend. You also hope (there it goes again) your investment will grow in value allowing you to eventually sell the shares for more than they cost.

What is the relationship between shareholders and the business? Are they, like the providers of loans, "third-party cold-blooded outsiders"? (see p.124.)
   Far from it. The shareholders own the business. When someone buys a share, what they are really buying is part ownership of that business. Of course we know that – but it is very easy to lose sight of this when working in a large organisation. Here you see your boss, and your boss' boss ... and sitting there at the top of the organisation, the Chief Exec and Board of Directors. From within the business it feels like they own it. After all, who decides whether we bid for the new contract, develop the new product or service, take people on or downsize, move work to another location? But the shareholders own the business and they

appoint the top team to run the business on their behalf.

What can the shareholders do if they don't like the decisions the board are making?

Replace them. Which explains why the board will want to keep the shareholders happy by running the business in such a way that they can deliver dividends and share price growth.

Share Price

What may individual shareholders do with their shares if they feel their investment is not performing well and are unable or unwilling to muster sufficient support to replace that top team?

Sell them.

What happens to the share price if people start to sell their shares?

It falls. A simple case of supply and demand. If more people want to buy than sell, the share price rises. If more want to sell than buy, the price falls. And what do companies become vulnerable to if their share price falls? Takeover. Because when one company buys another it doesn't buy the land, buildings, plant, equipment, inventory... although that's what it gets!- it buys the shares. Because if you own the shares you own the business. So if the share price falls the price tag for the business reduces, attracting potential predators.

So, share prices are determined purely and simply by supply and demand. But what about that statement accountants prepare called the Balance Sheet that lists the value of everything the company owns... the land, buildings, equipment, inventory...? Surely if you take that total value and divide it by the number of shares that must be the share price?

No. When you buy a share, you don't just buy a fraction of the things the company owns. What you are really buying is a share of the company's future financial performance. A share of its creativity to take the things it owns and use them to make goods or organise services and deliver them to a market and in so doing generate a stream of sales, profits and cash into the future.

Not all "assets" of the business are to be found on the Balance Sheet. For example, what do companies say time and time again is their biggest asset?

Their people. But we don't 'value' people and put them on the Balance Sheet (and perhaps interestingly therefore have to deal with the issue of how we should "depreciate" them over their useful life to the business....)

And what about the order book? When a company announces that it has won a large order what is likely to happen to the share price? It will probably go up as investors rush to buy into that future success. But nothing may yet have happened to affect the Balance Sheet. The business may not have even started to buy the necessary materials.

So, the share price is all about expectation and investors' opinions of the future financial performance of the business.

Which helps explain why share prices can be so volatile. And that volatility can create other false impressions about the financial position of the business.

You hear people say that as their company's share price is high the business must have lots of money around for salary increases and bonuses.

Not necessarily.

Take a simple example.

Alf has a great business idea. All he needs is £10,000 of capital. He approaches his friend Bert and persuades him to buy 10,000 £1 shares in the new business. Bert hands over the £10,000, Alf hands over the 10,000 share certificates and uses the £10,000 to rent some premises, buy some equipment ... and the business is up and running very successfully.

A year or so later Cecilia bumps into Bert and, having heard how well the business is doing (and knowing that Bert is about to move house and could do with releasing some cash), offers to buy the shares from Bert for £15,000. Not a bad return thinks Bert. So they shake hands and the deal is struck. The share price has risen from £1 to £1.50 but look what happens. Bert hands over the share certificates to Cecilia and Cecilia hands over the £15,000 to Bert. No extra money comes into the business. Alf just has the initial £10,000 that he has put to work in the business.

Donald dabbles in shares and he has heard on the grapevine that the business Alf is running is about to win a large order. So he offers to buy the shares from Cecilia for £2 per share. Note again what happens. Cecilia hands over the share certificates to Donald and Donald gives the £20,000 to Cecilia. The share price is now at twice its original value ... and yet there has been no increase in the share capital invested in the business.

Sadly, there is always one fall-guy in this and the large order goes dreadfully wrong. Ellie, a bit of a business-angel, who likes investing in struggling businesses offers to buy the shares from Donald for £1 each. Donald just wants out so the deal is struck. Ellie hands over the £10,000 to Donald and Donald hands her the share certificates. The share price has collapsed – and yet there is no reduction in the amount of capital invested in the business.

So, despite the dramatic headlines that accompany announcements of upswings or downturns in the stock market, increases or decreases in the value of shares do not affect the financial position of the business – what they do affect is the personal wealth of those fortunate (or unfortunate) enough to have been caught holding those bits of paper called share certificates.

[Of course, there are repercussions for the business of movements in share price. If they are rising, owners of the shares will be pleased with their investment and may be willing to put additional capital into the business should there be opportunities for growth. Banks too will be influenced in their lending decisions (and the risk they attach to them as reflected by the interest rates they charge on loans) by the confidence investors have in the future performance of the business as evidenced by the share price.]

Raising Additional Share Capital

Take the example of a business that issues 100,000 new shares. The shares have a nominal value (the value shown on the share certificate) of say £1 but will be sold at the current market price of for example £5. What will happen to the share price when the new shares are issued? Will it go up? Go down? Stay more or less the same? It can do any of these as it all depends on what the market believes the business will achieve with the additional £500,000 of capital.

As far as accounting for new share issues is concerned, share capital on the Balance Sheet is valued at its nominal value so "premiums" have to be accounted for elsewhere. In the example above cash will increase by £500,000 (top half of the Balance Sheet) but Share Capital (bottom half of the Balance Sheet), which is always shown at its nominal value, will only increase by £100,000. The problem is resolved by creating a "Share Premium Account" in which to put the £400,000 premium paid for the shares and which is included on the Balance Sheet under the heading "Reserves" (see p.23).

Appendix 2

Loans

Most businesses use loans as one of the ways to provide the long-term finance needed to support the investment in *Fixed Assets* and *Working Capital*. There's nothing wrong with borrowing money to help finance a business; most companies do just that. But there is everything wrong with borrowing too much money.

If you approach a potential lender for a loan, the first thing they will want to see is the business plan and, as businesses go to the wall not because they make a loss but because they run out of cash, they will look particularly carefully at your cash flow projections.

[If you're not sure why profit and cash flow are not the same thing take a look at Chapter 4, The Cash Flow Statement].

If they like the look of the business plan (and believe you have the managerial skills to deliver it) they may agree to lend the money.

Their business model is to make money out of lending money so they're going to be charging interest on the loan – and expecting repayment of the capital at some agreed future date.

When the business takes on a loan it signs a contract committing to make the agreed payments as and when they fall due. To make sure these terms are adhered to the lender will look for some form of security or collateral. If the business is unable to invest the money it has borrowed profitably, to generate the profits and cash to make the agreed payments, the lender may come in, sell off some of the business assets to recover the debt and there may be no business left.

This is 'third-party cold-blooded contractual money'. So borrowers need to be careful. Borrowing money increases the financial risk to the business. This shouldn't put you off borrowing money – but it should make you wary of just how much should be borrowed.

The relative proportions in which businesses are financed by loans as distinct from shareholder investment is referred to as gearing and is explained on p.71.

Appendix 3

Fixed Assets (or Non-current Assets)

What Are They?

If you make a list of all the things your business needs you'll find the items fall into two distinct categories. Some purchases are of a 'one-off' nature (e.g. equipment) whereas others are constantly consumed and replaced (e.g. materials). This appendix looks at the first category, known as Fixed Assets. These items (purchased through the Capital Expenditure process) are bought with the intention of keeping them.

[By contrast, items in the second category are purchased with the intention of pulling them through the business as fast as you can by turning them into the products or services your customers are willing to pay for. To learn more about this take a look at Appendix 4, Working Capital.]

Bought with the intention of keeping them? Why would you do this? Surely business is about buying items and selling them on at a profit?

The reason you buy fixed assets is because you're going to use them. They give you the capability of turning materials into the products or services the market wants. They provide the 'facilities', the 'processes', the 'tools to do the job'. Without them you could not make your products or deliver your services

A Strategic Choice

The authorisation process to gain approval to buy fixed assets can be extremely onerous (see Chapter 8, Capital Expenditure Appraisal). It is often assumed that this is just because items tend to be high-value. But it is more than this. When you choose your 'capability' you make a strategic decision that defines how you are going to do business. When you choose your land and buildings, you geographically locate your business. When you select equipment, you define the process you are going to use to turn materials into products or services. When you select your vehicles, you determine your distribution strategy. If you get these decisions wrong and your competitor gets them right, it can put you out of business. It is the cost to the business of getting it wrong that results in a capital expenditure appraisal process that is so challenging.

For most businesses the market sets the price for products or services based on the customer's perceived value of what is on offer. Customers care about the product or service that they receive, not about how cost-effectively their supplier has gone about their business. The customer will not pay a premium for your offering just because you choose to make it inefficiently and therefore wastefully. It is therefore up to you to keep focused on the market and continually align your business to meeting market needs in the most efficient way. You 'sell' these fixed assets to your customer in just the same way as you sell the materials you've used; both are integral aspects of the product or service they are purchasing. If you get it right, the customer will buy your products or services at a price that covers all your costs – including the cost of providing this capability.

The accountant's jargon of referring to these items as "fixed" assets may be unhelpful and misleading here. To most people 'fixed' implies something that doesn't change. This should not be the case with fixed assets and is not the impression accountants intend to convey. If there's any word that should be buzzing round businesses these days it's the word "challenge". This challenge applies to your fixed assets just as much as to anything else. As the market changes, it is important that your business continually realigns itself, looking for better ways of doing more with less. Standing still is rarely a sustainable option. It may take time and money to restructure your 'capability' but just shrugging your shoulders and making the best of a bad job is unlikely to be a realistic option.

Accounting Treatment

All accountants mean when they refer to certain assets as being "fixed" is that when they were purchased, it was believed these items would continue to bring value (in terms of a capability to make products or deliver services the market wants) to the business over a number of years and would therefore need to be accounted for differently.

If you want your profit figure to be meaningful you will want to compare the selling price for your products or services with a fair assessment of the costs that have been incurred in making them. It would therefore not be sensible to put all the cost of a fixed asset into the profit calculation in the year of purchase (and nothing into the other years that will also benefit from its use), as this would distort the results.

Profit would look dreadful in the year of purchase and artificially good for those subsequent years that were not carrying a 'fair' share of the costs. The accountant therefore spreads the cost of these fixed assets over their useful life and feeds a fair share into your business costs each year.

Take, for example, the purchase of a new piece of equipment costing £50,000 to be used to deliver a product or service (and therefore to help generate sales revenue) for the next 5 years. Rather than putting all the £50,000 cost into the calculation of profit in the first year and nothing into the following four years, the cost is spread fairly over the 5-year life of the asset and charged against profit each year as "depreciation" or "amortisation".

If the accountant used a "straight-line" method for depreciating the equipment, there would be a depreciation charge of £10,000 included as one of the business costs in each of the 5 years.

$$\frac{\text{Purchase price of equipment}}{\text{Useful life (Years)}} = \frac{£50,000}{5 \text{ years}} = £10,000 \text{ p.a.}$$

(Note that this is nothing to do with any financing decision to spread the payments for purchasing an asset over a number of years. That is a conversation about cash. Here we are talking about cost.)

As far as the Balance Sheet is concerned, fixed assets are valued at their cost less the cumulative depreciation charged to date. This "net" value is referred to as "Written-Down Value" (WDV), "Net Book Value" (NBV) or "Carrying amount".

In the case of the equipment in this example it would be valued for Balance Sheet purposes as follows:

	Year 1	Year 2	Year 3	Year 4	Year 5
	£	£	£	£	£
Cost	50,000	50,000	50,000	50,000	50,000
Cumulative Depreciation	10,000	20,000	30,000	40,000	50,000
NBV	40,000	30,000	20,000	10,000	0

For an explanation of some of the implications of the way fixed assets are accounted for and valued, see Chapter 2, Balance Sheet.

Appendix 4

Working Capital

Businesses buy in materials, spend money converting them into products or services and then sell them to their customers. Cash flows out of the business and then back in again. And, if you've got it right and can sell your products or services at a profit, the cash that eventually flows in exceeds the cash that you had to outlay.

But businesses rarely complete this process instantaneously. Unless you buy materials for cash, turn them into products or services and sell them for cash all on the same day, then at any point in time there will be money 'trapped' in your cash-to-cash cycle. And this investment, referred to as Working Capital, has to be financed.

The scale of the investment you need will depend on the way 'time' works in your business and the volume of products or services working their way round the cycle. It's helpful to look at the cycle one step at a time, starting with Cash.

The Working Capital Cycle
Cash is used to buy materials ....

that are then converted using people and other resources through work-in-progress or work-in-process (WIP) into finished goods or services.

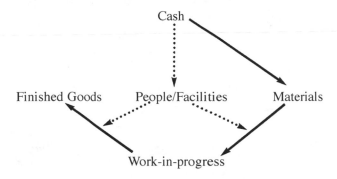

These goods or services are then delivered to customers ..

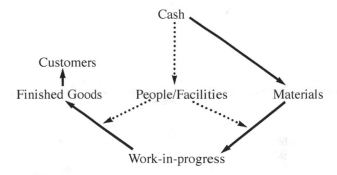

who will, after taking any agreed credit period, pay for them.

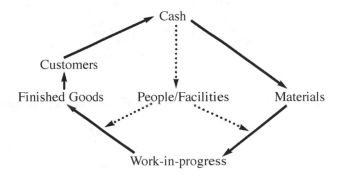

The amount of money tied up in this cycle of Cash back into Cash again is referred to by accountants as Current Assets.

For most businesses, life is fortunately not that simple as they rarely pay cash for materials. Instead, they negotiate credit from their suppliers. So a supplier delivers to the business which then runs as fast and furiously round the cycle as far as it can get ….

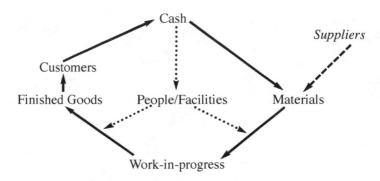

before having to pay the supplier's invoice.

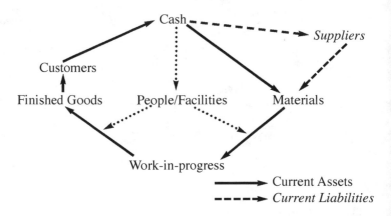

This allows the business to finance some of their Current Assets using other peoples' money. Accountants refer to such credit as Current Liabilities.

Therefore the amount of investment the business needs to find to finance the Working Capital cycle is:

Working Capital = Current Assets − Current Liabilities

(When accountants talk of "current" assets or liabilities they mean cash or things that will result in cash being received or paid out in the short-term.)

Time is Money

How much working capital the business needs is determined by time. Look back at the cycle and consider the example of a supermarket buying in some tinned beans from their supplier on 60 days credit.

No such thing as raw material or WIP, the tin goes straight on to the shelf in the store.

How long do goods sit on the shelf of a supermarket? Perhaps a couple of days. So, with 58 days left before the supermarket has to pay its suppliers, along comes the customer with his shopping trolley.

How many days credit have customers negotiated with their local supermarket? Even if they pay by cheque or credit card it is cash to the business almost straight away. What a lovely world to live in!

If only time worked the same way in all businesses …
A manufacturer of seals for the automotive sector also buys materials on 60 days credit from their suppliers. The processes the seals have to go through means that it takes about 30 days to finish the products that are then shipped out to customers who tend to pay on 30 day terms. Can you see how the business is receiving the cash for its products around the same time as it is paying its suppliers?

Then there is the manufacturer of complex components for the aerospace market. They too negotiate 60 days credit from their suppliers, but it takes about 6 months to manufacture their product so they have to finance it themselves throughout most of this time. They then deliver the components to customers who have negotiated payment terms often in excess of 120 days. Can you see the impact that 'time' has on the scale of the investment required by a business such as this?

Accounting Terminology

As far as the jargon is concerned, accountants refer to the total amount trapped in raw materials, WIP and finished goods as inventory (or stock). The amount you're waiting to receive from your customers is known as receivables (or debtors) and the amount you owe other people (e.g. suppliers) is known as payables (or creditors).

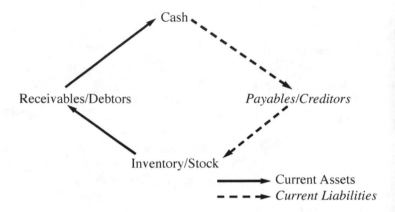

Hence the investment in working capital is:

Working Capital = (Inventory + Receivables + Cash) – Payables

Accounting Treatment

Under the accounting principle of prudency where accountants are required to take a conservative approach when valuing assets (see Chapter 2, The Balance Sheet), the components of working capital are valued as follows:

Inventory – at the <u>lower</u> of cost or net realisable value (what it could be sold for).
Receivables – at the amount believed to be collectable (i.e. excluding those invoices at risk of becoming bad debts).
Creditors – the amount owed
Cash – the sum of money in cash and at the bank.

For a more detailed explanation of the way working capital is valued and the implications of 'writing down' assets, see Chapter 2, The Balance Sheet.

Pedal Power

There is only one word on the cycle that accountants like.

Cash. Cash is king!

Accountants can do things with cash (pay people their wages and salaries, pay suppliers, pay the bank their interest, pay the taxman ...). They can't do this with anything else on the cycle. Everything else on the journey represents risk.

So how can you lure accountants to take on this risk?

There's one thing accountants like more than cash.

More cash.

If you are in business delivering a product or service on which you make a profit, every time you set out on the journey round the cycle and complete it successfully, you end up with more cash than you started with. Now you've got the accountants' attention. But there are still a few issues you'll need to focus on.

Don't stop till you get there!

There is only one step of the cycle that brings any real financial benefit to the business. The customer paying you. You invoice the customer when you ship the product or deliver the service – but all you are doing at this stage is transferring your resources into someone else's warehouse. Only when the customer pays you do you arrive at your destination. If you fail to complete this final step you may as well have saved yourself a load of time and effort and just sat in the corner of the office dropping £50 notes into the shredding machine. It's not just down to accountants to collect the cash after everyone else has moved on to getting the next contract fulfilled. You need to make sure that everyone understands that the job isn't finished until the customer pays for the work that has been done.

Don't hang around!

As soon as you move out of Cash, and embark on the hazardous journey round the cycle, you bring risk into the business. Any order commitment with your suppliers just makes this risk worse.

What if the market changes and you're caught holding money tied up in materials, goods or services that nobody wants? What if you need to modify your design? What if your customer goes out of business before he pays you?

It makes sense to plan the way you run your business so that you can whiz through the cycle as fast as you can to minimise the risk of being caught out if the circumstances change – and maximise the speed with which you can respond to opportunities such as stepping in to help a customer out when a competitor lets them down or where there is a sudden upturn in the market.

And as the faster you go round the cycle the less money you have trapped at any point in time, and as every £1 had to come from somewhere, that means lower financing costs – and therefore more profit!

Don't mess up!
Whilst it's great to think that every time you pedal around the cycle and complete it successfully you're going to generate profit and cash for the business, be honest with yourself, do you always get everything you do 'right first time'? Your customer rewards you for the things you get right; you pay the price when you get it wrong. Every time you stumble on your journey (for example by buying the wrong materials, or having to rectify work or repeat activities) you are incurring cost that your customer is not going to pay for. Again, that's akin to sitting in the office dropping £50 notes into the shredding machine. What a waste.

Appendix 5

Alternative Balance Sheet Formats

Format 1 (as used in the text – see Chapter 2)

	£	£
Fixed Assets		290,000
Working Capital		
Current Assets	285,000	
Less:		
Current Liabilities	75,000	
		210,000
Net Assets Employed		£500,000
Share Capital	48,000	
Retained Profits (or Reserves)	252,000	
Net Worth		300,000
Loans		200,000
Net Capital Employed		£500,000

Format 2

	£	£
Assets		
Non-current Assets[1]		290,000
Current Assets		285,000
Total Assets		£575,000
Equity and Liabilities		
Share Capital	48,000	
Reserves[2]	252,000	
Total Equity[3]		300,000
Loans		200,000
Current Liabilities		75,000
Total Equity and Liabilities		£575,000

Format 3

	£	£
Fixed Assets		290,000
Current Assets	285,000	
Current Liabilities	75,000	
Net Current Assets		210,000
Total Assets less Current liabilities		500,000
Loans		200,000
Net Assets		£300,000
Capital and Reserves[4]:		
Share Capital		48,000
Reserves		252,000
		£300,000

1 Another term for Fixed Assets
2 A collective term which includes Retained Profits (see p.23)
3 Another term for Net Worth or Shareholders' Funds
4 Another term for Net Worth or Shareholders' Funds

Appendix 6

Cash Flow Statement - Worked Example

Cash Flow Statement from p.50.

	£
Operating Profit	100,000
Depreciation	25,000
EBITDA	125,000
Increase in Inventory	(22,000)
Increase in Receivables	(29,000)
Increase in Payables	8,000
Cash Flow from Operating Activities	82,000
Interest Paid	(20,000)
Tax Paid	(12,000)
Capital Expenditure	(30,000)
Dividends Paid	(28,000)
Increase in Share Capital	3,000
(Decrease) in Cash	(5,000)

Overleaf is some information you'll need if you want to work through the details behind this Cash Flow Statement.

Profit and Loss Account for the Year Ended 31st December 20XX

	£
Sales	1,000,000
Cost of Sales	700,000
Gross Profit	300,000
Distribution costs	85,000
Administration expenses	115,000
Operating Profit	100,000
Interest	20,000
Profit Before Tax	80,000
Tax	16,000
Profit After Tax	64,000
Dividends	30,000
Retained Profit	34,000

Balance Sheet as at 31st December 20XX

	Previous Year		Current Year	
	£	£	£	£
Fixed Assets:				
Land and buildings		165,000		165,000
Equipment[1]		120,000		125,000
		285,000		290,000
Current Assets:				
Inventory		78,000		100,000
Receivables		151,000		180,000
Cash		10,000		5,000
		239,000		285,000
Current Liabilities:				
Trade Creditors[2]	35,000		43,000	
Interest	1,000		1,000	
Tax	12,000		16,000	
Dividend	13,000		15,000	
	61,000		75,000	
Working Capital		178,000		210,000
Net Assets Employed[3]		£463,000		£500,000
Share Capital	45,000		48,000	
Retained Profits[4]	218,000		252,000	
Net Worth		263,000		300,000
Loans		200,000		200,000
Net Capital Employed		£463,000		£500,000

1 The increase of £5,000 during the year comprises:
     – Purchase of new equipment (CAPEX) £30,000
     – Depreciation of all equipment £25,000
2 The amount owed to suppliers
3 Net Assets Employed = Fixed Assets + Working Capital
4 As this is a cumulative figure, the increase of £34,000 between the two statements
is the retained profit for the year (see Profit and Loss Account above)

The following sections will take you step-by-step through the workings behind the Cash Flow Statement shown on p139.

Cash Flow From Operating Activities

Start by working out how much cash has actually flowed in and out in arriving at the Operating Profit stage of the Profit and Loss Account (P&L).

If the sales invoiced during the period are £1,000,000 (see P&L) and receivables have increased by £29,000 (see movement on Balance Sheet from £151,000 to £180,000) then the amount of cash that has been collected from customers must be £971,000.

If the cost of the goods or services that have been sold is £700,000 (see P&L) and during this period inventory levels increased by £22,000 (from £78,000 to £100,000 as per Balance Sheet) then the cost incurred must have been £722,000. Included in the £700,000 cost is £25,000 depreciation (see footnote 1) that doesn't involve any cash flow so the cash that could potentially have been paid out for materials, labour and overhead is £697,000 (i.e. £722,000 - £25,000). If this is added to the cost of distribution and administration from the P&L of £200,000, there is a potential cash outflow of £897,000.

But if you look on the Balance Sheet you will see that the trade creditors figure increased by £8,000 (from £35,000 to £43,000). The business increased the amount of credit it was taking from its suppliers. Therefore the actual amount of cash paid out was not the £897,000 just calculated above, but £8,000 less than this, i.e. £889,000.

If you then compare the figures that you've just calculated for cash collected of £971,000 and cash paid out of £889,000 you'll have a net figure for the Cash Flow from Operating Activities of £82,000.

On the Cash Flow Statement these adjustments are encapsulated by taking EBITDA and the movements in Working Capital from the Balance Sheet.

	£
Operating Profit	100,000
Depreciation	25,000
EBITDA	125,000
Increase in Inventory	(22,000)
Increase in Receivables	(29,000)
Increase in Payables	8,000
Cash Flow from Operating Activities	82,000

Interest Paid

The interest owed at the start of the financial year is £1,000 (see Balance Sheet). During the year interest costs are £20,000 (see P&L) and £1,000 is owing at the end of the financial year (see Balance Sheet).

The amount paid is therefore:

	£
Amount owed at start of year	1,000
+ Amount charged in the year	20,000
- Amount owed at the end of the year	1,000
Amount paid	20,000

Tax Paid

The interest owed at the start of the financial year is £12,000 (see Balance Sheet). During the year tax costs are £16,000 (see P&L) and £16,000 is owing at the end of the financial year (see Balance Sheet).

The amount paid is therefore:

	£
Amount owed at start of year	12,000
+ Amount charged in the year	16,000
- Amount owed at the end of the year	16,000
Amount paid	12,000

Capital Expenditure

The amount paid for new equipment was £30,000 (see note 1 to Balance Sheet).

Dividend Paid

The dividend owed at the start of the financial year is £13,000 (see Balance Sheet). During the year dividend costs are £30,000 (see P&L) and £15,000 is owing at the end of the financial year (see Balance Sheet).

The amount paid is therefore:

	£
Amount owed at start of year	13,000
+ Amount charged in the year	30,000
- Amount owed at the end of the year	<u>15,000</u>
Amount paid	28,000

Share Capital

Share Capital increases from £45,000 to £48,000 (see Balance Sheet) raising an additional £3,000 cash.

Cash Flow

The statement balances to the £5,000 decrease in cash during the year (from £10,000 to £5,000 see Balance Sheet).

Appendix 7

Discounted Cash Flows

For the purposes of this explanation, assume interest rates are 10%.

If you were offered the choice of £1,000 now or £1,000 in a year's time which one are you going to choose? The £1,000 now – and not just because the giver might change their minds!

If you took the money now and put it in the bank you would have £1,100 by the end of the year.

So £1,000 now and £1,000 in a year's time are not worth the same to you. If on the other hand you were offered £1,000 now or £1,100 in a year's time there would be no rational reason for preferring one over the other – they would be 'worth' the same amount.

If you left the money on deposit, by the end of the second year you would have £1,210 (i.e. £1,100 + 10% or £1,100 x 110/100); the third year £1,331 (i.e. £1,210 + 10% or £1,210 x 110/100); and so on.

So if interest rates are 10% then £1,000 now or £1,331 in three years' time are worth the same amount. If you were to offer one person £1,000 and another £1,331 in three years' time you would be treating them equally.

When looking at project appraisal, instead of compounding cash flows to a future point in time, the opposite is done. By 'flipping over' the compounding factor (in this case 110/100 becomes 100/110) future cash flows are discounted back to their 'present value' – i.e. their equivalent in 'money today'. This then allows these present values to be compared with the cost of going ahead with the project (a cash outlay 'today') to

Anne Hawkins

see whether the project is financially worthwhile.

If a project offers a cash inflow of £1,000 in one year's time, that's worth the same to you as being given a cheque today for:

£1,000 x 100/110 = £909

[You know that's right because if you go into the bank today with £909 and earn 10% interest, when you check your statement in a year's time you will have £1,000.]

So £1,000 in one year's time is worth the same thing to you as being given £909 today. In other words, if interest rates are 10% then £909 is the "present value" of £1,000 in one year's time.

What about a project that rather than paying out £1,000 in one year's time, pays it out in two years' time? How much is that £1,000 worth in 'today's money terms'?

£1,000 x 100/110 x 100/110   = £ 826

Run it through your calculator to check. If you put £826 in the bank now and earn compound interest at 10% on it for two years you end up with £1,000 in your account. So if interest rates are 10%, the present value of £1,000 in two years' time is £826.

You've now established the "discount factors" to be applied to future money if interest rates are 10% :

One year's time :   1 x 100/110   = 0.909
Two year's time :   1 x 100/110 x 100/110 = 0.826

The good news is that you don't have to bash away on a calculator for hours to establish these discount factors – they're readily available in tables covering different interest rates and much longer timescales.
Just choose the rate you need and enter the factors into your calculation.

On the next page is the example from p.106.

146

	NCF	Discount Factor	NPV
	£	10%	£
Year 1	80,000	0.909	72,720
Year 2	150,000	0.826	123,900
Year 3	90,000	0.751	67,590
			264,210
		Initial Investment	250,000
		Project NPV	14,210

In Year 1, the cash inflow of £80,000 has a NPV of £72,720.
So if interest rates are 10%, the cash inflow the project will generate of
£80,000 in one year's time is equivalent to being given a cheque today
for £72,720.

Continue with the same argument for Years 2 and 3 then take a look at
that total NPV for the three years of £264,210. This tells you that going
ahead with a project that results in cash inflows of £80,000 in Year 1
then £150,000 in Year 2 and £90,000 in Year 3, is worth the same thing
as being given a cheque today for £264,210.

Would you be willing to outlay £250,000 to go ahead with a project that
would give you benefits equivalent to being given a cheque today for
£264,210?
The rational answer is yes. The business would be £14,210 'better off'
if you proceed with the project.

Appendix 8

Standard Costing

Standard costing is often used in conjunction with overhead absorption costing systems. "Standards" are set, usually at the beginning of the financial year, and are the expected or forecast costs.

There are usually:

- standard costs for the purchase price of materials;
- standard usage for that material;
- standard times for tasks to be carried out;
- standard rates at which people are to be paid to carry out those tasks;
- and a standard *overhead rate* to be applied to that work and those materials.

As with any forecast, all will not go according to plan. Actual costs incurred will not always match with those standards thereby creating "variances". Some of those variances will be favourable – e.g. purchasing materials at a cheaper price than forecast. Some will be adverse – e.g. taking longer to carry out a task than was predicted.

All actual costs are analysed into standards and variances with the inventory continuing on its journey through the business at its standard value with all the variances being 'thrown into a bucket' to be reported on separately.

The merits of such an approach are that where there are lots of different parts running through a business with the same part being used on different contracts it simplifies cost control and that the variance reports allows the management team to focus on 'exceptions'.

As external financial reports require inventory to be reported at actual rather than standard cost, an adjustment will be made to the value of inventory to include those variances that relate to costs that are still 'in the business'. Those variances that are attributed to goods or services that have been 'despatched' will adjust the cost of sales from standard to actual and will therefore be shown in the Profit and Loss Account.

(In reality, if the inventory value is low and the variances are small, this adjustment from standard to actual may not take place.)

Appendix 9

Product Life-Cyles

Here is a simplified life-cycle for a product:

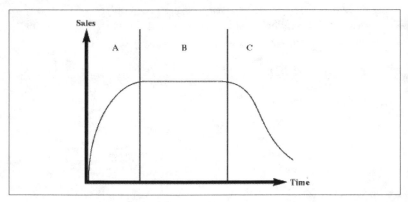

The 'A' stage, as you launch the new product, is often known as the "star"; products in the 'B' stage where you are selling in steady, relatively high volumes are spoken of as "cows"; and in the 'C' stage when demand for the product declines, products may be referred to as "dogs".

The financial performance of the business will be influenced by where your products are on that cycle.

Cash Flow
Look at the 5 levers (see p.53) that determine whether cash flows in or out of your business.

EBITDA
+ Movement in Working Capital:
    Δ Inventory
    Δ Receivables
    Δ Payables
+ <u>Capital Expenditure</u>
= Cash Flow

'A' Stage

At this 'rising star' stage profit is usually low as you have the costs of sorting out any teething problems.

Look back at that Working Capital cycle on p.45. The amount invested in the cycle will increase as you feed in cash to get the cycle turning but you will have little, if anything, back from your customers yet. And this is the time when you need to do all that capital expenditure to give yourself the capability to make the new product.

Hence cash tends to pour out of the business at this time. Businesses don't go under because they make a loss. They fail because they run out of cash.

Ironically just as everything looks great and a business is 'on the up' they're also financially extremely vulnerable.

For example, if your sales increase from £10,000 per month to £14,000 a month and credit terms to customers remain unchanged at net 60 days, an additional £8,000 cash will have to be found to finance the increase in receivables resulting from this success.

All too often businesses fail to predict the amount of cash they need to get through the 'A' stage. If they did, they would make sure they had everything organised so that they could get it through it as quickly and cost-effectively as possible (e.g. by making sure the design was sound) and also avoid taking too many products through the 'A' stage at once.

'B' Stage

Products in this stage should be your 'cash cows'. They're called cows because you ought to be able to 'milk' them to generate cash.

What do those cash levers look like now?

Profits should be high as you're now producing a proven product at a steady rate.

As the supply chain is now sorted and processes are under control inventory 'buffers' can be removed.

Credit terms with suppliers are being maintained and now that any quality and delivery issues have been resolved, payments from customers should be flowing in on a regular basis.

As for capital expenditure, there should be little other than the occasional bit of replacement kit.

Cash should be flowing in – and it's the cash from your "cows" that you need for those "stars" that are your future "cows"!

'C' Stage

You need to keep your "dogs" under control and watch those cash levers. Complexity breeds cost and if you fail to adapt your processes to those suitable for smaller volumes you may be making little, if any, profit. Even businesses that claim they "make all their money on spares" rather than original equipment because selling prices for spares are higher may be surprised by how much narrower that differential can be (see the section on costing below).

Well-managed, the investment in working capital should fall (although lemming-like, many fail to spot the edge of the precipice resulting in an initial increase in inventory as the business readjusts the supply chain to the lower levels of demand) and there should be little if any capital expenditure.

When the "dogs" stop generating cash it's time to cut their tails off.

Costing

One of the criticisms of overhead absorption costing (see p.87) is that cost rates fail to discriminate between those products that are easy to produce and those that cause disproportionate hassle.

Cost rates are averages, calculated by taking the total costs of a cost centre and dividing that by the number of hours work that the centre is expected to generate. Think about what goes into the cost of the cost centre. The costs of procurement, receiving, scheduling, supervisory payroll costs, production engineering... Does this example strike a chord with your business?

A range of products, including X and Y, travel through a cost centre that has a cost rate of £60 per hour.

Product X has been around for years. The supply chain works well. X is manufactured in a simple 'drum beat' fashion and sails through the cost centre like a dream. Each unit takes 10 minutes to machine therefore the costing system reports that it 'costs' the company £10 of overhead costs to make a unit of X.

Product Y on the other hand is a nightmare. Poorly designed and in low-demand, the material supplier struggles to produce the quality required. A group of supervisors and engineers huddle round the machine as the most skilled person on the shopfloor tries to nurse the product through the machining process. As it takes 10 minutes per unit to machine, product Y is also reported to have 'cost' the company £10 of overhead.

An extreme case. But inevitably there will be winners and losers from the costing system as a result of cross-subsidisation. Does this matter? It does if it encourages people to take the wrong decisions for the business.

'A' Stage

Products at this stage will typically be under-costed making it harder to justify the appropriate investment in up-front design and methods to make the learning curve faster and cheaper.

Setting targets for 'cost-down initiatives' and measuring whether they are achieved is difficult if the starting point isn't understood. Profit forecasts for periods of new product launch will be overstated and expectations unrealistically high.

'B' Stage

With products almost inevitably over-costed, there is a grave danger of killing off those cash-generating cows.

At this point in the life-cycle there is likely to be strong competition in the market and a downwards pressure on price. If costs are overstated this might encourage companies to pull out of what is, in reality, high-margin cash-generating business.

'C' Stage

At this stage products tend to be under-costed if costing systems fail to pick up the 'hassle' associated with managing variety. As volumes fall this becomes particularly pertinent. Processes that were well-aligned with the market at the 'B' stage might not be so for the 'C' stage and it may be appropriate to re-think how those market needs are met.

Businesses need to make sure that the market continues to pay a price that covers all the costs. Be sceptical when looking at profit margins and watch out for variations of the following:

- A customer rings up with an order for a spare part. (This is a part that, for simplicity, is brought in, re-packaged – the cost of which is to be ignored here – and then sold on.)
- The order quantity is one. The list price is £20 and, with the costing system showing that the part costs £10, a good margin appears to be being made. When the supplier is contacted he is happy to supply at a cost of £10 per unit but has a minimum order quantity of 10. The order is placed for the 10 items at a total cost of £100.
- When the item is sold on to the customer the records show a profit of £10 on the deal.
- But what about the £90 of stock now sitting on the shelf? A year later, when it is still sitting there, the accountant 'writes off' the £90 against current year profit.
- In reality there was no profit on the original order – the business made a loss of £80.

In these types of situation the commercial options need to be considered including:

- Can the price to the customer be increased?
- Can there be a minimum order quantity for our customers?

- Can the minimum order quantity from the supplier be renegotiated?
- Can we afford not to offer these types of products?

Certainly what the business should not be doing is to incentivise the sales team to aggressively sell 'one-offs' of this type – unless it's to get that potentially redundant stock off the shelf!

About the Author

Anne Hawkins started her career as an apprentice in a multinational engineering group where she qualified as an accountant. She then held senior positions in a range of sectors before starting her own training business and has developed an enviable reputation for explaining financial matters in simple terms. Passionate about her subject and the leverage to be gained by ensuring everyone in the organisation understands the financial implications of the choices they are making, Anne has also written a number of successful business books, including *Lean Means Beans* (2003), *100 Great Cost-Cutting Ideas* (2010) and is the co-writer of the *Balance Sheet Pocketbook* (2010).

Also by Leslie Scase

Fortuna's Deadly Shadow

FATAL SOLUTION

LESLIE SCASE

SEREN

Seren is the book imprint of
Poetry Wales Press Ltd,
4 Derwen Road, Bridgend, Wales, CF31 1LH

www.serenbooks.com
facebook.com/SerenBooks
Twitter: @SerenBooks

ISBN: 9781781726181
Ebook: 9781781726198

A CIP record for this title is available from the British Library.

The publisher acknowledges the financial assistance
of the Welsh Books Council.

The maps of Pontypridd and Cilfynydd from the 1890s are adaptations of
OS maps kindly provided by Pontypridd Library

Printed by Bell & Bain Ltd, Glasgow

To Rachel
The best daughter I could wish for

Pontypridd Town Centre c.1896

Pontypridd Station, Graig and Tumble Area

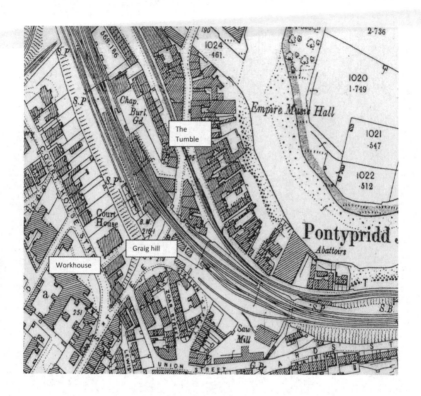

Cilfynydd
North end of the village, late 19th century

ONE

The mining village of Cilfynydd – two miles north
of Pontypridd – 23rd June 1894

George Butcher made his way reluctantly towards the pit head.
He trudged through the boggy ground, his boots collecting mud. As he felt the rain trickle down the back of his neck, he grumbled to his best friend.

'I don't know Dai, there's got to be more to life than this. Just enough to keep food in our bellies and a roof over our heads. I don't know how the married men manage.'

'Worry about that when it comes to it. You're too ugly and skinny to get married,' Dai teased. Then he became serious. 'Anyway, we can do bugger all about it. Last year's strike showed that. All we got was the risk of being cut up by the cavalry, the bastards. We can't do anything when half the mine owners are magistrates and can call in the troops.'

'Let's face it, here we are on a Saturday afternoon in the height of Summer when we should be having fun. Instead, we're going underground, to work like navvies until we go home in the middle of the night.'

'Well at least we'll be dry.'

'Too bloody dry. They haven't been watering the mine regularly and nothing is properly inspected.'

'Keep your voice down or you'll be sent home without pay.'

Other men were making their way to the pit-head ready for their afternoon shift, some to repair the underground roadway and others to clear up the dust. The great wheel was already turning, fetching the morning shift up from the bowels of the earth. Over fifteen hundred men had been working below ground, hacking coal with their mandrels; and loading the trucks pulled by sturdy, uncomplain-

ing pit ponies. There should have been a break between shifts for shot firing, the use of small explosive charges to loosen the coal seams. Today though, like so many other days, it was felt that the company could not allow the delay, due to the time already lost transporting the morning shift to the surface.

'We'll make it in the fifth cage I reckon,' guessed Dai. 'How many cages today Bert?' he asked of a workmate operating the winding mechanism.

'About thirteen, I think,' came the reply.

George nudged his friend. 'That's another thing. They've got no idea how many of us are going down or who we are. We could go missing down there and be lost for days.'

'Don't be daft, you miserable bugger. How could you get lost down there when your mates are all around you? What's the matter with you today?'

George ignored the question.

'I know,' laughed Dai. 'Sally Williams has given you the old heave-ho, hasn't she?' George's displeasure was written all over his face, which made Dai howl with laughter. 'Never mind *bach*, there's plenty more fish in the sea.'

Eventually all of the day shift had come up, skin and clothes blackened by coal dust, laughing and joking as they made their way home.

The cage started to take the afternoon shift down and the first twenty men packed inside. George and Dai were indeed in the fifth cage. As it descended, the two men glanced up to watch the sky slowly disappear from view as the cage went deeper into the dusty, claustrophobic world they would inhabit until they emerged to once again breathe fresh air.

With a resonant clang they reached the bottom of the shaft and the cage door screeched open, allowing the men to squeeze out and make their way down the narrow tunnel. The main roadway branched off at several points. The supports of each tunnel were checked: no-one wanted a roof-fall which might condemn them to a slow death by asphyxiation or a quicker one crushed by hundreds of tons of rock. George tried hard to banish such ideas from his mind. Then again, there was always the risk of explosion; and even

surviving a life in the pits gave no guarantee of a pleasant old age.

George shook himself out of his miserable reverie and followed Dai down a side tunnel, their way lit by Davy lamps. They passed underground stables for the pit ponies and George stopped for a moment to pat one and whisper gently in its ear. The animal looked back with doleful eyes before munching a mouthful of hay, content to have finished its eight-hour shift of pulling trucks along the underground rails. George caught up with Dai as the tunnel narrowed and they were forced to crouch. This was the section that they were assigned to thoroughly check by the dim light of the Davy lamps. Electric light had been fitted in the mine but the dynamo had been damaged a fortnight earlier and had not been repaired. Use of a naked flame underground was strictly forbidden, in theory, as was shot firing to clear pockets of gas when workers were present.

***

Mrs Evans was in her kitchen when the sound came. It was a slow rumble like thunder, followed by a second. Then the floor seemed to move and a plate fell from the table and shattered on the floor. For a moment her heart missed a beat. Very slowly she put down the cup she was drinking from and forced herself to remain calm, though deep inside fear gripped and would not go away. As if in a dream, she walked to the front door and opened it. Neighbours were already on the street and a wailing had started as wives, mothers and children old enough to understand, could no longer contain their emotions. Telling their children to stay indoors, the women, and the men not long returned from their shift, made their way towards the Albion Colliery.

***

The explosion came two hours into the shift. A handful of men working on the surface close to the shaft entrance heard the rumble, then the blast hurled them to the ground. In the mine's offices, manager Philip Jones was talking to the under manager, William Jones, who was also his son.

'*Iesu Mawr!*' he exclaimed, as the floor shook beneath them. The

younger man ran to the window overlooking the yard, where workers were already running towards the wheelhouse.

'It's an explosion. Quick Father, we need to get to the wheel-house.'

Soon both men were striding purposefully towards the mine shaft, their minds swept with panic at the serious impact an explosion might have on the colliery's profits. As they got nearer, one of the men ran to them, his face ashen.

'I reckon it's bad Mr Jones. The cage and the fan are damaged, but we can get them going again. Who do you want to join you in the rescue party?'

Father and son were shaken by the sudden realisation that they were expected to go underground to lead the search party. Finally, Philip Jones spoke.

'Get the cage fixed and find me as many firemen as you can. We will descend as soon as it is safe.'

As the man raced away, William Jones turned to his father. 'This will be on our heads. Everyone will hold us responsible.'

'Calm down William. We don't know what has caused the blast. It isn't our fault if the men don't look after their own safety. Lewis, the company agent, may well be held to account and I suppose some criticism might come our way. Let me worry about that. You are only the acting under manager, so I will make sure that nothing falls on you. Just pull yourself together.'

By the time the winding mechanism had been checked, workers from the day shift had begun to return. They watched as Philip Jones, William Jones, a pitman and three firemen entered the cage. The descent was painfully slow and the cage made an appalling noise as it now scraped against the sides of the shaft. Ten feet from the bottom, it came to a shuddering halt and would go no further, so ropes were lowered to allow the men to climb down. The air smelled of sulphur and they tried to cover their faces with handker-chiefs and scarves as they inspected the immediate area. The blast had thrown rocks, timbers, tram carts and other debris into the bottom of the shaft and clearing a way through became a difficult task, even with spades and crowbars. Slowly they made their way through the first hundred yards or so, where they saw the first bodies.

By then they had been below ground for some time and realised that considerable help would be needed to make further progress. By the time they were lifted to the surface, the men had been gone for two hours and concern had risen. Crowds of anxious onlookers waited for news of their workmates and loved ones. William Lewis, the company agent, arrived after the rescue party had descended and had taken charge. A second rescue party had been formed, with tools and medical provisions to help the injured. The carpenter's workshop was made ready to act as a makeshift hospital and a hayloft would be used as a temporary mortuary. Several doctors from the area had arrived and were ready to assist; and general order was maintained by police officers from Pontypridd, as the crowds continued to grow.

The second rescue party was able to move deeper into the mine, though it was badly hampered by fires from underground boilers damaged by the explosion. Soon they reached the first bodies, most badly burned and mutilated. However, they also found a number of men unconscious and injured, but nevertheless alive. News of the dead men reached the surface first, leading to wails of despondency among the large crowd, but when the second rescue team re-emerged and told of survivors, some hope returned. The Chief Constable of Glamorgan County Constabulary had arrived, together with Superintendent Jones from Pontypridd. Under their direction, the crowds were moved back to make more room for further rescue teams, which included local doctors. The sights that met the eyes of the search teams over the following hours would stay with them for the rest of their lives.

The bodies of men and boys lay strewn through the mine. Many had been mutilated by flying debris, their bodies horribly ripped and torn. Others lay as if in sleep, their internal organs smashed by the concussion from the blast, but leaving no external indication of the damage within. Some lay buried beneath tons of earth where timber roof supports had been blown away, and yet more had been asphyxiated. The rescue parties were also touched by the pitiful sight of the dead and dying pit ponies, of which there were more than a hundred.

The priority was to find and treat the few surviving men. It was

7.30 p.m. before the first survivors were brought to the surface. As they appeared, there was a great surge forward from the anxious crowd. The police cordon held firm and the injured were taken to the carpenter's shop to receive medical attention. As the cage brought up more survivors, hope sprang in the hearts of waiting relatives, but soon that was to fade. The slow procession of stretchers from the cage now started to go, not to the carpenter's shop, but to the hayloft which onlookers realised was being used as a mortuary. The crowd started to move forward again, desperate to see if their loved ones were among those brought to the surface.

Superintendent Jones raised his hands to indicate he wanted silence and made an announcement.

'We need to identify the injured men. We will select a small number to enter the hayloft and the carpenter's shop and then subsequently move on to further groups after they have finished. You will need to identify yourselves and give the name of the person for whom you are looking. Anyone trying to enter for anything other than a genuine reason will be arrested. I hope I make myself clear.'

After the Superintendent had finished speaking, small numbers were let through, and the solemn business of identification began. Inside both buildings there were scenes of despair, and ministers, vicars and the local Catholic priest tried to comfort the bereaved and the injured.

Mrs Evans was one of a group of four women let into the hayloft. Fear made her light headed as she walked forward unsteadily. There was a sudden cry of anguish next to her as young Sally Williams threw herself to the ground in tears as she recognised one of the bodies.

'Oh, George, I didn't mean to be angry with you. Oh, my love,' she cried.

Mrs Evans looked down with pity at the girl mourning her lost love, but then she saw what she had prayed she wouldn't. Lying in the hay, looking at peace, was her dear husband.

Inside the carpenter's shop most of the survivors were unconscious, though as they woke some began to scream. Suffering from burns and broken limbs, many would not make it through the night. The recovery of bodies continued for many hours and by midday

on Sunday a hundred corpses lay in the hayloft. The crowds did not disperse, rather they grew as sightseers began to arrive, having packed trains from Cardiff and then taken brakes and cabs from Pontypridd. On the Monday the hayloft was full and an initial Coroner's inquest was held at the New Inn in Pontypridd. Its purpose was for formal identification of the victims to enable warrants of internment to be issued. As bodies were taken to the inquest, the space created in the hayloft was filled with more corpses. During the proceedings it became evident that there would have to be an adjournment. The advice from the rescue parties was that it would take over two weeks to cover the whole extent of the mine; and they didn't know exactly how many bodies still needed to be recovered. The poor practices at the colliery meant there was no record of exactly how many miners had been underground, or indeed who they were. The estimates were between 250 and 290 dead, including seven of the sixteen original survivors The police were forced to issue notices asking for information on anybody who might be missing.

The legacy was one of immeasurable sorrow for the bereaved relatives, including literally hundreds of fatherless children, and a deep and lasting hatred for the colliery owners and the system that allowed such disasters to happen.

TWO

Two years later – Pontypridd, May 1896

Thomas Chard left his house on Gelliwastad Road in good humour.

It was a relatively mild February evening, a little chilly but not too uncomfortable. There was a fresh feel to the air, despite the slightly acrid smell of the smoke from coal fires that were now being lit around the town. Chard tucked his scarf inside his heavy woollen coat and waited for a carriage to pass before crossing the street. Heading in the direction of St. Catherine's Church, he anticipated passing a pleasant evening in convivial company.

It was over a year since Chard first arrived in Pontypridd as its new police inspector. From an inauspicious start, becoming embroiled in a brawl on his first night, he had through luck as much as judgement, been given credit for solving a number of serious crimes. From a disorientated English outsider in this close knit, rather strange community, he had become thoroughly assimilated.

Pontypridd, or Ponty as it was often known, had changed from not much more than a hamlet and river crossing point at the beginning of the previous century, to an industrial boomtown. Surrounded by a number of coal mines, an ironworks, steelworks and a chainworks, it was also the main market town for the Rhondda valleys. Additionally, it sat astride the main road and canal routes between Merthyr and Cardiff, and two railway networks connecting the coal producing Rhondda Valleys with the towns and ports of South Wales. There had been an influx of workers from other parts of Wales and also from England, Ireland and the continent, even as far as Eastern Europe. Some came to make their fortunes, others just to earn the basic necessities of life, something denied them in their homelands. Pontypridd was like a social experiment on a

massive scale and the area was slowly developing its own distinctive cultural identity.

Turning right past the church entrance, along a side street and over a railway bridge, it didn't take Chard long to reach the row of large, three storey houses overlooking the railway line, where his friend lived. Reminding himself of the number, Chard walked a little further and approached the front door. Seeing no bell pull gave a gentle knock. A petite woman in a navy-blue dress with a white collar opened the door. Her dark hair was arranged tidily and framed a face of unremarkable appearance, other than a pair of soulful brown eyes which Chard found rather attractive. She looked with a degree of disdain at the visitor. He was smartly dressed, of good deportment and had a pleasant demeanour, but his large sideburns and moustache she found unappealing.

'Thomas Chard to see Doctor Matthews,' he announced.

'Yes, Mr Chard, you are expected,' replied the woman. 'May I take your hat, coat and cane?'

Chard handed over his coat, scarf and new bowler hat, which he had only bought earlier that day, but declined the offer to take the cane. The woman turned and led the way down the hall where she stopped and knocked on the door, before entering.

'Mr Chard is here, Doctor Matthews.'

Chard entered the room to be greeted warmly by his host, a stout man of average height with a small waxed moustache and wavy brown hair brushed back.

'Thomas my friend, do come in and take a seat.'

'Ezekiel, it's good to see you, I was pleased to be invited tonight.'

'I see you've brought your recent purchase to show me,' said the doctor indicating the walking cane. 'I think you are probably glad to have got rid of the old one, despite its value.'

'Yes,' replied Chard. 'I returned it to the original owner. I should not have accepted it as a gift, regardless of the circumstances; and as things turned out....'

'Well, you did the right thing,' interrupted the doctor.

Chard had been given an expensive walking cane during a murder investigation the year before and although he had taken a liking to it, the circumstances made him uneasy about keeping it.

'What do you think of this one?' asked Chard handing over his new cane.

The doctor examined it, his nose twitching as he did so. It was a peculiar habit that reminded Chard of a rodent, perhaps because the little waxed moustache gave the impression of whiskers. He'd found it irritating when the men met during Chard's first case. It was only since Christmas, when they found at a social event that they shared interests, that their friendship had developed.

'Ebony and a solid brass knob handle. Weighty and quite functional I would imagine, particularly if you wanted to hit someone with it. I'll check future corpses at the mortuary just in case,' he joked.

'Well I am not going to send someone your way deliberately,' laughed Chard, 'though you are a bit short of trade.'

'True enough. My private practice is doing well but I don't feel I am earning the retainer that the police pay me. Only two suicides this year and not a sniff of a murder. Never mind though. It means I can rent this house and keep a small cottage back in my home town. You know I like to travel back to my beloved Swansea every now and then.'

'It looks very nice here, and you have acquired some help.'

'Oh, you mean my housekeeper, Mrs Murray. Yes, she came with excellent references; a widow you know, and very respectable,' he added. 'She has her own accommodation in the attic room and obviously it gives me some security knowing that the house isn't left empty when I am away.'

'Yes, that must be a relief. I don't have that reassurance, but then again I am rarely out of town.'

'How is your new residence?'

'Practical is how I would describe it. The house came up for rent on Gelliwastad Road, so it's close to the police station and within walking distance of everywhere I usually need to be. I've got a maid who comes in daily who was recommended by Gwen, so that was good enough for me.'

Gwen was the landlady of Chard's favourite public house, the Ivor Arms, and he trusted her implicitly.

'Are you thinking of settling down here permanently, perhaps

take a wife?' enquired Matthews.

Chard slightly reddened. 'The lady you saw me with over Christmas was just a dalliance, Ezekiel. I am only in my early thirties, there is no need for me to settle into married life yet.'

'Ah, I seem to have touched a raw nerve. I do apologise.'

'No need. It turned out that we weren't really suited. Ships that pass in the night and all that,' said Chard.

'Would you care for a sherry before we dine?' asked the doctor, changing the subject. He knew before asking that his guest would say yes and so began to pour from a decanter that sat on a small table next to his chair. Chard took the glass and savoured the dry fino sherry before raising a topic that would keep them engaged in intelligent conversation until dinner.

'How do you think things will develop in South Africa?'

'War once again, no doubt,' answered the doctor with conviction. 'It's been on the cards since the Jameson raid. I blame that idiot Rhodes.'

They settled into a discussion on the previous conflict with the Boers and how precariously the political situation was balanced, then moved on to the current conflict in the Sudan. Before they realised, an hour had passed, and Mrs Murray entered the parlour to announce that dinner was ready to be served.

The housekeeper produced a simple but tasty wild mushroom soup, followed by a delicious main course of roast pheasant accompanied by braised leeks and roast parsnips.

Whilst waiting for dessert the conversation turned to the subject of Mrs Murray.

'Your housekeeper certainly can cook, Ezekiel.'

Doctor Matthews smiled. 'Yes indeed, Thomas. She has a wonderful talent with herbs and makes jars of her own ingredients to flavour her dishes.'

'It's a wonder that she hasn't found another husband, or was her loss recent?' asked Chard.

'It happened two years ago. Unfortunately she lost her husband and her brother in the Albion Colliery disaster.'

'Ah, I see. It must have been terrible. When I first came here, I was warned by the Superintendent not to speak of it, as the men at

our station were involved in the aftermath and quite traumatised. I didn't really understand at first, but then last month, we had the disaster at Tylorstown.' Chard paused before continuing. 'When I witnessed the recovery of the bodies and the devastated relatives....'

'Yes, and when we think that the casualties at the Albion Colliery were far higher...'

'Did Mrs Murray at least have the comfort of the bodies being recovered?'

'Of her husband yes, but not the brother. He went missing on the morning of the disaster and never turned up, so it was assumed that as he was due to be working the shift, he must have been one of the poor souls buried underground for ever.'

'That is very sad,' commented Chard

'Yes, indeed – '

The two men abruptly ceased their conversation as Mrs Murray entered the room with two generous servings of apple pudding

No sooner had Chard taken a spoonful of the inviting dessert than the meal was interrupted by a knock at the front door. They listened to Mrs Murray walk down the hall and there followed a mumbled sound of voices. Soon the housekeeper entered the dining room to report on the interruption.

'Mr Chard, there is a police constable at the door and he says that he needs to speak to you urgently.'

With a look of disappointment Chard put down his spoon, excused himself to the doctor and made his way to the front door.

'What is it Constable Scudamore?' he asked warily.

'Sorry to interrupt you sir,' replied Scudamore. 'You mentioned to Sergeant Humphreys that you would be here if something urgent cropped up.'

'I did indeed. What is so urgent?'

'There's been a fire at a workshop in Cilfynydd. A body was found inside sir, and the circumstances are suspicious. Sergeant Humphreys thought you would want to come straight away.'

***

By the time Chard and Constable Scudamore arrived in Howell Street, Cilfynydd, the wooden workshop had virtually burned to the

ground. The light from the flickering embers revealed that the wall of the stone-built house alongside had been blackened by the blaze. Two constables stood guard, and a small number of bystanders had gathered a few dozen yards down the street.

'The fire was discovered earlier this evening when it hadn't been going long. Neighbours tried to put it out, but it caught hold fast and there was nothing they could do. The fire brigade was sent for but they arrived too late to do anything,' explained Scudamore.

'You mentioned a dead body,' prompted Chard.

'It's over there, Inspector, under that blanket. It isn't a pleasant sight.'

Chard wandered across to the blanket which lay next to a pile of charred wood, and with a degree of apprehension used his walking cane to lift up the edge of the material.

'Ugh!' he grunted when he saw what remained of the victim's upper body.

'Burnt to a crisp sir,' commented Scudamore.

'Yes, I can see that Constable. What started the fire?'

'The firemen seemed to think that it was an overturned oil lamp.'

'Well they usually know what they are talking about.'

'Yes sir, but then there were his cries for help.'

'Why, what did he say?'

'That's the point, absolutely nothing sir. His body was found right behind the door when it eventually collapsed, yet when the fire was raging there was no cry for help.'

'Perhaps he was overcome with the smoke, Constable.'

'Except as I mentioned earlier, the blaze was first spotted before it had really taken hold.'

'If he was right behind the door then one might also presume that he could have let himself out. What was the state of the door lock?'

'Badly damaged by the heat, but the firemen could tell that it had been locked. It could of course have been locked from the inside, but so far there has not been any sign of a key. Then again, in this bad light it could easily have been missed. It will have to wait until morning.'

'Who was the poor beggar?' asked Chard.

'Name of Hughes sir.'

'It was even money it would be Hughes, Evans, Davies, Williams or Jones,' muttered Chard who was frequently frustrated in his enquiries by the prevalence of certain surnames in the area, which often caused confusion. 'Let me guess, his first name is David or William,' suggested the inspector sarcastically, as they seemed to be the most popular Christian names.

'Good guess sir, it's William. He lives in the next street.'

'Any relatives?'

'A wife sir, the local minister is with her, together with a couple of neighbours. She was working at a pub in town when the blaze was reported.'

'Very well, I will leave talking to her for the moment.' Chard paused in thought before continuing. 'I want to speak with whoever reported the fire and the owner of the house next door. Afterwards, I want you to make door to door enquiries to ask if anyone saw anything suspicious. In the meantime, the corpse can be sent to the mortuary for Doctor Matthews to take a look at.'

***

Constable Scudamore knocked on the door before stepping aside for his inspector. It was opened by a pale, frail-looking man, clean shaven with unruly dark hair. The hallway was dimly lit but the houseowner recognised the uniform of Constable Scudamore behind the inspector.

'My constable tells me that you are Gareth Dixon, the owner of this house. I am Inspector Chard, may we come in?'

'We can talk fine here on the doorstep,' answered the man belligerently.

'You seem a little unfriendly Mr Dixon. I appreciate that having a fire next door must have been a little unsettling, but a man has died you know.'

'Yes, having a fire next door is unsettling, I could have lost everything. The fire brigade made me get out of the house until they were sure that it wouldn't catch alight. But, I don't forget things and I will never forgive your lot for what happened three years ago.'

Chard looked quizzically at Constable Scudamore who said 'Hauliers' strike at the pits sir.'

'That's right. You let the troops get at us. We were just striking for fair pay and better conditions but in you came, backing the colliery owners.'

'Well Mr Dixon, I personally did not come to Pontypridd until last year, but the police are public servants and if they were ordered to keep the peace, then their duty would have been to obey.'

'That's as maybe, but my sister went missing at the time and despite me demanding that you look into it, nothing was done. The police were too bloody concerned with breaking the strike.'

Scudamore leaned forward and whispered into his superior's ear. 'We did look into it sir, and it was considered that she had just run away from home. Nothing sinister there.'

Chard spoke to the man in a conciliatory a tone. 'I am sorry about your past relationship with the police, but I do need to ask you some questions about what happened this evening. If you just answer them, we will be on our way.'

'Very well, but you aren't coming in. We'll do it right here.'

The inspector gave a grunt of disapproval and scratched his sideburns before beginning. 'Who told you that the workshop next door was on fire?'

'Mrs Griffiths, the local busybody. I heard a hammering at the door and I could smell burning before I opened it.'

'It was Mrs Griffiths that raised the general alarm sir,' volunteered Constable Scudamore.

'Did you hear anything unusual before that?' continued the inspector.

'No there was nothing,' Dixon replied in a smarmy fashion, 'but then again you haven't asked me the right question.'

'Very well,' responded an irritated Chard, 'what should I have asked you?'

'You should have asked if I heard anything usual.'

'Talk sense man!'

'I am talking sense. That noisy bastard was a nuisance and early evening he would normally have been banging away with his tools. This evening there was not a sound after about five o'clock. So, I didn't hear anything unusual but neither did I hear anything that was usual.'

'I see, that is useful,' conceded the inspector, 'but it is also very clear that you had no particular liking for Mr Hughes.'

'Couldn't stand him and neither could a few others in the village. He always used to be very reasonable about getting paid for his work, but recently it's been cash in hand before he does anything. Very abrupt too, or so I've heard. I wouldn't know myself because we haven't spoken for months.'

'I don't think that your attitude is very charitable considering the man is dead.'

'That's not my problem is it? Will that be all?'

'For now, Mr. Dixon, for now,' repeated Chard before turning away with Constable Scudamore following behind. They heard Dixon's door slam as they walked down the street towards an elderly woman in an old coat who stood waiting, with a thick shawl wrapped around her head and shoulders to give extra warmth.

'This is Mrs Griffiths who discovered the fire,' said Scudamore by means of introduction.

'Very pleased to meet you Mrs Griffiths, I am Inspector Chard. I hope you might be able to help me with my enquiries.'

'Only too pleased to help. There's not much that I don't know,' stated the woman confidently. 'Not that I'm a gossip mind,' she added.

'Thank you. Now when did you notice the fire?'

'Well, I had noticed old Mr. Jones go up the road, hadn't I? Poor old soul, it's the dust on his lungs, he hasn't been well for ages. It takes for ever for him to get to the end of the street.'

'What time would that be?'

'Sometime after five o'clock then wasn't it?'

'Can you be more precise? I mean you must have been out on the street yourself so what time did you set off?'

'My old man has a bad cough so I was off to see Mrs Evans, wasn't I?'

Chard was becoming irritable. 'Very well Mrs Griffiths, why were you going to see Mrs Evans and how does that help us establish the time?'

The woman looked at Chard as though he was simple minded. 'I was going to Mrs Evans to get something for my old man's cough,

like I said. We don't have enough money for doctors around here do we? We all have little gardens and grow our own natural remedies. I was short of a few bits and bobs so I was going to get some dried herbs from Mrs Evans. That's how I know what time it was.'

'What was the time?'

'It was definitely sometime after five because I saw Mr Jones. I told you that didn't I?'

Chard grimaced and decided a different tack.

'Very well, did you notice anyone else about at the time?'

'The light was very poor, but yes. There was Mrs Davies out with her little boy, horrible little thing as he is. Always pulling jibs.'

Chard glanced at Constable Scudamore who assisted by saying, 'pulling faces, sir.'

'Then there was Mr Phillips from the grocer's shop, going about his business. He had his window smashed the other day, didn't he? Now then, we also had Mrs Evans.'

'The one that you were going to see?' asked Chard.

'No, different Mrs Evans. We have four in our street. There was someone I didn't know, a scruffy looking man in a long coat. There were two men talking together, but they were too far away to see properly. Then young Tommy Jones, he is nearly twelve so will be down the pit soon.'

'Is that all?'

'Apart from Mrs Pearce's children, she lets them run riot you know, not that I'm one to talk.'

Chard turned to Constable Scudamore. 'Tomorrow morning trace everyone this lady has mentioned and see if they know anything.'

'Can I go now?' asked Mrs Griffiths.

'Just one or two more questions. Did people get on with Mr Hughes, I mean was he popular?'

'I am not one to cleck on others,' said Mrs Griffiths hesitantly.

'She means tell tales,' added Scudamore helpfully, for even after a year Chard was still unfamiliar with the local idioms.

'To be truthful, for I cannot tell a lie, Mr Hughes was not a particularly pleasant man. The only person who got on with him was his wife, and he was besotted with her.' continued Mrs Griffiths. 'No-

one else had much of a good word to say about him and he had been very mean spirited of late.'

'So Mr Dixon told me,' said Chard.

'There's another grumpy bugger. Those two didn't get on at all. Why are you asking though?' asked the woman with keen interest. 'Do you think the fire started deliberately? You can tell me. I won't tell a soul.'

'We are keeping an open mind Mrs Griffiths so I wouldn't jump to any conclusions. Thank you for your help.'

Turning away the inspector led Constable Scudamore out of earshot. 'If this is murder then it doesn't make sense. By the sounds of it he was unpopular but why not just slit his throat one evening? Why do it in daylight and then burn down the workshop?'

'No idea sir,' answered the constable, rubbing his chin.

'There is evil here Constable, I can feel it in the air, but I will uncover it, you mark my words.'

THREE

Barry Docks –

The Offices of the Barry Railway Company

Jeremiah Davies continued to work on a meaningless document, purportedly on the subject of new safety procedures to be introduced the following month. Not that they would actually be introduced, nor would he himself be around to enforce them, but it was important that it should appear that he was busy. There was a knock on his office door and a young clerk entered.

'I am going now Mr Davies, if that is alright with yourself. Is there anything you require?' he asked.

'No, I will be working late but you may go, Oswald.'

'Thank you, sir.'

'Before you go though, has Mr Cornwall left the building?'

'Yes Mr Davies,' replied the clerk. 'All the directors have now gone home.'

'Thank you. That will be all.'

The clerk closed the door behind him leaving Davies with a satisfied smile on his face. He would show them. Twenty years he had put into this company and yet, despite all the promises, they had failed to appoint him to the board of directors. Davies put his pen down, stood up and walked towards the window. He was an uninspiring figure, small of frame with a tendency to stoop, greasy black hair that lay flat on his scalp and a face that seemed to exude an aura of deceit. Davies was aware of his failings, but equally he felt he should be valued for what he had brought to the company, for its profits would not have flourished without his intellect. His attention to detail and the ability to influence third parties through bribes and other forms of coercion, had helped to make the Barry Railway Company the successful enterprise that it had become.

Davies gazed through the window at the bustling scene below. Barry was a thriving commercial port thanks to the export of coal and it was the company's trains that were largely responsible for the sheer volume of black gold that passed through the docks each day. Not that the Barry Railway Company had a monopoly on the transport of coal, for there was a bitter rivalry with the Taff Vale Railway. At least they knew how to reward people they valued, he thought.

Davies walked back to his desk and opened the top left-hand drawer, from which he extracted a small tin box. He opened it and took out a key, examining it for flaws, though he already knew there were none. It had taken weeks to get hold of the original and make a wax impression. Obtaining a copy had been much quicker, for he knew plenty of artisans in the docks area that would make copies of keys from such impressions, with no questions asked. Davies picked up his briefcase which he had left by the coat stand, opened the door and looked out onto the second-floor landing of the building. It was quite empty, as it normally would be at this time in the evening. He stepped out and then paused, listening for footsteps on the stairwell, before making his way to the Chairman's office. Just to be on the safe side Davies knocked before trying the door handle. As he had expected, it was locked, and so he took out his key and inserted it in the lock, turning it gently. Davies's heart beat faster, for if someone appeared now it would be difficult to conjure up an explanation for his actions. With a click which sounded unnaturally loud, the door eased open. Taking extreme care, he entered and ever so slowly and gently closed the door behind him. The Chairman's office was lavishly furnished with a deep pile carpet, ornate light fittings and a large, highly polished, mahogany desk inlaid with ivory. Behind the desk was a painting and behind that, Davies knew, was a wall safe.

It had taken weeks to get an opportunity to watch Cornwall open the safe and observe the combination. Now was the time to find out if his observations had been accurate. He walked confidently towards the picture behind the desk, because there was no turning back now. If caught he would have no excuse for having entered the room, and once the safe was revealed his motive would be obvious. Placing the picture carefully on the floor, Davies took a piece of paper out of his pocket and read the note he had made of the likely

combination. Putting his ear against the cold steel of the safe door he began to turn the combination lock, listening for the tell-tale clicks that would indicate that his numbers were correct. After five success-ful clicks the safe door sprang open and Davies had access to the documents that he was after.

Pulling out a large bundle, he placed them on the mahogany desk and looked for the information he needed. After ten minutes he selected a dozen papers and placed the rest back in the safe, but did not fully close its door. Then Davies took some sheets of paper from his briefcase, and started to make handwritten copies of the documents that he had selected. He felt his pulse quicken for fear of discovery, even though he suspected that the night watchman would be unlikely to try the office door. The task took much longer than he anticipated and it was over an hour before he finished writing. Sweat dripped from his brow and he had palpitations as he feared the outcome if he was discovered. Tomorrow Cornwall would notice he was missing, but it would take a few days to work out that he had left the company for its bitterest rival. Even then they wouldn't know that he was betraying their commercial secrets. Putting the copies into his briefcase, Davies went back to the safe to return the originals. As he placed them inside, he heard footsteps coming up the stairs and onto the landing. Losing concentration, some of the papers to slipped onto the floor and he froze. The footsteps moved across the landing, and stopped directly outside the office door. A match was struck, followed by silence, before the footsteps started once more. Davies breathed a sigh of relief as they retreated down the staircase. Hurriedly he picked up the fallen papers and tried to put them back in the right order. As he did so, Davies noticed a page of correspon-dence that he hadn't been looking for, but the importance of which he recognised immediately. His nerves were shredded and his prior-ity was to get out as fast as possible. There was no time to make a copy, yet this was the ultimate insurance against things going badly. There was a chance that its absence would be noticed, but it was a risk worth taking. Davies stuffed the paper into his jacket, closed the safe and replaced the painting. He paused at the office door and listened carefully, before exiting quietly and locking it behind him. Pulling himself together, Davies walked down the staircase as

normally as possible. As he came to the entrance hall, he was noticed by the night watchman who panicked and tried to hide his cigarette behind his back.

'Sorry sir, I thought everyone had gone home. I know I shouldn't be smoking. It won't happen again,' he blurted.

'Just see that it doesn't, Dobbs,' replied Davies who promptly walked out of the building into the salt sea air of the docks.

***

Benjamin Armstrong, chairman of the Taff Vale Railway drummed his fingers impatiently on the desk. It had taken weeks of clandestine meetings between his man Jennings and Jeremiah Davies to persuade the latter to betray his company. Not that he liked Davies, if he betrayed his current employers then he could do the same again. Yet it was important to get Davies to join the Taff Vale Railway to demonstrate that he was capable of pulling off such an important commercial coup. He got up and walked to the window. Cardiff's Queen Street was busy with the evening trade and Armstrong watched, as below the office window people hurried to and fro, filling the public houses and restaurants.

The importance of this matter was not so much the commercial well-being of the Taff Vale Railway, it was about his survival as chairman of the board. A year ago, there had not been the merest suggestion that Armstrong would be appointed. However, in-fighting between the directors of the company had been so destructive, that eventually they had to agree on someone that none of them considered a threat. A small man, short of stature with a hare lip, Armstrong had never been considered as having the commanding presence necessary in a leader. All the other directors, particularly Bowen and Wilkinson, who nominated him, thought they would be able to influence him. They were proved wrong, and having discovered their error, discussions were taking place behind closed doors to replace him.

'I'll show them,' Armstrong vowed to himself as he walked back to the desk. Before he could sit there was a knock at the door.

'Enter,' commanded the chairman, with the hopeful expectation that this would be the promised arrival of Davies.

'Mr Jeremiah Davies to see you Mr Armstrong,' announced the clerk, disgruntled at having been ordered to work extra hours that evening.

The visitor was led in and Armstrong crossed the room to shake his hand.

'Mr Davies, please come and take a seat.'

'I am delighted to meet you in person Mr Armstrong,' replied Davies. 'Mr Jennings has explained that it would be mutually beneficial for me to join your company.'

'I believe in rewarding good people, those that are loyal to me,' emphasised the chairman. 'In truth, I was hoping that you would have agreed to join our company at an earlier date.'

Davies tapped the briefcase that he held on his lap. 'I wanted to wait until I could obtain access to sensitive documents, which I have copied for you. I believe that they will prove my loyalty to you.'

Armstrong reflected that they also proved his disloyalty to his former employers, but declined to make the point. 'Then let me see what information they contain.'

Davies started to open the briefcase but then paused. 'There is the matter of my position here....'

'You will initially be paid a retainer as a special consultant answering only to myself, as does Jennings. However, as soon as I fight off the planned attempt to remove myself as chairman you will be found a place on the board of directors.'

Davies looked concerned. 'Your position is at risk? You do realise that I have gambled everything on coming here?'

'Calm yourself Mr Davies, my position is definitely not at risk. The attempt to remove me will fail, rest assured. I will remain as chairman and I intend that you will play a great part in that. Now let me see the papers.'

Davies handed over the documents and Armstrong started to read them. Eventually he put them down with a satisfied smile. 'I was not expecting you to have done this. You have done well Mr Davies, very well indeed. Cornwall will be furious if he finds out I have these.'

'Hopefully he won't find out. My only concern is if I failed to put the papers back in the right order. Some of them slipped on the

floor when I was putting them back in the safe and I had to act quickly. He might notice and put two and two together.'

'In which case Mr Davies, I suggest you remove yourself from Cardiff. Cornwall is a vengeful man, most inclined to ensure that anyone who crosses him will regret it. Don't go too far mind. I want you in easy reach, perhaps Pontypridd would be convenient?'

'Yes, perhaps that would be advisable, I will go this very evening,' agreed Davies.

Armstrong watched his new employee leave the room and sat back with a self-satisfied smile. Davies had been useful but he would of course never be allowed on the board of directors. Still, that was his fault for being so treacherous.

FOUR

Chard pushed away his plate with a contented sigh. 'That was delicious Lucy, you are forgiven for being late.'

'Thank you, Mr Chard. It won't happen again. They called me in to work an extra night at the pub and I was ever so tired.'

'I know. Just don't let it become a habit.'

'Yes, Mr Chard,' answered the rosy-cheeked young maid as she cleared away the breakfast dishes.

The inspector had employed Lucy on the strong recommendation of the landlady of his favourite pub, the Ivor Arms, where she had a part-time job as a scullery maid. In addition, Lucy occasionally worked as a barmaid in the Tredegar Arms. Chard had wondered if the girl would be reliable enough to employ, but she had turned out to be honest and hardworking, if a little rough around the edges. He even trusted her enough to give her a key to the house, with the understanding that she arrived early each weekday morning to cook his breakfast and then perform the household tasks he needed by midday. Chard tended to eat out during the rest of the day or secretly (for it would be looked on with dismay by his colleagues) cook something himself.

The inspector got up from the table and went upstairs to finish putting on his uniform. The previous evening had been the first time that he had attended a crime scene out of uniform in months. When he had arrived in Pontypridd, Chard had hoped that there would be a fairly relaxed attitude to dress, as had been the case at his previous station in Shrewsbury. However, Superintendent Jones, his new superior, was not a man to allow what he referred to as 'a lack of respect for the constabulary'. After giving his sideburns and moustache a quick comb, Chard put on his navy-blue jacket with black braid, then took his peaked cap from the hook on the back of his bedroom door. He adjusted the cap on his head and took a final look in the mirror before descending the staircase. With a call to the

maid to let her know he was leaving, Chard set off on the short walk to the police station.

A chill wind blew as Chard strode along Gelliwastad Road, but at least the weather was dry and the winter sun shone out of a pale blue sky. He crossed the road and glanced up at the spire of St Catherine's church which cast its shadow across the grey stone walls of the police station. As he entered the yard, the inspector tried to block out the noise of the workmens' hammers, as they made yet more changes to the building. The work had been constant for the last few weeks as the planned expansion of the premises took shape.

'Good morning sir,' greeted the desk sergeant, whose missing front teeth gave him a rather grotesque appearance when he smiled.

'Good morning Sergeant Humphreys. Is the Superintendent in yet?'

'Yes, Inspector, and he asked me to let you know that he wants to see you in his office once you've settled in.'

'Oh well, at least it isn't too serious or it would have been an urgent summons,' joked Chard.

'I think it might be to do with us sergeants,' commented Humphreys, turning away to write in a ledger.

Puzzled, Chard went into the common room where the huge frame of Sergeant Morris stood by the noticeboard giving instructions to a small group of constables.

'Right then lads, apart from a couple of broken shop windows the main thing to look out for is any trouble between the railway workers. If you see any group of Taff Vale men gathering near a group of Barry Railway men, then break it up before anything starts or it could soon get out of hand. Do I make myself clear?' he boomed.

'Yes Sergeant,' came the group response.

Chard saw that among the group were Constable Jenkins, an accomplished amateur boxer known as 'Fisty' to his colleagues; Constable Billy Matthews, tall and solidly built with no moustache but a clump of beard on his chin, an incorrigible joker; Constable Morgan, of average height but stocky with muttonchop whiskers, the best rugby player in the station, who was looking rather gloomy for some reason; and Constable Davies who was of substantial

proportions and not terribly fit, due to a fondness of pies and pastries. Standing to one side was a tall, lanky blond-haired constable who Chard did not recognise. And one constable that according to the duty roster should have been present, wasn't.

'Sergeant, where is Constable Jackson? I was sure he was on town patrol today,' enquired the inspector.

'If you don't mind me saying so sir, I think that the Superintendent would rather break it to you himself,' replied the huge sergeant morosely.

'Very well Sergeant. I will be seeing him soon, so I will hear it from him,' responded Chard scratching his sideburns in thought.

From the sergeant's response he assumed that something unfortunate had happened to Constable Jackson; though the possibility that the ill-mannered, sadistic brute of an officer had come to harm hardly filled Chard with dismay. The inspector went into his office and glanced at the papers on his desk to make sure that nothing urgent had come in for his attention. Then, he absent-mindedly brushed his jacket with the back of his hand, straightened his posture, took a deep breath, and left the room headed in the direction of Superintendent Jones's office.

When he got there, he found the door open, so with a polite knock he entered and found his superior sat at his desk looking supremely pleased with himself. He was a commanding figure with bushy sideburns and a resplendent moustache, and he did not suffer fools gladly.

'Ah, Chard, take a seat. I felt it was time to review our progress on re-organising the station. Fortunately, in my other role as Deputy Chief Constable I have been able to make further advancements of which you will be unaware.'

Chard looked at his Superintendent with a degree of concern. The possibility that major decisions had been taken without his prior involvement could have disappointing results.

'I await with interest sir,' replied the inspector.

'Let us recap what has been achieved over the last six months,' continued Superintendent Jones. 'Firstly, the station has been expanded as far as it can be. We have more cells to cope with miscreants and also better stabling to allow an additional horse drawn van

and a gig. We will still retain stabling for another gig and my own steed at the White Hart. Also, a telephone is being installed with the promise that on this occasion it will actually be a reliable service and not something that keeps breaking down.'

'Yet, there are only a handful in the town so I doubt it will be much use,' interjected Chard.

'Perhaps,' conceded the superintendent, 'but it is the future. At least it will improve communication with the other divisions who are also gaining the facility. In addition, the temporary mortuary at the workhouse infirmary has now been fully equipped to a high standard, so that it can also be used for our medical examinations of suspicious deaths.'

'Yes sir, I had dinner with Doctor Matthews yesterday evening. He said how satisfactory he has found the arrangements.'

Superintendent Jones sniffed. 'That is largely because we are paying him a reasonable retainer, yet he has not had much opportunity to earn it.'

'Don't worry sir, I sent a corpse up to the mortuary last night so that will give him something to do,' joked Chard.

'Death is not an amusing topic,' reprimanded Superintendent Jones. 'What are the circumstances?'

'Fire in a carpenter's workshop sir. It is possible that the victim had been locked in, though it is too early to say. I intend speaking to the widow this afternoon and I will know more once a post mortem has been carried out.'

'Very well, keep me informed if anything develops. Now, about the changes....'

'I understand there might be something affecting the sergeants?' prompted Chard.

'Well yes, that's one minor change. I will put it in context. Thanks to the success of your investigations last year, plus pressure from our Member of Parliament and the new local authority, we have as you are aware, gained a significant increase in our complement of officers. On paper we now should have twenty-eight constables and three sergeants in the Pontypridd Division.'

'Even if we actually had all the posts filled it is still not much to police a population of thirty-five thousand,' interrupted Chard.

'Quite,' agreed the Superintendent. 'As I was about to say, when you came last year, we had a rather informal arrangement whereby the outlying villages could knock on the door of a local constable's home in cases of emergency. That was of course if they had a constable living nearby, which wasn't always the case. My plan is to create a number of subsidiary stations which will help us to become more efficient. However, that may take some time to come about.'

The Superintendent got up from his desk and started to pace back and fore as he continued to explain his plans.

'We have, as you know, just finished putting a more formal arrangement in place whereby we have renovated an unoccupied dwelling at Treforest. It will initially be manned by three of our new constables, one of whom is experienced, having been transferred from another division and two others that are not. The new station will therefore require a degree of extra supervision.'

'Sorry to interrupt sir, but Sergeant Morris has all he can cope with.'

'I totally agree Chard, so if I may continue....'

'Sorry sir,' apologised the inspector.

'I have given the matter some thought and I have decided that we need to make changes. We were already one sergeant down when you arrived last year and since then Sergeant Humphreys and Sergeant Morris have been under tremendous pressure. Thankfully Sergeant Humphreys, despite being close to retirement and preferring the role of desk sergeant, has stepped up to the mark. I also am aware that you have coped with a tremendous workload yourself, not only with regard to administration, but also in accompanying constables when a sergeant has not been available. You have even come in overnight on occasion, when the constable covering the night desk has had to deal with something requiring a senior hand.'

'That hasn't been a problem sir. I only live a short distance away.'

'None the less, you are to be commended for your diligence,' replied the superintendent who stopped pacing and stared directly into Chard's eyes.

The inspector had a feeling of foreboding. The superintendent rarely gave him a direct compliment and he suspected that he was being lined up for some unpleasant news.

'However,' continued the superintendent, 'as on paper we should have three sergeants and only actually have two, I have had to do something about it. My first bit of news for you is that we do have a new one.'

'Who is the sergeant?' queried Chard.

'I have appointed one of our current constables on the basis of seniority.'

'That would be Scudamore I assume, sir?'

'No, though there were only a few weeks in it. The senior man was Constable Jackson, or as I should now correctly say, Sergeant Jackson.'

'Oh no sir!' exclaimed Chard. 'I was told that there would be news about Jackson, but I thought it was to do with an accident. You cannot be serious.'

The superintendent raised a cautionary hand. 'Stop there, Inspector! I know you aren't keen on the man, but he has served his time and earned his chance. The matter is not for discussion.'

Chard knew from experience that arguing would be a complete waste of breath. So despite the loathing he felt about the sadistic Jackson, he pursued the matter no further.

'Very well sir,' he conceded.

'Good, now let us move on to the constables. We now have Constable Temple who has started today….'

'Would he be the tall blond-haired officer I noticed?' interrupted Chard.

'That's correct. He is quite experienced and was previously at this station going back about four years ago. Temple was transferred to 'A' Division in Merthyr Tydfil when there was an urgent need to switch resources to that god-forsaken town. He knows this area well and will be an invaluable addition.'

'Good news then sir.'

'Yes, it is, and I have kept the best news until last of all.'

'Before you continue sir, I don't suppose it relates to more resources so that we can have a detective department like in some other forces?'

'Inspector Chard,' began the Superintendent, rising from his seat, 'I am continuously aware that you do not like wearing uniform

and want to follow the relaxed practices of your former station in Shrewsbury, but I have standards. If we were somewhat awash with resources and you were to repeat your results of last year then I might consider it, but as for now....' the Superintendent slammed his fist down on the desk for effect which made Chard jump, '...it is out of the question.'

Chard watched Superintendent Jones walk to the window, taking a look out. After an uncomfortable pause the superintendent returned to the desk and looked down at his inspector. In a calm voice and with a hint of a smile he resumed the discussion.

'I did say that I had saved the best news to last. As I mentioned earlier, I have been aware that these past months you have been working extremely hard, particularly with regard to your administrative duties.'

'I have indeed sir. I occasionally have some assistance from Sergeant Humphreys and Constable Morgan but I am stretched.'

'Yes, I know. I am also aware that you find administration extremely tiresome, and I have to admit that you do seem more suited to the more active aspects of your position. The good news is that I have gained agreement that another inspector will join us. It may take some considerable time because we will want to get the right man. I will be looking for an experienced leader of men, with ambitions of advancement. Someone who in order to assist any future promotion needs more evidence of being able to administer the running of a busy station. Therefore, he could handle the vast majority of your administration duties, leaving you free to do a little more in respect of investigating any serious crimes. I trust that will please you?'

'I am sure that will be fine sir,' answered Chard.

'Good, then I think that is about all I have to tell you, so please carry on with your duties.'

Chard left his superior's office with his mind in a whirl. A new constable, the bad news about Jackson's promotion, but best of all the sheer bliss that another inspector would free him from the mountain of paperwork that was the bane of his life.

As the inspector walked to his office, he passed Constable Morgan in deep discussion with his cousin, Constable Matthews.

'Constable Morgan, you can accompany me to Cilfynydd this afternoon to take notes. I will be speaking with the widow of the poor fellow who died last night.'

'What about Constable Scudamore who is out there already, if you don't mind me asking sir?'

'I do mind you asking, but on this occasion I will explain myself. I like consistency and whoever takes the notes of the interview will also take notes when I visit the mortuary which, as Scudamore might still be tied up with other duties, means you.'

'Yes sir, sorry for asking.'

'What is the matter with you today Morgan, you are looking glum. Is it to do with May?' asked Chard. He was aware of the constable's relationship with the young clerk who had been stabbed a year earlier.

'No sir. Everything's fine.'

'Is it to do with the new man, Constable Temple?'

'I would rather not say sir. He worked here some years ago.'

'Yes, so I understand,' commented Chard a little curious at Morgan's evasive reply. 'Is he a local man?' continued the Inspector.

'No. He ran away from home and travelled about before ending up here,' answered Morgan. The constable spoke abruptly, clearly wanting the conversation to end.

'He has even been to China,' interjected a grinning Matthews who was still standing close by.

'Has he really?' questioned Chard. 'Fascinating, I must ask him about it.' The inspector paused, before mentioning the bad news that he had been given. 'On another matter, I assume you've heard about Jackson?'

'He was the first to let us know, shouting his mouth off,' commented Matthews.

'I appreciate your misgivings but we all have to accept that he is now a sergeant and so that is the last insolent comment that I can allow. Perhaps he might become a changed man,' added the inspector, without believing it for one moment.

FIVE

Ernest Wilkinson winced, as his dining companion stuffed another piece of sirloin steak into his mouth using the point of his knife.

'Steady on old chap you'll end up with indigestion,' he cautioned, though his concern was largely embarrassment, rather than a genuine interest in the health of the shaggy-haired, ill-mannered man who shared his table.

'Nonsense, you could do with following my example and building yourself up Ernest. There are tough times ahead and one needs to be well fortified,' he replied rather loudly, causing other diners in the opulent restaurant to turn and stare.

'Keep your voice down Hector, you are drawing attention to our conversation,' warned Wilkinson. There were times he absolutely despaired of Hector Bowen. He was undoubtedly an intelligent man, having graduated from Oxford, but he seemed to revel in playing the buffoon. The clothes Bowen wore had been made in Savile Row, yet he somehow seemed to contrive a look that suggested he had dressed whilst blindfolded. Wilkinson watched whilst Bowen gestured to a pretty young waitress. The girl came to his side and Bowen indicated that she should bend down that he might whisper something in her ear. She complied, only to straighten up a moment later, red-faced with embarrassment, before rushing out of the room. Bowen smiled as he noticed the stern look on Wilkinson's face.

'Well, you never know your luck, do you?' he shrugged. In truth he liked to shock Wilkinson, who played the upper-class gent to perfection. He dressed the part too, with his elegant tailoring, slim upright frame and a monocle which Bowen suspected was only an affectation.

'Please take this matter seriously, Hector.'

Bowen took another mouthful of steak, and washed it down with a glass of claret whilst Wilkinson waited patiently for a response.

'Very well,' he finally conceded. 'We know what we have to do. As allies, we have made Armstrong, so we can also break him.'

'It has become necessary,' agreed Wilkinson. 'The beggar was only supposed to hang around long enough to steady the boat before disappearing into obscurity, leaving me – I mean us – to take over.'

Bowen had caught the slip, but ignored it. They both knew that each disliked the other, and that the removal of Armstrong would leave them fighting for power; but for the moment it was in their interests to maintain their alliance.

'We had no option at the time of course,' added Bowen, who was now speaking at a low volume much appreciated by his ally. 'The shareholders and their representatives were moving towards the idea that we should merge with the Barry Railway Company. The inoffensive Armstrong meant that those wavering between our stance of remaining independent and the pro-merger lobby, had what they felt was a safe pair of hands.'

Wilkinson ate a morsel of food from his plate before continuing. 'Under our unwritten agreement, now that the pressure for merger has eased and the majority share our view, he should stand down. My concern is that he is simply not leadership material. Where is the strong figure that we need to lead us forward? We have no direction, no iron fist. No, now is the time for better men to take the lead.'

'Agreed, but when exactly is the time to call for a vote of no confidence?'

'I propose that if this afternoon's board meeting is the usual vacuous, boring event with our so-called leader spouting the same insipid claptrap, then we shall put forward our views and assess the mood of our fellow directors. If they appear to be on our side then we will make our play.'

***

'Dammit!' cursed Constable Morgan, as he was forced to pull on the reins of the gig suddenly, to avoid colliding with the rear of a horse-drawn omnibus.

'Calm down Constable, you were going too fast anyway,' reprimanded Inspector Chard.

The road through the town was busy, and an overladen cart had

caused the omnibus to slow almost to a stop in the middle of the New Bridge over the River Taff. It was impossible to move around it due to the number of vehicles coming from the other direction. After a few minutes the cart made its way off the bridge, turning into a side street along the river; leaving those who had been held up free to continue, past the canal basin and, in the case of the policemen, uphill to join the road to Cilfynydd.

'The new man seems to have got under your skin, Constable Morgan. Is there anything I should know about?' asked Chard.

'Sinner and me don't get on. That's all sir. I would rather not discuss it.'

'Sinner?'

'It's what we call him,' replied Morgan who made it clear from his expression that it was an unwelcome subject.

Chard looked quizzically at his constable. Morgan had indeed been a little out of sorts in recent weeks, but clearly he had become more morose. With his full mutton chop whiskers, which belied his young age, he could look quite stern. However, he would usually break into a frequent smile or laugh at one of Constable Matthews's ridiculous jokes. Something was definitely not right, but Chard decided it was a matter that was perhaps better left for another time.

The village of Cilfynydd, often referred to as Cil by the locals, was just over two miles away from Pontypridd town. Before the Albion Colliery had opened there it had just been a small hamlet, but now a number of parallel streets of houses for the miners lined the hillside. When the policemen arrived, Chard felt inexplicably uneasy. A sense of tragedy seemed to settle on the streets like an invisible cloak.

'Let's go past the site of the fire first,' suggested Chard.

Morgan swung the gig into Howell Street, and as they approached the burnt out remains of the workshop a familiar, unwelcome sight greeted them.

'What the hell…?' muttered Chard as he got down from the gig.

'Jackson, what are you doing here?' asked the inspector.

Jackson was standing with another constable next to the ruined property, and he gave a grin as he turned around.

'It's Sergeant Jackson if you don't mind sir.'

'Not until you've put your stripes on it isn't,' responded Chard with ill humour. 'Where is Constable Scudamore? He was supposed to be taking statements today.'

'Ah, well he was sir, but I felt that instead it would be useful experience for one of the newer constables under my instruction. I appraised Constable Scudamore of my promotion and said that Constable Connelly and I would finish the statements. I will get them back to you in good time, Inspector. We were just about to go and see the widow.'

Chard seethed inwardly. Jackson had clearly sought out Scudamore solely to gloat over his own promotion.

'Very well Jackson, you may continue with the statements of bystanders but you will go nowhere near the widow. I will be talking to her myself. Do I make myself clear?'

'As you wish sir,' answered Jackson.

'Good, and make sure your stripes are on by the next time you go on duty.'

Jackson gave a nod and then walked away with Constable Connelly in tow.

Chard gave a grunt of satisfaction as he watched them leave, then turned to Morgan, 'I want another look around what is left of the workshop. The light is better than yesterday evening.'

The sour-faced constable joined the inspector as he walked into the blackened ruins and pulled aside pieces of burnt timber.

'Nothing much to help us here, sir. Just fire damaged tools and furniture.'

'Perhaps, but keep looking,' insisted the inspector. 'Try and find a key.'

Chard scratched his sideburns in thought, then bent down to pick up some pieces of twisted metal. Prodding away some burnt detritus he picked up some pieces of glass, then another metallic object. 'Put these in the gig Constable,' he ordered, before continuing his search. A few minutes later he came across another item of interest which he passed to the constable. 'That'll do us, I think.'

'Important evidence sir?' queried Morgan.

'Possibly, I'm not sure yet. Let's make our way to the victim's house,' answered Chard thoughtfully.

***

In the boardroom of the Taff Vale Railway things were becoming fractious. The Chairman, Benjamin Armstrong, had taken some considerable time delivering a monologue on the company's current financial position to the directors. Strangely, it seemed as if he was deliberately being more languid than usual in his presentation; it was almost as if he wanted to annoy the more impatient directors into openly challenging his authority. Even the more restrained Wilkinson had started to drum his fingers on the table, and the impetuous Hector Bowen could clearly barely contain himself.

It wasn't long before Bowen, unable to hold back any longer, spoke out.

'Now look here Armstrong, there are a number of us here who find it curious that you have failed to address our prime concern. Namely the inroads that our rival, the Barry Railway Company, has been making into our markets. The majority of us want urgent action to disrupt their trade and bring them to their knees, but I have my suspicions that you are now more inclined towards some form of merger. If that is the case then you should step down.'

The outburst resulted in a chorus of agreement from several of the men sat around the table.

'Nonsense,' responded Armstrong, who did not look the least bit unsettled by the interruption.

Ernest Wilkinson stood up and adjusted his monocle. 'In that case, why did you allow them to start running a passenger service on part of our railway line? Instead of a basic loading bay they have now built a full station, and it opens officially next month. It was bad enough challenging us with their freight service, but now passengers as well? It really is too much!'

Armstrong smiled beatifically. 'Gentlemen, gentlemen. Please calm down. I had no option but to allow the BRC to run a passenger service on part of our line. It was political pressure from parliament.'

'Nevertheless, unless you can show us that you intend fighting against the BRC, then there will have to be a vote of no confidence,' stated Wilkinson as he sat back down, to mutterings of agreement from most of the other directors.

'Perhaps I do need to put some of you at ease,' said Armstrong

with a smile. 'Jennings! Bring the papers.'

At the command, a smartly dressed, tall young man with an arrogant expression stepped forward holding a briefcase.

Armstrong took the briefcase and fetched out a sheaf of papers. 'This, gentlemen, should satisfy your concerns. You may have heard of an employee of BRC by the name of Jeremiah Davies. He is one of their strategists and it would be a tremendous blow if he was to leave their company.'

Several directors acknowledged the remark with a nod.

Armstrong smiled. 'Well he has now left their company. I am pleased to announce that thanks to my own personal intervention he is now one of our employees. Furthermore, as an even greater coup, I now have copies of BRC's business plans and commercial agreements. They will of course remain in my possession, but we now have the whip hand.'

To the consternation of Bowen and Wilkinson there were whoops of delight from a number of directors, and the mood of the room changed dramatically.

'To celebrate this major accomplishment, I have ordered a couple of bottles of Dom Perignon, so if you would all care to go into the next room....'

As the meeting broke up, Armstrong beckoned to his aide, Jennings. Taking him to one side he whispered, 'I need someone followed. Come to my office in an hour and I will give you the details.'

***

Chard stood outside the house on Cilfynydd Road and shivered involuntarily. It wasn't the cold wind; he had a sensation of foreboding. Visiting the bereaved was never something to which he looked forward. A waggonette drove past on the main road from Merthyr to Pontypridd with four or five passengers, but otherwise the road was quiet. Two women stood talking on the pavement, both dressed largely in black and wrapped up in thick layers of clothing against the chill. There were no men in sight. They were either at the colliery, in bed awaiting their next shift, or already in their graves.

Constable Morgan gave a loud knock on the door of the solidly

built stone terraced house, then stood aside for the inspector. Eventually the door was opened by a lady of mature years, who stood with upright posture and a firm stare. She looked the uniformed inspector up and down before waving him into the house. '*Dewch i mewn.*'

'I understand "come in", Mrs Hughes but my Welsh is very limited,' informed the inspector. 'Let me introduce myself, I am Inspector Chard, and this is Constable Morgan.'

'Very well, we can speak in English but let me correct your assumption. I am Mrs Evans, not Mrs Hughes. Please come into the parlour,' the woman responded rather abruptly.

The door into the parlour was pushed open and revealed a young woman dressed in black. The widow stared blankly into space, a small blue bottle dangling from one hand. She would have been regarded as pretty, were it not for her red-rimmed eyes and the tears that silently streaked down her cheeks. Chard had been in the presence of grief-stricken spouses in the past. It was not a pleasant situation to be in, and in a way, he was grateful that the woman didn't seem to realise that they had entered the room.

Mrs Evans tapped the inspector on the shoulder and led both policemen through to a neat and tidy kitchen. A wooden table laid with dishes and cutlery stood on one side. Well-made shelves against another wall (no doubt the handicraft of the deceased carpenter) displayed neatly stacked pots and pans with small bottles of dried herbs above. Larger utensils hung from hooks close to the back door, and there was a heavy aroma of carbolic soap from the large sink by the kitchen window.

'I've given her something to calm down,' explained Mrs Evans.

'It must have come as quite a shock,' said Chard kindly.

Mrs Evans gave a sigh and seemed to relax slightly. 'Yes, it was. She is devastated. I must apologise if I was rather abrupt with you. It has been difficult.'

'I am sure it has, Mrs Evans. I take it that you and Mrs Hughes are close friends. Are there any relatives?'

'None, I am afraid. Her parents passed away with typhoid two years ago, not long after the colliery disaster. The poor thing has suffered a lot in her young life. Tell me Inspector, why are you taking such an interest in all this, if you don't mind me asking?'

'Just routine, Mrs Evans. No doubt the fire was caused by accident, but as there was a fatality we are obliged to investigate the matter to some degree,' replied Chard.

'Do you know what caused the accident?' asked Mrs Hughes.

'It is too early to say. Perhaps an overturned lamp but we cannot be certain at this point. Was Mr Hughes a popular man?'

Mrs Evans shrugged. 'He could be a bit short at times and recently he had fallen out with some people by refusing to give them credit. Then there's the man who lives next door to the workshop'

'Mr Dixon?'

'Yes, that's him. They have never got on.'

Chard glanced out of the corner of his eye and was pleased to see that Constable Morgan had been quietly making notes.

'Were you near the workshop when the fire was first noticed? I ask in case you might have spotted anything unusual.'

'I am afraid not, Inspector. The first I knew about it was when I heard shouting in the street and went to see what all the fuss was about. By then the place was burning fiercely.'

'I see. Well, thank you very much anyway. You have been most helpful. I will still need to speak to Mrs Hughes though.'

'She's too upset to talk at the moment, as you've seen.'

'I agree,' replied the inspector. 'There will be a post mortem of course, so I am prepared to wait a little longer.'

'Thank you, Inspector, I'm sure that would be best. May I show you to the door?'

The policemen walked back through the house and out to the gig, Mrs Evans watching them from the front door.

As they set off Chard asked his constable, 'What was your impression of Mrs Evans?'

'Seems alright. A bit moody I suppose, but then so are all women.'

The inspector thought carefully before deciding to venture into what he felt might be a topic relevant to Morgan's comment.

'I know you don't get on with the new constable, but you've not seemed your usual self for a while now, and Temple only turned up recently. Is it to do with May?'

Morgan went very quiet and seemed to be on the point of

answering on several occasions, but kept silent for a further mile before finally speaking up.

'She is just too difficult to cope with sir. We started walking out together when she had recovered enough from her injuries. I thought everything was going fine, but then she started going into these moods. She goes sullen and quiet and I can't get a conversation out of her.'

'Perhaps May is still suffering from the shock of it all,' suggested Chard.

'Maybe, but it isn't as if I haven't tried to help. I gave her some cocaine to help buck up her spirits but then she stopped taking it. She is just impossible.'

'Have patience Constable.'

'No, I'm sorry but I am going to have to break things off. I've had enough.'

SIX

The thick wooden door was stiff. Chard put his shoulder to it, gave a good shove, and it opened with a loud creak. As he entered the warm, stone-flagged room its clientele momentarily glanced in his direction before resuming their conversations. Almost immediately the inspector felt himself relax. This was his refuge where he could enjoy good conversation and forget the day-to-day troubles of police work. The Ivor Arms was situated just out of the town centre, between the New Bridge and the canal basin area, with its back to Ynysangharad Fields. Unusually for most public houses, there was little residual stale smell of tobacco smoke. Gwen, the landlady, was not keen on smoking around the bar and although not banned, she would tend to give 'the look' which usually deterred those who wanted to light up.

'Good evening, Thomas,' she greeted him.

Chard smiled at the cheerful yet imposing figure behind the bar. She was a sturdily built woman with an enormous bosom respectably contained within what must be a corset of remarkably sturdy construction, beneath her tightly buttoned blouse. Gwen had been the first friendly face that he had come across when he arrived in Ponty the previous year. One of the kindest people that he had ever met, the inspector had insisted that if he came into the pub out of uniform, she should treat him no different to any other customer.

'Hello Gwen, where's Gwyn tonight?' asked Chard, surprised, yet delighted that her regular barman, who could be exceedingly grumpy, was absent.

'Miserable old bugger has left,' answered Gwen with a rueful smile. 'He has gone to run a pub in Cardiff. I'll miss him.' The landlady gave Chard a wink 'I don't suppose you fancy a change of career Thomas?' she teased.

'The barman is a noble profession, but no. I am happy as I am,' answered Chard smiling.

'I suppose I'd better serve you then,' sighed Gwen, pretending to be surprised at his refusal of the offer. "Pint of bitter?"'

"Yes please," answered Chard putting his money on the bar. Whilst Gwen poured his pint Chard looked across to where three of his regular drinking companions were deep in conversation.

Taking his pint, Chard wandered over to his friends, curious to discover what topic was engaging them so deeply.

'Well, you've got to and that's an end to it,' insisted the youngest of the three, a stoutly built man in his thirties with dark receding hair. Owner of the best hansom cab in town, he was known as Will Horses to his friends.

'But I can't. I just can't bring myself to do it,' replied one of his companions. He took a large mouthful of beer, swallowed and shook his head in refusal. The man who spoke wore round framed spectacles and had grey streaks in his dark hair that gave him a distinguished appearance. David Meredith, known to his friends as Dai Books, had worked for several years as a librarian for Lady Llanover, a great patron of Welsh arts and culture.

'Will is right, Dai. No option is there butty? You have to eat. Things aren't going to be the same. That's life, isn't it?'

The third member of the group, Dic Jenkins, looked quite disreputable. He wore a long shabby coat and displayed a drooping black moustache beneath an enormous bulbous nose. Chard knew that his Superintendent would not approve of his social interaction with many of the pub's patrons. What the reaction would be if he knew that Dic Jenkins was one of them, the inspector shuddered to think. Chard gave a little cough, causing Will to glance in his direction.

'*Shwmae* Mr Chard,' he greeted.

Although the inspector had offered them to use his Christian name when out of uniform, his drinking companions insisted that they felt more comfortable addressing him formally.

'*Shwmae* all,' replied the inspector. 'It appears you are discussing something of great concern.'

Dai Books looked forlorn. 'You don't know the half of it.'

Will chipped in. 'He's out of a job.'

'Really?' queried Chard. 'I thought that your position was secure.'

'I thought so too,' replied Dai sadly. 'Even when Lady Llanover

passed away last month I believed that all would be well. There is so much work to be done. For a long time now, I have been travelling over to Monmouth, staying for a few days at a time to catalogue the vast collection of books and manuscripts. Then I would fetch some bits and pieces back to Ponty to do some translating. Ideal for me and of course it gave me regular breaks from my missus.'

'So, what has gone wrong?'

'Go on, tell him,' encouraged Dic.

'It's the heirs to the Llanover estate,' continued Dai. 'They have been looking at the accounts and decided that they can find someone else in the local area to do my work. That would mean they wouldn't have to pay for my travel or accommodation. I can continue for the next few weeks as I am in the middle of translating a twelfth century manuscript, but when I've finished, that will be it.'

'What will you do?' asked Chard, genuinely concerned.

'That is what we were discussing,' spoke up Dic.

'I have to admit that there aren't many positions available for librarians. Though I am sure one will come up in Cardiff eventually.'

'Eventually isn't going to give you money now though is it mun? You need security and a job,' said Will sagely.

'Yes, and you know what that means,' added Dic.

'But I can't. I would hate it,' responded Dai, taking another large mouthful of beer.

'What are you talking about?' asked Chard. 'With your qualifications they aren't suggesting that you apply for a job at the chainworks are they?'

'Worse. Far worse,' shivered Dai. 'They want me to go teaching!'

'Yes, teaching, that's it for you Dai. New Board School opening up this year on Tyfica Road. Posts being advertised this very week. You must apply. No doubt about it,' insisted Will.

Chard could not help but smile at Dai's discomfort.

'It is not a matter of amusement Mr Chard,' snapped Dai. 'I can't abide children. I would be most ill-suited. *Iesu Mawr!*' he exclaimed loudly.

There was a sudden loud smack as Gwen's firm hand slapped angrily on the wooden counter of the bar.

'Oi! Dai Books. There will be no blasphemy in this public house. Any more and I'll kick your arse out of the door myself,' she threatened, while making a quick sign of the cross.

'Sorry Gwen,' apologised the librarian. He turned to his companions. 'Look, I'll think about it, but please change the conversation to something else.'

There was silence for a moment, then Dic addressed the inspector. 'You'll be going to the game tomorrow then Mr Chard.'

'What game?'

'What game! You're pulling my leg. He is, isn't he lads?' replied Dic nudging the other two.

'Rugby of course,' clarified Dai Books, pleased that he was no longer the centre of the conversation.

'It's a big game. Ponty against Neath. There should be a good crowd, and there will be a collection to raise money for the Tylorstown widows and orphans,' explained Will.

'Yes, and your constable is playing in it. One of the centres is injured and I understand he has been asked to step in,' added Dai.

'Aye, Constable Morgan. It's a feather in his cap to have been asked. A real honour,' emphasised Dic.

'I was with him today and he didn't say anything about it. Then again, he seems to have a lot of things on his mind at the moment.'

'We're all going, so why not come with us Mr Chard,' suggested Will.

Chard scratched his sideburns and considered, 'Oh why not? What harm could it do?'

***

Hector Bowen made his way down the dark side street in the Grangetown area of Cardiff. The air was thick with the cloying smell of coal dust, for the evening temperature had dropped and most homes had lit their fires. The gas lamps had not been lit, whether from damage or failure by the lighterman he did not know or care. There were figures that watched him, possibly rogues or vagabonds, but they stayed clear of the burly individual who walked confidently with the swagger of a pugilist. A cap pulled down over his eyes and a nondescript long coat hid Bowen's identity: he did not want to be recognised.

Damn and blast that Jeremiah Davies. Why the hell couldn't he have stayed with the BRC? he thought. It really fucked up things today. We had Armstrong. I was sure of it. I won't forget this. That bastard Davies will pay for it.

Deep in thought of how he would repay both Armstrong and Davies, Bowen nearly stumbled on a raised manhole cover.

'Damn and blast!' he cursed, before looking around to see if he had been heard, or if indeed he was being followed. There was no-one else in sight. With a grunt of satisfaction, he moved on. He would quench his desire for violence with some vicious fun tonight. Not that he would be violent, but cruel, oh yes!

A turn into another street and a few dozen paces took him to an alley that led between the back gardens of two streets. The path was unkempt and Bowen had to tread carefully to pick his way through without catching his leg on discarded timber from broken fences, or stubbing his toe on the occasional stone. Eventually, he came to a gate which he recognised from a previous visit. Carefully he pressed the metal catch and pushed it open, for he knew that the bolt on the rear was broken.

Taking extra care to be quiet he moved his large frame as stealthily as possible down the garden path until he reached the back door of the terraced house.

Grinning to himself, he knocked gently on the door. There was no reply.

He rapped a little harder. Still no reply.

'Open up you little slut,' he whispered as he rapped once more, even harder.

Finally, he heard some steps approach from the other side of the door and then stop.

Bowen waited, his anger rising as he waited.

'I know you are there. Open up!' he snarled, as loudly as he dared without attracting attention from the adjacent houses.

'Who is it?' asked a tremulous voice.

'You know damn well who it is! I said I would return on this night, so don't delay further. Just open the door.'

There was another pause, then there was the sound of a bolt being drawn back and the turning of a key in the lock. Slowly the

door started to open, but before the occupant could pull it fully open, Bowen shoved his way in. He quickly turned and pushed the door shut with both hands before turning the key in the lock. Slowly he turned to face the person he had come to torment.

'Oh, please don't touch me. I don't want this,' begged the young dark-skinned woman. She wore a grey dress of cheap fabric and in her left hand she clasped a child's blanket. 'I've only just seen to the baby and settled him down in the next room,' she pleaded.

'Good, then the creature won't hear what I am going to do to you, or what I am going to make you do to me,' snorted Bowen.

'I shan't!' argued the woman defiantly. 'I cried for days after you came to me before and it was so hard to hide the shame from my husband.'

'If you don't do what I want, or if you tell your husband, then you will know what will happen. How many darkies do you think get a position on the railways like him? One word from me and he will be out on his ear. Perhaps he will have been caught stealing as an added bonus. Either way he won't get employed again. Certainly not well enough to pay the rent on this house.'

'You wouldn't,' cried the woman with tears streaming down her face.

'You know I would my dear,' answered Bowen cruelly. He felt the surge of sexual excitement resulting from the torment of his poor victim. 'You would be out on the streets, perhaps with your husband in prison. Then what? I will tell you Mrs Torres. It will be the workhouse for you and the child, if it lives that long.'

The woman went silent and just stood there, the tears now dripping from her face and onto the flagstone floor.

'That's better,' murmured Bowen lecherously, satisfied with her acquiescence. He reached into his pocket and retrieved a small glass bottle half full of liquid. Undoing a small catch with his fingernail, thereby removing the top of the container, he handed it to the weeping wife and mother that stood obediently before him.

'Drink it,' he commanded.

'What is it?'

'Just a little something made up by a chemist of my acquaintance. He often concocts this and that at my instruction. This little potion

will make you, shall we say, slightly more agreeable to my demands. You know I have my certain preferences and given your distaste for them; this will make it a little easier for both of us.'

The woman reluctantly took the bottle and swallowed the contents down in one go. It tasted sweet, not unpleasantly so, but she nevertheless felt her stomach churn with revulsion as she raised her eyes to look directly at Bowen.

It only took a few moments before the room started to appear distorted and her limbs felt heavy. Everything seemed to have a dreamlike quality and although she tried to speak, no words would come forth.

'Don't worry my dear. By the time your husband comes home from his night shift you will be as right as rain,' said Bowen softly. 'But for now. you are my plaything,' he added with an evil sneer, as he reached towards the terrified woman.

SEVEN

Thaddeus Cornwall, chairman of the Barry Railway Company, strode into the company offices looking, as always, as if the rest of humanity was beneath his contempt. A tall balding figure with a short yet full grey moustache, he tended to lean forward as he walked, giving the impression that time was money and there was a need to progress as quickly as possible.

The doorman's 'Good Morning' was ignored, as were similar greetings from the various staff who hastily moved out of his way. Striding up the stairs two at a time, to the landing that led to his office, he finally acknowledged a 'good morning' with a 'Perkins, fetch me some refreshment!'

Entering the office, he removed his coat before going to his desk. It had been a good business trip. The company was extraordinarily successful. Having developed Barry Docks as well as its railway network, the BRC now carried a large percentage of minerals for export and dividends of over ten per cent for investors were being achieved. Yet, there was one fly in the ointment, the Taff Vale Railway. Something had to be done, but plans were afoot.

Taking some notes for a forthcoming speech from his jacket pocket, Cornwall took down the painting behind his desk. He entered the combination of the wall safe and pulled open the door.

'Damn it!' he cursed as a pile of papers fell out onto the floor.

He picked up the papers and placed them on his desk, when there was a knock on his office door.

'Wait!' he shouted.

Leaving the papers on the desk, Cornwall closed the door of the safe and replaced the painting.

'Come in!'

In walked Perkins, his junior clerk, carrying a tray bearing a silver tea service with a Wedgwood cup and saucer. He put down the tray on the desk and turned to leave.

'Send Mr Davies in,' commanded Cornwall.

'He isn't here sir,' replied Perkins timidly.

'What do you mean he isn't here?'

'I am afraid he hasn't been in since you left the other day, Mr Cornwall.'

'Is he ill?'

'No idea sir. There has been no message.'

'Well send someone around to his house!'

'Yes sir,' agreed the clerk and hurriedly left the room.

Cornwall sat with furrowed brow, and then started to sift through the papers on his desk. 'They shouldn't have fallen out like that when I opened the door,' he thought. With growing concern, he went through the papers. He gave a sigh of relief on finding them all there, but then he realised.

'The bloody document has gone. When I find who's taken it, I'll have him skinned alive!' he cried aloud. Cornwall threw the papers into the safe, locked it, rushed to a small table in a corner of the room, and picked up the telephone.

***

'Go off duty Constable Morgan. I can manage without you. You should have told me about this afternoon's match,' said Inspector Chard kindly.

'What about the mortuary sir? I thought you wanted me to accompany you.'

'I can manage Constable. I understand that it will be an honour for you to play today and I will be coming to watch.'

'You will sir?' asked Morgan, surprised by his superior's interest.

'Yes. I have never been to a game, so I am sure it will be an education.'

'I'll go then, if you are sure sir,' replied Morgan, clearly thankful, but still in low spirits.

Chard watched him go. The decision to send him home to prepare was not solely based on consideration for the rugby match. The inspector wanted to try and get to the bottom of the animosity between Morgan and the new constable, John Temple,

As soon as Morgan left, he gestured to Sergeant Morris.

'Sergeant, I am going up to the mortuary. Is Constable Temple free at the moment?'

'He's just doing some paperwork sir. If you want him to accompany you, I am sure he would be delighted,' replied the huge sergeant.

Chard nodded his approval and in a few moments Constable Temple was standing to attention at the door of his office.

For the first time, Chard was able to take a good look at the lanky new officer. He was slightly taken aback to see that the young constable had evidently suffered a major accident on the right-hand side of his face. He had a severe burn which left scarred, puckered skin. The result was disconcerting as it was such a contrast to his otherwise well-defined facial features. Aware of the uncomfortable pause before speaking, the inspector gave an embarrassed cough and addressed the constable.

'I understand you have worked here before, so obviously you will be familiar with the area.'

'Yes, sir. I know it very well.'

'Your accent. From North Wales I take it?'

'Yes sir, from Anglesey,' answered Temple, surprised that the inspector, who was obviously English, knew the difference. 'I came down here looking for work and I sort of drifted into the job.'

'Well Constable, you can accompany me up to the workhouse infirmary. I want to see what Doctor Matthews has made of the corpse I sent him.'

It was perhaps half a mile to the workhouse, and as the inspector was feeling in need of exercise the two men walked. The morning was cold, and Chard was grateful for the warmth provided by his uniform jacket. They walked briskly across the bridge that led to the larger of the two town railway stations, situated on the junction known as the Tumble. From there, the officers walked underneath a railway bridge and up the steep hill known as the Graig.

As they walked, Chard felt he should make amends for having stared at Temple's disfigurement by engaging him in conversation.

'I understand you have some experience of China, Constable.'

'That's correct sir,' answered the Temple, without expanding any further.

'How did you find the people?'

'Thieving bastards sir.'

'Really?' answered Chard, surprised at the vehemence of the reply. 'I understood them to be clever and law abiding.'

'Thick as shit and wouldn't turn my back on them,' answered Temple. 'Of course, it's not their fault. It's the poverty that causes it. Their housing is terrible and they have very little to eat.'

'What do they eat? Rice I suppose?'

Temple glanced at his inspector with a quizzical look on his face.

'No sir, of course not. Bread and potatoes.'

Chard did not reply to such a ridiculous comment. Clearly Constable Temple was trying to play him for a fool, or had never been to China and was just making things up. They walked on in silence.

***

The workhouse was a large complex set behind high stone walls. It existed to provide subsistence-level food and accommodation for the homeless and destitute. In return the inmates submitted to a rigid regime that deprived them of basic freedoms. This was deliberate, for the object was to dissuade anyone from entering the workhouse unless they were truly desperate. Drab uniform clothing was provided, the sexes were separated, and all inmates were expected to work hard to earn their keep. Reforms had been passed so that workhouses were now far more compassionate than they had been in earlier decades, when they had often been worse than prisons. Nevertheless, the social stigma of being forced to enter the workhouse was still a powerful deterrent to poor people who strove to survive by their own means.

Sitting separately within the walls was the infirmary block. Although built primarily to treat the sick inmates of the workhouse, it had over the decades, become a valuable asset to the town as a whole. Many people were unable to afford a doctor and relied on their own remedies, or on various patent medicines sold in the market instead. Some doctors took on a few cases on a charitable basis. However, when more treatment was required, the nearest hospital was in the town of Porth several miles away. The infirmary at the workhouse,

under the direction of Doctor Henderson, could set broken bones, address dislocations and identify diseases. As the workhouse housed the poor, ill-nourished, old and infirm, deaths occurred frequently at the infirmary and corpses had been stored in a 'cold room'. Through the influence of Superintendent Jones, the 'cold room' had now been provisioned as a mortuary with full facilities.

When Chard and his constable entered the infirmary, they were taken straight to the office of Doctor Henderson. 'We need to let Dr Henderson know that we are here, out of politeness,' he explained.

However, the portly Doctor Henderson was not there. In his office, filing some papers in a storage cabinet, stood a young woman with auburn hair, in a white blouse and grey patterned skirt. She turned as they entered.

'Inspector Chard. I am afraid Doctor Henderson is out at the moment. Doctor Matthews is in the mortuary if that is of any help.'

Chard noticed that the young clerk spoke in a monotone. The fire in her eyes and the vibrancy, which he had found so irritating when they had met in the previous year, was missing.

'Thank you, Miss Roper. I only wanted to advise Doctor Henderson that we were here.

Miss Roper nodded and returned to her work without a word.

Constable Temple had noticed that she hadn't stared at his disfigurement and as they walked through the infirmary ward to the mortuary, he ventured a comment.

'A very attractive young lady.'

'Unfortunately, she suffered a terrible experience last year. I think it has affected her deeply,' confided Chard.

'Very pretty nonetheless.'

'She has been walking out with Constable Morgan, so don't get any ideas,' cautioned Chard, as they stepped into the mortuary.

They were immediately struck by the strong smell of disinfectant that permeated the white-tiled room. Standing by a table was the unmistakeable frame of Doctor Matthews, shirtsleeves rolled up, writing in a small notebook. He turned as they approached, a welcoming smile on his face.

'Ah, good morning Inspector Chard,' he greeted, keeping the salutation formal as the inspector had a constable in tow.

'Good morning Doctor Matthews. Do you have anything of interest for us?'

'In relation to the poor burnt chap you mean? Well, let's take a look, shall we?'

The table in front of him was covered by a white sheet and the doctor pulled it back with a flourish to reveal a grisly sight.

Chard looked away instinctively.

'Sorry Inspector, I forgot that you are not as inured to these sights as I am,' apologised Matthews.

Chard regained his composure and turned back to look at the blackened corpse which seemed to have shrunk and curled up in the heat.

'Not very pleasant I grant you,' continued the doctor. 'Revealing though.'

'In what way?'

The doctor's nose twitched above his thin waxed moustache, 'I believe you have a murder on your hands.'

'You mean he was killed and then the premises were set alight to hide the crime? How can you tell a cause of death from what's left of him?'

'Let me correct you, Inspector. It was the flames, or perhaps the smoke, that killed him. I believe he was alive when the fire started.'

'Please explain yourself, Doctor.'

With a self-satisfied look on his face, Doctor Matthews pointed to a small metal tray alongside the table and taking a pair of tweezers, extracted something from it.

He held the tweezers up to the light that came from the single window in the room and gestured Chard to look.

'You see those fibres?'

Chard nodded.

'I found these burnt into what blackened tissue remaining around the wrist area. I believe the man's hands had been tied.'

'Did you find anything in the mouth? My original suspicions arose because allegedly nobody heard him call for help.'

'I found nothing,' answered Matthews, 'but that doesn't mean there wasn't anything, mark you.'

'Damn it. I'm going to have a busy time of it then. I have the

widow to speak to and I need to ensure that the evidence is all in one place. I was hoping to see the rugby match this afternoon.'

'I am looking forward to it myself. Surely you can still go, Inspector? Presumably one of your constables can be delegated to ensure that the evidence is in one place?'

Constable Temple, who had been taking notes, spoke up. 'I would be happy to do that sir,' he volunteered.

'I would also imagine that the widow would prefer to wait a little before being interviewed formally. Surely it can wait until Monday morning?'

Chard hesitated, unsure whether he should delay, but then gave in.

'Very well then. I'll see you later Doctor.'

It was a decision he would regret.

***

The town centre was extremely busy. It was a full market day and the population of Pontypridd swelled many times over, as people from miles away came to buy and sell their goods. In addition to the permanent stalls of the indoor market, others had been set up along the length of Market Street and Church Street. The other streets of the town also bustled as pedestrians dodged the horse-drawn omnibuses, brakes, gigs and other vehicles that brought yet more shoppers and sightseers.

Amidst the thronging crowds, a thin, greasy-haired, stooped figure made his way towards a tobacconist's shop, where he intended to treat himself to some expensive cigars.

Jeremiah Davies had settled in at his lodgings in the County Hotel. It was a decent enough premises, though not as well furnished as he would have liked. He was just a few feet from the shop door when someone tapped him on the shoulder.

'Jeremiah! How are you old chap, and what are you doing here of all places?'

He turned and with a shout of delight exclaimed, 'Theodore! My old friend. I had forgotten that you live in the area.'

The man to whom he spoke was rotund and well-dressed. He sported a thick coat over a dark grey suit, with waistcoat and gold

watch chain. Clean shaven and jolly, he also wore a black bowler hat which he removed and waved in pleasure.

Davies shook his hand. 'I have left the service of the Barry Railway Company this very week. They failed to appreciate me, so I have taken up a position with the Taff Vale Railway.'

'Ho, ho! You will not be popular with your former employers I take it'

'Correct, Theodore. That is why I have moved out of Cardiff for the time being until it blows over.'

The jolly-faced man frowned. 'Just be careful that the Taff Vale Railway doesn't let you down mind,' he cautioned.

Davies gave a sly smile. 'Don't worry my friend. I have insurance,' he confided, tapping the side of his nose.

His friend looked reassured. '*Da iawn*! Very good!' he repeated in English. 'We must meet up soon and you can tell me all about it properly. What about this time next week eh? Where are you staying?'

'The County Hotel.'

'Excellent, excellent! I will call on you at midday next Saturday.'

With that the two men shook hands and parted. Davies entered the tobacconist's shop unaware that he was being watched. The new employee of the Taff Vale Railway looked forward to the promised meeting. He was unaware that it would be the last time that the two friends would ever meet.

EIGHT

Inspector Chard had decided to walk to the rugby ground despite the cold weather. He wore a thick woollen jacket beneath his coat and his scarf was pulled up over his chin. With the brim of his bowler hat pulled down over his eyes, he was barely recognisable. Lacking gloves, he had left his cane behind so he could keep his hands warm inside his pockets. The weather had turned colder, overcast and generally more miserable and Chard was regretting his decision to stand at a rugby match. At least the walk would warm him. As he progressed out of the town and onto the Tram Road, he noticed a familiar figure ahead. Increasing his stride, he made ground on the man. Once within earshot Chard pulled down his scarf a little and called out. The man turned, and then waited for the inspector to catch up.

'Thomas! I am glad you kept to your decision to come.'

'Well to be honest I am starting to regret it, but I am glad to catch you alone Ezekiel. I wanted to talk to you at the mortuary, but it was difficult with Constable Temple present.'

'Please be my guest, Thomas. You've got me quite intrigued.'

'It's nothing to do with the case. I just wanted to ask you about May Roper. She clearly is not herself.'

The doctor shook his head sadly. 'I was talking to Doctor Henderson earlier this morning. In my opinion she is still in shock from that bad experience last year. She needs patience and understanding. Time will be the healer.'

'Is there no medication that can help?'

'Not that I would advise, though Doctor Henderson would no doubt be prepared to prescribe something to calm her down if she experienced periods of hysteria. Whether or not he has done, I couldn't say. She is his own patient and her details remain confidential between them.'

Chard was silent for a while as they walked on, noting the many

vehicles passing them by, filled with spectators going to Taff Vale Park.

'Constable Morgan told me that he had given her some cocaine, but Doctor Henderson told her to stop taking it.'

'I imagine that would be correct. I know many doctors would commend the constable, but both Doctor Henderson and I agree that it is too easy to become dependent on it. No, time will cure it. You mark my words.'

Taff Vale Park had been built as a sports ground on land owned by the Taff Vale Ironworks. The chairman of the ironworks, James Roberts, was also the chairman of the Town Council and keen to provide facilities for the community. Initially just an empty field, the rugby pitch was now surrounded by rail barriers. On one long side of the pitch there was a large terrace with a covered grandstand in the centre, straddling the players' entrance.

As the doctor and inspector made their way through the gathering crowd towards the ground entrance, he felt a tap on the shoulder.

'*Shwmae* Mr Chard,' came a familiar voice.

Chard turned to see, the familiar bulbous nose and drooping moustache of Dic Jenkins. Following close behind were Will Horses and Dai Books, both wrapped up in warm clothing and wearing Dai caps.

'Where's Gwen gone?' asked Will.

They all looked back at the crowd behind them and Chard could not help but grin as Gwen started to make her way forward. The only woman in the crowd, the brawny landlady pushed and shoved the men around her, ignoring their loud complaints until she caught up with her friends.

Chard glanced at Dr Matthews who looked bemused.

'Some fine acquaintances of mine,' he explained.

Before he could say anything further there was a surge in the crowd and they were carried towards the gates, where those without tickets were required to throw their admittance into a bucket held by the gate keepers.

'I have a ticket for the grandstand Thomas, so I will see you after the game,' shouted the doctor over the noise of the crowd.

'You come with us Mr. Chard, we'll see you alright mun,' reassured Dic Jenkins.

Once inside the ground, the small group bustled their way across to the terrace next to the grandstand. The higher section of terrace at the back had a better view and was already full. Although they had to settle for a place at ground level, it was at least close to the pitch.

There was a feeling of high anticipation, and the excitement of the crowd grew as kick-off approached. The pitch appeared in excellent condition as Chard surveyed the scene. Behind the goalposts to his right could be seen the smoke from the chimneys of the ironworks in the distance. Directly across the field, there were few spectators and no terrace, just the trees that bounded the river bank. Behind the posts to the left, latecomers were still coming to watch the encounter.

Suddenly there was a roar of expectation from the spectators as the teams began to emerge from the changing rooms. They were accompanied by a strong smell of liniment, rubbed into the limbs of the combatants to prevent muscle strains.

Neath entered the pitch first, all in black with a white Maltese cross on their jerseys. They were greeted by a polite round of applause together with shouts of approval from a large number of Neath supporters that had arrived by train. Then came Pontypridd, led by their captain, young Jack Morgan, who looked diminutive but extremely athletic. The usual jerseys with narrow cardinal and black hoops had been replaced by a kit with very broad black and white hoops to better distinguish the two teams. Their appearance was accompanied by loud cheers from the home crowd, rising to a crescendo when their international forward, Ernest George took to the field.

The teams lined up for the kick off, the eight larger, heavier forwards of each team facing each other, with the seven lighter, faster, backs spread across the open field.

Chard saw Constable Morgan set up in his position alongside the other centre, Jack Morgan. The constable was a little taller than his captain, heavier and of a sturdier build, but he looked anxious.

In Chard's opinion, the first half of the game was not terribly memorable, other than the fact that it felt bone-numbingly cold. When Neath had possession, they tended to kick the ball out of play

further up field, to get a good position for an attack. Their plan was flawed, as Pontypridd had a very tall forward with a long moustache and wild hair, who (through liberal use of his elbow) won every ball that was thrown into play. Conversely, Ponty would make their way with ball in hand only to be stopped twenty yards out through infringements by Neath. Each time a penalty was awarded, and on the first occasion it was Constable Idris Morgan who was called on to kick for goal. He missed. On the second occasion he also missed. The third time, Chard felt that with the ball directly in front of the posts, he couldn't possibly miss. He did.

'Morgan what are you doing?' exclaimed Chard loudly.

A rather intoxicated supporter behind him tapped Chard on the shoulder.

'"ere, do you know him?' he asked, his breath heavy with the smell of stale beer.

'Never seen him before in my life!' joked the inspector.

Fortunately for Ponty, they changed their kicker and by half time they had scored two penalty kicks and a converted try, giving a lead of 11-0.

At half time the teams gathered around their respective managers near the touchline and Chard could hear the impassioned talk being given to the Neath team.

'Now then boys, you are fighting hard, I'll take my hat off to you!' The manager emphasised this by literally removing the bowler hat that he wore and waving it at them. 'But that bugger at the line-out needs taking care of. Raise the game boys. Raise the game! I want more fight, more fire, more *hwyl*!'

That was where the trouble started.

The teams kicked off for the second half and at the very next throw-in one of the Neath forwards grabbed the Ponty line-out expert, pulling him back before he had a chance to jump for the ball. The Ponty player swung his fist, resulting in a crunch and a tooth flying in the air to land several feet away. Meanwhile the ball was in play further along the field. Nursing his jaw, the Neath player appealed to the linesman, only to receive the curt response, 'Well, you shouldn't have been holding him.'

There were laughs and jeers from the home crowd and indigna-

tion from the visiting supporters. At the next scrummage the Neath team retaliated by their front row calling 'Send one through.' On the command a second-row player sent a punch from behind into the unprotected face of an opponent. Both teams then set too in a free for all, with the referee and both linesmen attempting to calm things down. Chard was only too aware that things were getting tense in the crowd too.

Someone nudged Dai Books and pointed towards a particularly noisy group of supporters a few yards away

'*Roedd rhw ffwl wedi taflu potel ar y cae.*'

'*Ie mae nhw I gyd wedi meddwi,*' responded Dai.

'What was that all about?' asked Chard.

'Nothing really. Those drunk idiots have just thrown a bottle on the pitch.'

'I don't like the feel of this,' chipped in Dic, who had an instinct for trouble.

Their attention turned back to the pitch as the ball was dropped on the ground, only for a Neath player to throw himself over it to prevent Ponty from gaining possession.

He regretted it, for there was a flurry of metal studs as the pack of Ponty forwards trampled over him, rucking his body out of the way.

'There was a stamp in there!' shouted an irate Neath supporter.

'Shut up!' came a response.

Chard was aware that some pushing and shoving was starting to take place around him. He looked at his friends. Will was looking wary, Dic anxious, Dai Books appeared calm, but Gwen was standing silently with arms folded. The inspector had seen that grim expression on her face before, when she was about to throw someone out of the pub.

Back on the pitch, the Pontypridd left winger was running forward with the ball tucked under his arm, when his opposite number threw a rigid arm out to catch him across the neck. He went down like a sack of potatoes.

'You dirty bastard!' erupted Gwen, her face full of fury.

'Go home and do the washing up, woman!' yelled someone behind.

That was it. The landlady, turned and launched herself towards the unfortunate heckler. Fighting having already broken out amongst the players on the pitch, Gwen's action was the signal for chaos to break out on the terrace.

'Look after her,' shouted Chard to his friends, glancing around at them. True to form Dic Jenkins had already disappeared.

Chard felt his legs move involuntarily as the surge of the crowd, pushed him sideways and caused him to lose his footing. Suddenly he was falling with someone above him, his head hit the stone terrace, and he blacked out.

***

When Chard awoke, he found himself laying on a bed in a strange room. His head hurt like fury and his vision took some time to clear. Suddenly a twitching little waxed moustache appeared over him as Doctor Matthews leaned over to take a look.

'What happened?' asked the inspector.

'The match was abandoned. It will have to be replayed.'

'I'm not talking about the match, Ezekiel,' snapped his patient.

'Now calm down Thomas. I am only pulling your leg. There was a bit of a kerfuffle, cuts and bruises and no-one really hurt.'

Chard grunted and tried to sit up, only for the room to start revolving. He gave up and lay down again.

'Apart from you of course,' continued the doctor. You were at the bottom of a pile of bodies and hit your head on the terrace.'

'What about Gwen?'

Matthews laughed. 'I don't think a battleship could damage that lady. She's fine. In fact, she helped me get you here, undress you and put you into bed.'

Chard felt his face redden with embarrassment. 'Where exactly am I?'

'In a spare bedroom of my house. I needed to fetch you here so that I could stitch you up properly.'

'Gwen will let your maid know of your situation. Since she only attends you for part of the day you must stay here instead. Mrs Murray lives in and will make sure that you are cared for properly over the next week.'

'The next week?' queried Chard in alarm. 'What do you mean? I am in the middle of an investigation.' He tried once more to sit up, only to give up and lie back groaning.

'Sorry Thomas, but you are not going to be investigating anything for a few days. You were out cold for quite some time. Then you were delirious and in a lot of pain so I sedated you for the journey back here.'

'I may possibly need to rest for a day,' conceded the inspector.

'More than that. I am concerned that there may be some after effects. Bed rest for four or five days then, if I am satisfied, you can get back on your feet. You can resume your duties on the following Monday. I will speak to Superintendent Jones myself.'

'I can't just drop a murder investigation,' appealed the inspector.

'You are not dropping it, just delaying it a little. Although quite large, Cilfynydd is a close-knit village. If anyone suddenly disappears, it will be noticed, then you will know they are likely to be the guilty party. If no-one disappears then your suspects will still be there to be interviewed. A few days won't make any difference. No, my friend, you must rest. I insist. The constabulary must manage without you. I am sure that they will find someone suitable to cover for you.'

NINE

On Monday morning, having had an early visit from Doctor Matthews, an irritable Superintendent Jones gestured for Sergeant Jackson to come into his office.

'It appears that the inspector has been caught up in a disturbance. He will be off duty for the whole of this week.'

'Sorry to hear that, sir,' lied Jackson.

'Doctor Matthews is of the opinion that the victim of the fire in Cilfynydd was murdered. He will be giving evidence at the inquest this week.' The superintendent slammed the desk with his fist. 'I cannot have everything come to a complete stop just because Inspector Chard has got himself involved in an unseemly brawl.'

'If there's anything I can do to help, sir?' offered the newly appointed sergeant.

'Find out how far the inspector has got with his investigation, and if there is anything that you think needs doing, get it done. At least everything will then be up to date for him when he returns next week,' ordered the superintendent.

Jackson gave an obsequious smile. 'Only too pleased to help sir.'

***

Later that afternoon, Sergeant Jackson stood outside the door of the widow, Mrs Hughes. Having discovered that Chard had not yet interviewed her, he had advised Superintendent Jones, and suggested that it should be done immediately. Jackson had wanted to visit her on his own, but the superintendent had insisted that a constable accompany him and allocated Constable Morgan to the task.

The weather had become even colder and both policemen wore thick, heavy coats.

'Just keep your mouth shut and only write down what I want you to,' ordered the sergeant.

Morgan did not reply.

The sergeant hammered on the door with unnecessary force with his fist. Soon they could hear footsteps on the tiled floor of the hallway and the door was opened by a young woman. She wore a dark grey dress edged in black, a cheap necklace of black beads and a small black woollen shawl over her shoulders. Her attractive face was very pale, with bags under her red-rimmed eyes.

She looked the men up and down. 'Come in,' she offered, turning away and leading them into the house.

Constable Morgan closed the door behind them and followed the sergeant into the parlour. There were dying embers of a fire in the grate and the room remained warm.

'I see you are not in mourning,' commented the sergeant impolitely.

'There is no option. I no longer have an income from my poor dear husband,' she explained. Morgan noticed a tear start to form in the corner of her eye. 'His workshop and tools are all destroyed. I have to go out to work to have enough money to eat.'

'Still, you should surely be in black, with your husband not yet put in the ground?' tormented the sergeant.

'I work in a public house, Sergeant,' she snapped back. 'I doubt that my employers would be very happy if I turned up in widows' weeds. This dress is the closest that I could manage. They have been very kind to me as it is, even paying me this past week. In fact, I cannot speak to you for very long, as I have to go to work within the next hour.'

'You will talk to me for as long as I say you will,' answered the sergeant aggressively.

'It doesn't seem very seemly for a new widow to be working at night in a public house,' he continued.

'I will ask them to change my shifts so that I will no longer have to work in the evenings and come home at night to an empty home.'

The pointless bullying of the sergeant made Morgan uncomfortable.

'You were going to ask the lady if she knew of anyone who bore a grudge against her husband, Sergeant,' interrupted the constable.

Jackson turned to look at Morgan with loathing. Then he looked back at Mrs Hughes.

'Yes, Mrs Hughes. As MY constable...' he paused, having emphasised to Morgan that he was in charge, '... here was saying. Do you know of anyone that might have wished your husband any harm?'

'Why do you ask? Surely the fire was an accident?'

'We think perhaps not.' Jackson indicated to Constable Morgan that he could now start to take notes.

'How can you be sure?' asked the widow. 'I have been told that the inquest isn't until Thursday.'

Jackson ignored the remark. 'I will ask you once again. Did anyone have any cause to harm your husband?'

'No. He was a good man.'

'He didn't have any disagreements at all?'

'Well he didn't get on very well with Mr. Dixon who lives in the house next to the workshop. Also, I know that a few customers have been late paying. No-one would want to harm him though. It must have been an accident.'

'What about you?' snapped the sergeant.

'What do you mean? What are you inferring?' asked the widow, upset.

Constable Morgan looked on uncomfortably, but unable to intervene.

'Did you have disagreements with your husband?'

A tear started to form in the young woman's eye. 'Only what is normal in a marriage. Everybody argues.'

'What about?'

'Things have been very tight over the past few months. William worked at the carpenter's shop at the colliery from time to time, as well as having his own little business here. But somehow, he still found himself short of money.'

'Really?' asked the sergeant incredulously. 'Are you sure you weren't arguing because he was seeing another woman?'

'Don't you dare suggest a thing!' answered the widow angrily. 'He was a kind, faithful husband.'

'Remind me, how old was he?'

'Forty-eight, Sergeant.'

Jackson rubbed his chin. 'More than double your age.'

'Yes, what of it?'

'Perhaps you fancied younger, lustier company,' leered the sergeant.

The widow's eyes were red-rimmed and she was barely holding back the tears. She formed as if to shout, but regained her composure so as not to give the sergeant any satisfaction.

'My William was a good, kind man, who took me in after I suffered a bereavement. I had no-one to care or provide for me. I would do anything to have him back.'

'When did you last see him?'

'On the day of the fire. I took him a cup of tea before I went off to work for the evening. I was in Pontypridd when the fire started,' she sobbed. 'I wasn't there to save him.' Unable to hold back the floods of tears that had welled up inside, the widow put her head in her hands and wept uncontrollably.

Unsure what to do, the bullish sergeant gave a grunt and gestured to Constable Morgan that they should leave.

***

Inspector Chard lay with eyes closed, listening to the crackle of the fire when the door creaked open. He looked across the room to see Mrs Murray enter carrying a bowl of warm water.

'Time for a wash and to change your dressing,' she announced.

'Where is Doctor Matthews?'

'He has other patients you know,' retorted the petite housekeeper.

Chard had slept for most of the previous day, woken only to be spoon-fed some broth by Mrs Murray, and to have his dressing changed by the doctor.

'I'll get up and…'

'No, you won't. You will do as you are told. Wait there whilst I get fresh dressings.'

The housekeeper returned a few minutes later and proceeded to tend to Chard's head wound.

'Doctor Matthews instructed me to change your dressing every morning. It hardly requires any medical training to keep a cut clean,' she explained as she bathed the cut before placing a cotton pad and re-bandaging the inspector's head. 'He will want to see how it's getting along this evening.'

The woman reached for the bowl of water, and took out a wet flannel. 'It's still warm enough for a wash.'

Before Chard could say anything, his carer had rubbed the flannel over his face and then started to pull back the bedclothes. Instinctively, the inspector made a grab with his left arm and pulled the blankets close into his body.

'Mrs Murray! What do you think you are doing?' he cried.

'Giving you a wash. Doctor Matthews's instruction was to keep you clean. You didn't have one yesterday as we didn't want to disturb you.'

'Give the flannel to me. I can manage myself.'

'Mr Chard, you are being ridiculous. I am a widow and not unfamiliar with the human body.'

'It isn't seemly,' argued the inspector.

'Very well then, if you insist.'

Chard took the flannel and with difficulty managed to clean himself beneath the blankets, though it made him feel a little dizzy.

Mrs Murray looked disapprovingly. 'I will go now and let you rest, but I will be back in an hour to feed you some soup. Doctor Matthews will be told how obstinate you have been.'

***

Constable Idris Morgan stamped his feet on the pavement to get some warmth into his legs. Sergeant Jackson had insisted that he stay walking the beat around Cilfynydd until nightfall. Then he would have to walk back to the station before finishing his shift. His patrol had been uneventful, with few people out on the streets in the cold weather.

As soon as the light had faded sufficiently for the constable to consider he had done enough, he started to make his way out of Cilfynydd and back towards Pontypridd. There was sleet in the air and the occasional frozen particle stung his face. As he passed a small ironmonger's shop at the edge of the village, Morgan noticed that the front door was slightly ajar. It wasn't out of the ordinary, but this was a cold evening; and although the light was now exceedingly poor, no light shone inside the premises.

Morgan gently pushed the door open.

'Hello, anyone in?' he called.

There was no reply.

Morgan drew his truncheon and cautiously stepped inside. His foot connected with an overturned wooden crate causing him to stumble.

'Is anyone there?' he called.

There was a groan in reply which came from beyond the shop counter. As Morgan's eyes became accustomed to the darkness he gradually made sense of the shadowy shapes in the room. Edging forward towards the counter, with truncheon raised, he peered behind it. He could just make out the figure of a man lying on the floor. Morgan reached out a hand to help, only to get a surprising response.

'Get away! Who are you?'

'Police Constable Morgan. It's alright, you must have had an accident. I'll light a lamp.'

'There's no need,' replied the man, getting unsteadily to his feet. 'I've just had a bit of a fall reaching for something.'

'Wait a moment. Don't move around too much,' answered Morgan who had noticed the outline of an oil lamp at the far end of the counter. Taking matches from his pocket, the constable lit the lamp and looked at the injured man. He was elderly, with grey hair and his face was badly bruised.

'How did you fall?' asked the constable. "It looks like you landed on your face.'

'It's my fault. I should have lit the lamp first.'

'Are you sure that you haven't been assaulted? I can see that a few things have been turned over. I nearly fell over a crate when I came in.'

'I had some deliveries today and I didn't stack things properly. They must have fallen over,' answered the shopkeeper unconvincingly.

'Come now. Tell me what happened.'

'I am telling you. Thank you for your assistance Constable, but I am perfectly alright. Please go.'

Morgan tried several more times to talk to the shopkeeper, but to no avail. Giving up, he made some notes in his pocketbook, then set off on the long walk back to the station.

***

Next day, Chard was pleased to be told by Doctor Matthews that he could at last sit up, and also receive visitors. As a result, in the afternoon he had been made a huge fuss of by Gwen, who had arrived with some flowers and fruit. Mrs Murray had stayed in the room whilst Gwen chattered away, telling Chard all the gossip she knew and saying a prayer for his speedy recovery. Eventually, Mrs Murray politely reminded Gwen that the inspector needed to rest and so, after another quick prayer, the landlady returned to the Ivor Arms.

'Mrs Williams seems very nice,' commented Mrs Murray.

'Salt of the earth, as they say,' replied Chard.

'It's a pity you weren't a bit more presentable.'

'How do you mean?'

'I'll be back,' answered the housekeeper, who left the room.

Ten minutes later she returned with a bowl of hot water, which she put to one side before taking some items from her apron pocket.

'What are you doing? I've had a wash this morning,' said a puzzled Chard.

'But not a shave. You are starting to look like a tramp, Mr Chard.'

'My razor is at my house and even if I had it, you would have to help me to the mirror,' reasoned the inspector.

'I have a razor. It was my Jack's and as for helping you to the mirror, you know that you mustn't get up yet. I will shave you.'

'You will do no such thing!' answered Chard indignantly.

'I have shaved my Jack before now and I have a steady hand. Doctor Matthews made me promise to look after you as best as I can and you are in no position to argue.'

Chard reluctantly let the housekeeper bathe his face and apply soap, but tensed visibly when she produced the cut-throat razor and held it to his skin.

'Are you sure that you don't want me to shave off those awful sideburns? They are becoming rather old-fashioned.'

'No leave them!' replied Chard with difficulty, not wanting to move his mouth whilst the razor scraped against his skin.

Mrs Murray grimaced, 'Very well, but I will get a scissors to trim them and your moustache as well. They should at least be neat and tidy.'

Eventually, the housekeeper finished and Chard gave a sigh of relieve. His face felt clean and soft to the touch and rather begrudgingly, he complimented Mrs Murray on her efforts.

'As I said, I shaved my dear husband on occasion.'

Chard didn't quite know the right thing to say next. 'I am sorry for your loss. Doctor Matthews explained that he was one of the men at the Albion Colliery.'

'Yes, not all the victims of the disaster were from Cilfynydd. We lived in Pontypridd and my Jack would travel out there every day for his shift. It was a sad time. I lost my brother as well.'

'So Doctor Matthews said. I am so sorry.'

'I hate Cilfynydd as a place and I hate the Albion Steam Coal Company even more. The company was responsible for all those deaths, but nothing was done.'

'Was there no formal enquiry?'

Mrs Murray laughed mirthlessly. 'Yes, there was. In fact, the government clearly wanted a prosecution but they didn't know the power that the coal companies have here. The chairman of the enquiry gave a ten pound fine to the manager of the mine, a two pound fine to a minor employee, and dismissed the case against the under manager.'

'What about the company and its owners?'

'The chairman threw out the charges against the company and its owners on a technicality. I was in the court room that day and I could have killed him. The prosecutor was livid. If the charges had stood, then perhaps we wouldn't have had the disaster in Tylorstown last month.'

'Terrible for a second disaster to happen so soon.'

'I had just about come to terms with things when suddenly Tylorstown fetched it all back. I know I won't have been the only one, but I am afraid that I became rather hysterical for a day or two, and the doctor had to give me some medication to help me pull myself together.'

Mrs Murray suddenly felt aware that she had been talking of issues that were too personal to share. 'I am sorry Mr Chard. I shouldn't...'

'It's alright. Call me Thomas...'

***

The following evening that Chard received another guest, this time one whose impressive physique filled the doorframe.

'Sergeant Morris! How nice to see you!'

'Nice to see you too sir. It looks as though you are on the mend.'

'Yes, I have been able to sit up today without dizziness. Hopefully the doctor will remove the stitches tomorrow and let me walk about. How are things at the station?'

'The superintendent sends his best regards sir. He would have come himself but has an important function that he has to attend. It's in London, keeping him away until Monday'

'I expect he isn't very pleased that I got caught up in the trouble at the rugby match.'

The sergeant rubbed his beard, not sure what to say.

'It's alright Sergeant, no need to comment,' continued Chard. 'How are work matters?'

The sergeant remained hesitant and paused a little before responding. 'Superintendent Jones asked Sergeant Jackson to take over the Cilfynydd investigation in your absence.'

The dismay was plain on the inspector's face as Sergeant Morris went on.

'So far Jackson has interviewed the widow and after the inquest tomorrow he reckons that he will be able to solve the case and make an arrest.'

'I don't want him anywhere near the case,' said Chard, alarmed at the prospect.

Sergeant Morris, who was as aware of Jackson's failings as the inspector nodded in agreement.

'Unfortunately, with the Superintendent absent, there's no-one to stop him,' commented the sergeant.

'Sergeant, please find Mrs Murray and ask her to fetch me pen and paper. I will write a direct order telling him to take no action until I return on Monday.'

The sergeant did as he was asked and re-appeared with the writing equipment.

'I understand that you took Constable Temple with you up to the mortuary sir,' said the sergeant as Chard started to write.

'Yes, I don't quite know what to make of him,' replied the inspector. 'He seemed reasonable enough, but frankly I was rather annoyed.'

'In what way, sir?'

Chard stopped writing whilst he replied.

'I had been told that he had experience of China, so I naturally enough asked him about it. He confirmed that he had been there but then started talking nonsense. He was obviously lying.'

Sergeant Morris looked thoughtful but then his expression changed as if some realisation had dawned.

'May I ask who told you about Constable Temple and China sir?'

'Constable Matthews.'

The sergeant raised his eyebrows.

'Yes,' continued Chard, 'I know he is a joker Sergeant, but Temple confirmed it.'

There was a suppressed smile on Sergeant Morris's lips as he replied. 'I think you will find that China is the name given to a particularly rough and disreputable area of Merthyr Tydfil. Temple would have had to go there when he was at 'A' Division.'

'Oh,' responded Chard. He returned to writing his instructions feeling a little foolish.

'I think I can foresee Constable Matthews having to do night shifts for the next two weeks,' commiserated the sergeant.

'On another matter, it appears that Morgan and Temple don't get on. Why is that?' asked Chard, keen to change the topic.

'Temple was injured during an arrest when he was stationed here before. That's how he has that burn scar on his face. At the time he reckoned that Morgan could have helped him but ran away. Nonsense of course, he actually fetched the help which saved Temple. There was a lot of discord at the time, but hopefully it's all in the past.'

Satisfied with the explanation, Chard finished writing and handed the instruction for Jackson over to Sergeant Morris.

'Thank you, sir. I'll be on my way now. We all hope to see you back on Monday.'

Chard watched the big man leave and thought back on the day. Mrs Murray, or Alice as he now knew her name to be, had spent as

much time between her duties as possible, sitting and talking with him. The things they discussed were frivolous, inconsequential, but they had made them both smile and laugh together. He felt content.

It was some hours later when Chard was ready for sleep that Alice came to check his wound dressing.

'It's healing nicely. I am sure the doctor will remove the stitches tomorrow,' smiled Alice.

As she settled his head back on the pillow her lips came close to his. Suddenly, unexpectedly, he kissed her. There was a slight pause as she did not pull away, but then she did. The moment was over. Alice turned in silence and left the room.

TEN

Jeremiah Davies raised his glass to Theodore Clark and congratulated him on such comfortable surroundings. Having had a pint of beer at the bar, they had taken their second round of drinks to a quiet area of the Butchers Arms to have a private discussion. They settled into a pair of elegantly carved chairs with plush red cushioned seats, their drinks on a small polished oak table between them.

'I have become a regular patron here, you know. This is my table, kept for me and anyone I wish to entertain,' boasted Clark. 'They keep my favourite cigars behind the bar and I was even consulted on the choice of new paintwork for the entrance,' he bragged.

'Truly, I am impressed, Theodore. I had only intended to stay in Pontypridd for a short while, but perhaps I may stay longer.'

'Has there been any contact from your former employer?'

Davies shook his head. 'None, I am relieved to say.'

'So, you made the right decision to move to the Taff Vale Railway?'

Davies grimaced. 'To be frank Theodore, I have been a little disappointed. I thought they could be trusted but…'

Clark leant forward in his seat. 'You seem unsure…'

Davies put his drink down, and explained his concerns, unaware that he was being observed by two thick-set men in tweed suits at a nearby table.

'I had a visit in the week from a chap called Jennings, a personal factotum of Benjamin Armstrong, chairman of the Taff Vale Railway. He came to give me some money.'

'Well that can't be bad,' interrupted Clark with some jollity.

'Unfortunately, as I engaged him in discussion, I got the distinct impression that the promise to install me on the board of directors will not be honoured. I have a way of seeing through lies, but it appears that my skills failed me when dealing with Armstrong.'

'You made the wrong decision then?' queried Clark with some concern.

'Not entirely. I do hold a trump card. I sent Jennings away with a message for Armstrong. Just one sentence, "I have the document".'

'What does that mean?' asked Clark, intrigued.

Davies laughed. 'Nothing … and everything,' he answered mysteriously.

'Well your business is your business. You always were one for complicated matters, unlike myself. I like the simple things in life, like comfort, a good drink and, of course, excellent food.' Clark rubbed his stomach as he continued. 'Talking of which, I feel like a nice cake or two. Let us take a stroll into Market Street for some sustenance and then perhaps you would care to join me for my afternoon constitutional.'

'I see no reason why not,' agreed Davies.

The two friends got up and left the Butchers Arms, followed seconds later by the two men in tweed suits.

***

Chard stood hesitantly outside his front door. His head ached, though not excessively, and stitches had been taken out by Doctor Matthews on Thursday. By the evening, Chard had been walking satisfactorily and on the Friday afternoon the doctor had taken him back to his home. After a good night's sleep, the inspector felt he should try a walk into the town unaccompanied. Although he no longer felt any dizziness, it was reassuring to have his walking cane for support. After taking a few steps and deciding that he wasn't going to suddenly keel over, Chard reflected on the past few days. He pursed his lips, then gave an audible sigh of disappointment as he thought about the kiss with Alice. She had not spoken a word since then and had only entered his room when Doctor Matthews was present.

As he continued towards the town centre, the street became busier. A Saturday in Pontypridd was always the same, as thousands of shoppers flooded the town from the Rhondda valleys and far beyond. Rather than walk down the centre of Church Street, which seemed to be jammed solid with shoppers, he took the stretch of

pavement that ran behind one of the long lines of stalls. This still necessitated squeezing past people coming in the other direction who had the same idea. A strong waft of freshly baked pastries hit his senses as the pavement passed by one of the entrances to the indoor market, and made Chard feel hungry. Determined to have at least something to satisfy his appetite, he headed for a smart little teashop in Market Street.

***

'What can I get your gentlemen?' asked the waitress.

'A pot of tea for two, and please show us the cakestand. I am in the mood for a nice slice of cake. The bigger the better,' replied Theodore Clark. 'Victoria sponge if you have it,' he added.

'I assume you are of the same mind, Jeremiah,' he asked his friend.

'Perhaps just a small slice of cake for me,' responded Davies.

The waitress nodded and walked off, almost bumping into the two men in tweed suits who had just entered. They glanced at Davies and Clark before taking the only unoccupied table in the room.

***

A few minutes later Thomas Chard also entered the Silver Teapot. Going from the chilly, noisy street market to the warm tearoom temporarily made his head swim. He stood for a moment to steady himself and take in his surroundings.

There didn't seem to be a table free. Closest to him were several four-seater tables occupied in the main by families. An elderly couple sat further inside the room drinking tea, then two men in tweed who seemed deep in conversation. Beyond them two men of the cloth were debating some matter in an animated fashion. In a far corner sat another two men, one with a jolly, florid complexion who was eating a large slice of cake and the other, thin with greasy hair who was sipping tea. Next to them, a woman sat with her back to Chard. The chair facing her was empty.

'I am sorry sir, but I am afraid we are full up,' advised one of the waitresses.

'That's perfectly alright. Perhaps I will come back later.'

On hearing his voice, the solitary woman turned in her seat. She blushed and look flustered. It was Alice. Ignoring the waitress, the inspector walked forward. Alice got up to leave.

'Alice, please don't go. Let us just sit a while.'

She hesitated for a moment, before sitting down, allowing Chard to take the seat facing her.

'I want to apologise,' said Chard earnestly. 'It was completely inappropriate of me to do what I did.'

Before Alice could reply, one of the waitresses came to take his order.

Irritated by the interruption and without taking his eyes off Alice, Chard quickly snapped an order for the first things that came into his head.

'A fresh pot of tea for two with Welsh cakes please.'

'Certainly sir,' said the waitress.

Something in the voice made Chard look up, and he was taken aback with surprise.

'Mrs Evans?' he asked rhetorically on recognising the friend of the widow from Cilfynydd.

'Yes Inspector?'

'Sorry, I was just surprised to see you here.'

'I am afraid I have to work somewhere, Inspector. I have no husband to keep a roof over my head since the disaster.'

'Yes, of course,' replied Chard apologetically.

'I will be back shortly with your order,' said Mrs Evans turning on her heel.

'So, another unfortunate like myself, widowed by the Albion colliery,' commented Alice.

'Yes. We met when I was investigating the fire at Cilfynydd.'

'You mean the murder at Cilfynydd. I overheard Doctor Matthews telling you about the inquest before you left us.'

'Yes, well hopefully, apart from the odd bit of dizziness every so often, I feel I should be able to resume my enquiries on Monday morning.'

There was an awkward silence before Alice spoke.

'That was the first time I had kissed a man since I lost my husband. I felt, still feel, guilty.'

'My profound apologies once again. As I said, my actions were inappropriate. Please forgive me.'

Another silence followed.

'I do, Thomas.'

They started to chat about mundane matters and were soon lost in conversation. They did not notice the occupants of the next table get up and leave, closely followed by the two men in tweed suits.

***

'Of course, those in the medical profession don't really know what they are talking about,' confided Theodore Clark to his friend as they pushed their way through the crowds in Market Street and onto Taff Street.

'Really Theodore? In what way do you mean?'

'My physician says that I am overweight and that I need to take a constitutional every day, nonsense really.' Clark paused as they crossed the road between a builder's cart and a waggonette, avoiding a pile of horse manure on the cobbles.

'True,' he continued, 'I have had to buy a couple of new suits recently but in my opinion, there is too much moisture in a gentleman's wardrobe.'

'I don't follow....' frowned a puzzled Davies.

'It shrinks the clothes,' informed Clark with a smile and a wink.

'Yet you do take a daily walk, as you are today.'

'My physician and I came to a compromise. When I take a constitutional, which is most days, I start it with a beer, then I have some cake. Sufficiently fortified, I walk to the end of town, over the bridge and down through Ynysangharad Fields to the confluence of the Taff and Rhondda rivers. I then retrace my steps and return to the Butchers Arms. A final beer finishes my exercise for the day and I go home a healthy man,' explained Clark.

Jeremiah Davies shook his head in disbelief at his friend's carefree attitude. And he envied him for it.

'You noticed our fine drinking fountain I take it?' said Clark, pointing to a truly magnificent edifice in the centre of Penuel Square.

'Truly a work of consummate skill. It's very impressive.'

'It was only completed last year. As a leading member of the community I was of course invited to the opening,' boasted Clark, puffing out his chest.

'I am sure the town is very grateful for a public supply of clean water.'

'Most homes have clean water, but in some poorer parts we have had contamination which has led to outbreaks of typhoid. The water from the fountain though is so pure. Come…' Clark gripped Davies by the elbow and guided him across the busy road towards the fountain.

'I know it's a cold day, but you must taste the water,' he insisted.

The raised paving by the fountain was crowded with shoppers waiting for a gap in the traffic to cross the street. Clark pushed through them towards one of the four drinking basins. As he reached forward a slender man in a long grey coat bumped into him, blocking his way.

'How dare you sir?' objected Clark.

The man moved away without a word, leaving the way free for the two friends. Clark put some water in the palm of his hand and took it to his lips.

'Try it, Jeremiah. It is most refreshing.'

Davies followed suit and nodded in appreciation.

'Now then,' sighed Clark, 'I must now begin my daily exercise. You need not accompany me if you do not wish to do so,' he commented in a kindly manner. 'Not everyone is of my own robust constitution.'

The smaller, thinner man smiled. 'I think I should be able to manage it just this once,' he replied, unaware what fate had in store.

ELEVEN

'I do believe the afternoon is getting even chillier,' announced Theodore Clark to his companion.

The two friends had strolled to the northern end of the town, turned right and crossed the bridge to the other side of the river. A short walk had taken them past the Maltsters Arms and into Ynysangharad Fields on the eastern bank of the river .

The path through the fields was well established. In summer months the fields were used by many locals for walking and picnics. Even in winter it was a popular route to take a relaxing walk on the weekend.

'I agree. I feel as if the cold has really got into my bones. I can't stop myself from shivering,' replied Davies despite his thick heavy overcoat.

Clark was just about to respond when something flew through the air and struck his bowler hat. There was a shout of triumph and jeers that were unintelligible to Davies, from behind a nearby tree.

'What was that? What is going on?' he demanded.

'Those bastards just threw a lump of dog shit!' spluttered a red-faced Clark. 'I'll have you in prison for that you scum!' he shouted after two scruffily dressed youths who ran laughing into the distance.

'I am afraid there's nothing we can do,' mollified Davies. 'We wouldn't be able to catch them,' he added, relieved that there would be no physical confrontation.

Clark looked around to ensure that no-one else was around to witness his discomfiture before inspecting his hat and replying.

'Very well, but I will report it to the police when we get back into town. I recognised one of those miscreants and they will regret their actions. You mark my words. It has left me feeling quite flushed.'

'I fully understand Theodore. I can feel my heart pounding. It must be the shock,' agreed Davies, his face pale. 'The sooner we get back to town the better.'

The two friends walked on, but they had not gone far before Davies called a halt. 'Sorry Theodore but I am a little breathless,' he complained.

Clark turned to reply just as Davies bent over with a groan, grasping his stomach.

'What is the matter Jeremiah?'

'My innards. God, I feel like vomiting,' came the reply through clenched teeth.

'I feel a little out of sorts myself,' replied Clark, concerned at his friend's discomfort, but all too aware of the griping taking hold of his own stomach.

Davies felt the nausea sweep over him as he vomited over a patch of snowdrops growing next to the path. Unsure what to do, Clark looked around for assistance.

'Hey, you there!' he yelled at a couple of men several dozen yards behind them, partially obscured by a tree. 'Please help us!' The two men, both dressed in tweed, turned away and moved out of sight.

The effort of having called out left Clark feeling exhausted and the strength drained out of his legs. Noticing a ramshackle wooden bench just a short distance along the path, he grabbed Davies by the arm and pulled him towards it.

'We need to sit down and rest,' he gasped.

'I feel faint,' replied Davies as they reached the bench. 'Oh, the pain!' he added as another spasm hit his stomach.

There was no reply from Clark as he also started to experience stomach pains and was desperately trying not to vomit.

'My chest, I can't... breathe...' continued Davies as Clark's fight to maintain control of his bowels was lost. Sat on the bench, neither man could move their limbs or call for help. Davies finally closed his eyes, leant against his friend and breathed his last.

***

It was well into the evening when the call came. Inspector Chard was sitting in his armchair by a crackling fire, reading *The Time Machine*, the latest novel by H.G. Wells, whilst sipping a cup of tea. It had been a quite wonderful day. His head hardly ached at all, there was one more day to fully relax, and best of all Alice Murray had

agreed to accompany him to the theatre later in the week. On top of that, there was the Cilfynydd murder to get his teeth into first thing on Monday morning, and he was relishing the thought.

It was with surprise, if not consternation, that the inspector reacted to the loud banging on his door.

'Who the hell can that be?' he muttered, putting his book down.

When Chard opened his front door, he was surprised to see Constable Scudamore.

'Sorry to interrupt your evening sir, but Sergeant Morris instructed me to find you.'

'Why? What's so urgent?'

'We found two men collapsed on a park bench late this afternoon and took them up to the infirmary. A message from Doctor Henderson arrived not long ago, insisting that you be called at once.'

'I see. Very well, I will just be a moment,' assented Chard, aware that the doctor would not send for him unless it was important.

Having put on his coat against the chill of the night, the inspector fell in step alongside Constable Scudamore as they made their way to the infirmary.

Their route took them via the Tumble, where the night was starting to get busy. With over half a dozen bustling pubs located in the vicinity, a Saturday night was usually raucous, though the worst of behaviour was not yet on show. Currently, the loudest noise was being made by a Salvation Army brass band playing 'Bringing in the Sheaves' outside the Half Moon. An ardent lady member was haranguing prospective patrons of the pub whilst thrusting leaflets at them, condemning the demon drink. On a Saturday night it was a task doomed to failure but Chard admired her spirit.

The policemen strode onwards, up the hill, with coat collars turned up against the sleet that was now falling, until they reached the workhouse gates. One of the watchmen, probably an ex-inmate himself, had been instructed to expect them, for the gates opened as soon as they approached.

'Doctor Henderson is expecting you in the infirmary, officers,' advised the man, standing to attention, one sleeve of his coat clearly empty of a limb.

'A former soldier,' thought Chard, aware that many disabled

military men ended up in workhouses at some point in their lives.

They found Doctor Henderson in his office. He was drumming his fingers on the desk, deep in thought. On noticing his visitors, he raised his corpulent frame out of the chair and greeted them glumly.

'Sorry to have to drag you up here, but we have a problem.'

'In what way Doctor? I didn't notice anything untoward as we came through.'

'That's because I deemed it necessary for a storeroom to be cleared out and a bed put in it,' explained the doctor. 'It was late afternoon when I received two rather unfortunate cases, carried in by your officers. One was dead on arrival and the other damn well near it. The deceased is in the mortuary, the other gentleman is very ill and in the storeroom. I felt it wise to isolate him.'

'What happened to them?' asked Chard.

'That's the problem. I don't know. They were well dressed and presumably must have been taking a walk in Ynysangharad Fields. So, whatever struck them down affected them suddenly. Neither typhoid or dysentery kill you that quickly.'

'Can the surviving man talk?'

'No. He is barely breathing. Whatever it is, has affected his digestive system and his heart rate, as well as his respiratory system.'

'Will he pull through?'

The doctor shrugged. 'Maybe. Only time will tell. I can't send him on to the hospital for two reasons. Firstly, he is too weak to move; and secondly, it might spread contagion. Since the smallpox outbreak at the Cardiff Workhouse we have been instructed not to risk moving any patients that might have any sort of infectious disease. We will know more from the body of the dead man, but I assume you will want Doctor Matthews to do a post mortem.'

'Yes, I doubt we'll get hold of him tonight. I recall that he was going to a function in Cardiff. However, if this is potentially a risk to public health, we'll have to spoil his Sunday. Do we know who the men involved are?'

The doctor stroked his grey moustache. 'I have never seen the dead man before, but he had papers on him that indicate he was a Jeremiah Davies. The surviving fellow is Theodore Clark, a well-known public figure.'

'If he is well-known, then it shouldn't be too hard to track down where he lives and who he has been in contact with.' The inspector turned to Constable Scudamore. 'I think we've got a busy time ahead of us.'

***

Tomos Edwards looked at the clock and sighed. Only 1 a.m. and still most of the night to go until he could finish work and go home. Not that being a night porter at the County Hotel was in any way arduous. It was just boring. Tomos looked at the keys hanging on the board behind the reception desk. All the guests were in their rooms bar one. Presumably they had decided to have a very late night on the town.

Stretching and yawning loudly, the night porter decided to relieve the monotony by taking a walk to see how many guests had left out their shoes for cleaning. Taking care to tread lightly, the only noise the jangling of the master keys attached to his belt, Tomos made his way up to the first floor. As he passed the third door on the landing, he thought he heard the sound of breaking glass. Putting his ear to the door he heard other sounds, whispered voices and the banging of furniture.

Tomos realised that this was the room of the guest who had gone out earlier in the day but had not returned. He knocked the door and listened. The noise inside stopped.

'Is everything all right in there?'

There was no response, so Tomos rattled the door handle.

'I'm coming in,' called the porter as he inserted the key.

This time there was a response, as he could hear urgent mutterings, and the sound of something being knocked over.

Tomos pushed the door open in time to see a figure climbing out through the window.

'Oi! what's going on?'

No sooner had the porter called out, than he felt a blow strike him across the side of the face that nearly floored him. A second intruder, too slow to get to the window, had placed himself behind the door and thrown a punch.

'Oh, like that is it, you bastard,' responded Tomos, who unfortu-

nately for his assailant was up for a fight. Aiming low, he struck at the intruder's groin doubling him up, and then fetched his knee up to try and catch him in the face. But his opponent had other ideas. Somehow he evaded the blow and grabbed the porter's standing leg. Over Tomos went, a side table toppling to the floor, a jug of water shattering. Now the intruder was on top of him, aiming punches at his face, some of which connected with considerable force.

'What's going on?' came a voice from the landing. Heavy footsteps and hurried conversation could be heard outside. Tomos's attacker paused his assault as he realised that hotel guests had been woken by the noise. With a snarl, he threw one more punch before running for the open window.

Tomos wasn't giving up, and as the fugitive climbed through the window he grabbed at the man's jacket. Punching Tomos once more, the intruder made his escape, leaving the porter with just a button and torn threads grasped in his hand.

TWELVE

Chard stepped out of his house with a degree of trepidation. Without warning it had snowed overnight. Not a heavy fall, but what had come down had frozen, leaving the pavements covered in a layer of ice. Carefully he tested his footing, only too aware that the sight of a police inspector in full uniform falling on his backside would cause great hilarity.

The bells of St. Catherine's Church had ceased their call to morning service and Gelliwastad Road was thankfully free of pedestrians and vehicles. Trying to appear nonchalant, Chard made his way along the pavement, a thin layer of ice crunching underfoot. As he walked, the inspector reflected on the events of the previous evening.

Having left the infirmary with Constable Scudamore, they had found a worried Mrs Clark at the police station. A plump, kind-faced lady, she was clearly shaken, her nervous state making her stumble over her words. Apparently, it was not unusual for her husband to change his plans without telling her, but he was always home for his evening meal. He had said that he was going to meet an old friend at the Butcher's Arms, but that was as much as she knew. When they explained what had happened, it was only with difficulty that they persuaded the distressed lady not to go straight to the infirmary. Eventually Chard convinced her to wait until the following day, as her husband was in no state to receive a visitor.

The inspector's thoughts were interrupted as he heard a giggle. Looking up he saw a girl walking towards him, pushing a bicycle along the icy pavement.

'That's a lot safer than riding it miss,' he commented.

'I tried and I fell off, but I didn't hurt myself. It was so funny,' laughed the girl with an infectious smile.

As she passed by, Chard found himself chuckling for no reason other than seeing the delight on the girl's face at something so simple and innocent.

'I don't think Ezekiel is going to be as amused,' he thought to himself. A constable had been told to wait outside Doctor Matthews' house until he returned home, to request his attendance at the infirmary as early as possible on Sunday morning. Chard had received a note just after breakfast advising that the doctor had returned home at 2 a.m., and that on receiving the request had responded with some detailed medical language. In short, the doctor would attend after a late breakfast and not before.

Sunday mornings were usually quiet in the town once the church and chapel services had started, but it was strange to see the Tumble so empty of vehicles. As Chard passed in front of the railway station, he noticed a sturdily built woman carrying a handbag approaching. Only a few feet from the inspector the woman started to slip and barely regained her balance. Chard wondered whether to rush forward and lend a hand, aware that woman might be offended at the suggestion that she couldn't manage on her own.

'It's alright, Officer,' the woman said with a smile, having noticed the concern on his face. 'Just take care of yourself if you're headed up the Graig.'

Indeed, the walk up the Graig Hill towards the workhouse was extremely precarious and Chard had to judge each footstep carefully. It was with a sense of relief that he finally made his way through the gates of the workhouse and into the infirmary.

When he found Doctor Henderson, he looked very harassed.

'How is the patient?'

'No change,' replied the doctor. 'I've had his wife here this morning and she wasn't happy that I wouldn't let her go to his bedside.'

'I can understand her wanting to go to him.'

'So can I Inspector, but I still haven't discovered what is wrong with him. He may be suffering from something contagious. I had a most difficult time trying to explain this to Mrs Clark, who is a most persistent lady. If I don't let her go to the bedside, or agree to transfer him to Porth Hospital tomorrow, then she has threatened to go to the newspapers.'

'I see,' commented Chard, scratching his sideburns thoughtfully. 'I don't suppose Doctor Matthews has turned up yet?'

'You'll find him in the mortuary, but go carefully for he is not in the best of moods.'

The inspector thanked the doctor and made his way to the mortuary. On this occasion it wasn't the usual clinical smell of the white tiled room that assaulted his senses. Instead it was a sweet, sickly smell that nearly turned his stomach.

'There you are Thomas,' came the curt greeting.

Doctor Matthews stood over a metal table on which lay the cadaver of Jeremiah Davies. In his bloodied hands he held a large lump of organic material that he placed into a glass bowl. The doctor's face looked very pale and he had bags under his eyes.

'A Sunday morning! A bloody Sunday morning! Do you not have any respect for a man's day of rest Thomas?'

'Sorry Ezekiel,' apologised Chard, quite taken aback.

'I had a fine evening's entertainment, then I come home to find one of your men waiting for me, demanding that I come here this morning…. It's just not on Thomas.'

'As I said Ezekiel, I am sorry. I didn't think you would be so annoyed.'

'Annoyed, annoyed,' he repeated. 'Yes, I am bloody well annoyed, and do you know why I am annoyed?'

'Because I've interrupted your Sunday morning?'

'Partly because of that, but mainly because I don't know what I'm dealing with here,' replied the doctor, his nose twitching furiously.

'How do you mean?'

'Come closer, Thomas. It's only a dead body, it can't hurt you.'

Chard felt his stomach churn as he approached the table. The cadaver had been cut open to reveal the inner organs, at least those that hadn't already been lifted out and put into the large glass bowl.

'I know the cause of death, respiratory paralysis. What I don't know is what caused it, as well as the evident effect on the digestive system and some apparent damage to the heart.'

'Is it some kind of disease?'

'Not one that I've come across that can suddenly take two men down in such a short space of time. Potentially it is a case of poison, but if so, I can't find any evidence of it. There are no obvious

symptoms of arsenic or cyanide poisoning, of that I am confident.'

'What can I do?' asked the inspector, suddenly worried by the enormity of the problem now presenting itself.

'If it is a disease, then the chances are there will be more fatalities and fairly soon, so I will put the hospital on alert. If it is a poison, then we need to know if these men were specifically poisoned, or if there is a wider risk to the population. Find out where this man and the survivor spent their time in the few hours before they were taken ill,' demanded the doctor.

'Few hours? Surely poison of this severity would be fast acting?'

'Not necessarily, it depends on what was used, if indeed it is a poison.' The doctor pointed to some glass jars on a shelf. 'I have taken samples of their vomit and excreta for analysis.'

'I will question the man in the infirmary as soon as Doctor Henderson will allow,' said Chard.

'I wouldn't count on him being in a fit state to be questioned for a few days. That is if he pulls through,' cautioned Matthews.

'In which case we'll have to do it the hard way. We know that Mr Clark was meeting the poor chap on your table at the Butcher's Arms, so that's where we'll start. I'll get my constables on it straight away.'

The inspector turned to leave, but as he did so he glanced at the face of the cadaver, and then paused.

'I've seen that man before, and recently at that.'

'Where?' asked the doctor.

'I don't know. According to Doctor Henderson there were papers on him that indicated he was Jeremiah Davies but the name means nothing to me. I think I'll ask Doctor Henderson if I can see the man Clark, in case I recognise him also.'

A few minutes later, the Inspector stood in the doorway of the makeshift isolation room, and stared at the face of the unconscious man on the bed.

Then the recognition came.

***

It was Doctor Matthews' namesake who walked into the Butcher's Arms at midday. There was only skeleton staffing at the police station

on a Sunday and Constable Matthews felt aggrieved that he had been ordered out on to the icy streets by a belligerent Inspector Chard.

'He isn't due to be back on duty until tomorrow anyway,' grumbled the constable to himself. 'It's just because he fell for my little joke about China.'

Constable Matthews had been given three specific tasks. First, he was to speak to the manager of the Silver Teapot in Market Street, to take down any details about two customers that had subsequently been taken ill the previous day. Secondly, he was to ask about the same two men at the Butcher's Arms; and finally he was to take down details of an attempted burglary at the County Hotel that had just been notified.

The first task had been a complete failure: the café was closed on a Sunday. At least that meant he could enter the comfortable warmth of the Butcher's Arms. Although selling alcohol was forbidden on a Sunday, the saloon bar was open for a couple of hours at midday to serve food and soft drinks. Unused to seeing a policeman entering the premises on a Sunday, the landlord came out from behind the bar to greet him.

'How can I help you Officer?'

'Do you know a man called Theodore Clark?'

'Yes, I do. He was in here yesterday.'

'Who was he with?'

'Someone I've never seen before. Thin looking, quite well dressed. What is this all about?'

'Anyone else with them?'

'No. Why?'

'What did they have to eat or drink?'

'I didn't serve them, it was one of the barmaids; but assuming Mr Clark had his usual, it would have been a pint or two of beer. Come now Constable, what is this about?'

'I am afraid that Mr Clark and his companion were taken ill yesterday and we are just checking on their movements.'

The landlord bristled and went red in the face. 'Are you suggesting that there is something wrong with my beer?'

'No sir, just doing my duty.'

'There is nothing wrong with my beer!' said the landlord forcibly. He turned back to the bar, pulled a small measure of bitter into a glass and swallowed it back. 'You see, nothing wrong with that,' he barked, challenging the policeman to disagree.

Constable Matthews remembered his instructions from the inspector, 'Whatever you do, be discreet'. Apologising, and thanking the landlord for his assistance, he beat a hasty retreat.

The third task was also of limited success. The night porter who discovered the burglary was off duty, but the manager of the hotel did at least give the constable a button and loose threads that had been torn from the jacket of one of the intruders. Comforted that he had done everything that had been asked of him, Constable Matthews looked forward to getting back into the warm station. His lack of concentration meant that he wasn't aware of the frozen dog turd under his foot, until he was sliding to the ground.

'Bugger!' he exclaimed.

THIRTEEN

When Superintendent Jones arrived at the police station early on Monday morning, he was surprised to find Inspector Chard already waiting outside his office.

'Good morning Inspector. Glad to see you up and about. Fully fit I trust?'

'Yes sir, a slight ache but otherwise fine.'

'Well, the slight ache might remind you not to get involved in any more brawls. Your past record is hardly distinguished in that respect.'

Chard ignored the mild reprimand and came straight to the point. 'I am afraid we have an issue of major importance to deal with sir, and it cannot wait.'

The superintendent looked quizzically at Chard, then indicated that they should go into the office. He led the way, leaving Chard to close the door firmly behind them.

'Very well, you have my full attention. What is it?'

'Two businessmen were found collapsed on a bench in Ynysang-harad Fields late Saturday afternoon. One is dead, the other is fighting for his life.'

Superintendent Jones stroked his bushy moustache. 'Do we know the identities of the men?'

'The one who died is a Jeremiah Davies. He appears to be new to the town and was staying at the County Hotel. The other man is Theodore Clark. I didn't recognise him at first but then I recalled seeing him at the courthouse.'

'Yes,' interrupted the superintendent. 'Of course, you would have done. He is one of the magistrates.'

'That's right sir, though he has not sat on any of my cases. I also recalled seeing him Saturday afternoon, at which time he was perfectly well.'

'So, what happened to these men?'

'That's the problem sir, we don't know. Doctor Matthews has had

the dead man on the slab and cannot work out whether we are talking about a contagious illness or some kind of poison. I fear that there may be a risk to public health in either case.'

'Have there been any other cases reported?'

'None as far as I know.'

'You say you saw Clark earlier that day and he was well. Was he with the other man, Davies?' queried the superintendent.

'He was sat in the Silver Teapot with someone. I can't say for certain it was Davies, but I think it is fair to assume that it was.'

'So whatever afflicted them happened after that.'

'Possibly. However, if it was a disease then in theory it may have been contracted days earlier, though I doubt it,' replied Chard pensively.

'Why do you say that?'

'Because we would definitely have had other cases by now.'

'Of course. What if it was poison?'

'By all accounts the effects were extremely violent, which would suggest to me that they would have been poisoned whilst in Ynysangharad Fields; but that is just supposition. Unless Doctor Matthews can identify a poison, we can only guess. Some poisons can apparently take hours to take effect.'

The superintendent began to pace up and down, his face expressing deep concern.

'Frankly it isn't the possibility of an unidentified poison that causes me the most concern, it is disease. I share your view that we might have had other cases by now if it was disease, but what if you are wrong? If these men were only the first of some epidemic or other, then the consequences could be terrible. We've had enough typhoid in the area. There is smallpox in Cardiff and now we might have something else.'

'I really think that poison is the more likely sir. There is also something else that happened on the weekend that may be relevant.'

The superintendent stopped pacing. 'Well, spit it out Inspector.'

'On Saturday night the hotel room of Jeremiah Davies was broken into. The night porter interrupted the burglary and got some bruising for his trouble.'

'A coincidence?'

'I don't like coincidences, sir.'

Superintendent paused in thought for a moment. 'That's all well and good, but we must act on the worst possible outcome. I must warn the Town Clerk of the possibility of an epidemic so that we can make emergency arrangements. In the meantime, you need to find out where the men could have contracted whatever it was afflicted them.'

'We know that they met at the Butcher's Arms and I saw them later at the Silver Teapot, so that's a start. Constable Matthews visited both premises yesterday, but the former was closed as it was a Sunday. He also got a far from welcome reception at the Butcher's Arms, but he did get some questions answered.'

'Not good enough Inspector. Close both premises down for forty-eight hours whilst we investigate. I will get a public health order from the Council to authorise it. Then get the constables asking around the town to try and trace where Clark and Davies went after the Silver Teapot.'

'Yes sir, I will get the men on to it,' answered Chard with a degree of hesitation in his voice.

'You appear to have something more to say Inspector.'

'I need to carry on with the murder investigation regarding the body found in the fire at Cilfynydd.'

'No. Give it to a constable. You know my views anyway. An inspector is there to inspect what the constables do, not to waste time investigating. I don't mind giving you leeway when there is nothing else urgent going on, but I need you to oversee and direct our men in addressing this other problem. That will be all Inspector,' concluded the superintendent with a dismissive gesture.

Chard knew better than to argue with his superior officer when his mind was made up. The superintendent was clearly worried, which no doubt was the reason for his abruptness. Nevertheless it was a very sour-faced Chard who approached Sergeants Morris and Jackson a few moments later.

'Sergeant Morris,' growled the inspector.

'Yes Inspector?' responded the genial giant with a pleasant smile.

'Take two constables and inform the landlord of the Butcher's Arms that his bar is to be closed for up to forty-eight hours. He can

serve food but no beer. Take a half pint sample from each open cask and fetch them back to the station. Tell him we are conducting an investigation and that any complaints should be made in writing. We will of course reimburse him for the samples we take. Stand no nonsense from him.'

'Anything else sir?'

'Not from yourself Sergeant Morris, but as for you Sergeant Jackson....'

Jackson scowled but came to attention, staring over Chard's shoulder to avoid direct eye contact.

'I want you,' continued the inspector, 'to go to the Silver Teapot with one of your constables. Find the proprietor and tell him that due to a police investigation it will be necessary to close the premises for up to forty-eight hours. Interview the staff that were on duty on Saturday and try to find out if they remember serving the two men who were later taken ill. Both were well dressed. One was thin, the other quite the opposite. The larger man, Theodore Clark, may have been known to them. I want to know what they consumed and details of anyone that interacted with them.'

'Yes sir,' came the unenthusiastic response.

'In addition,' added Chard, 'send half a dozen men out to ask around the town if anyone saw the two men between the time they left the Silver Teapot and the time they were found in Ynysangharad Fields. Whilst they are doing that, send someone to get Sergeant Humphreys out of bed. I am cancelling his night shift and giving it to a constable. I need him back here to help co-ordinate things.'

As both sergeants turned to go, Chard called after them. 'I forgot to add, be discreet!' he ordered.

Still feeling disgruntled, Chard marched towards his office, passing constables Matthews and Scudamore on the way. 'Constable Matthews, due to exigencies of the service you are now on a double shift. Tonight, you will have the desk instead of Sergeant Humphreys.'

Matthews groaned.

'Constable Scudamore,' continued the inspector.

'Yes Inspector,' replied the older, ginger haired constable.

'Come into my office and bring your notebook.'

Chard led the way then closed the door behind them.

'I've got a little job for you Constable.'

Scudamore raised his eyebrows expectantly as Chard went on to explain.

'I need you to go through all of the interview notes taken by Sergeant Jackson and his constables. Compare them with your own notes that were taken when we first arrived on the scene of the fire. I want to know anything that might be worth a second look. I am going out for a while so you can make use of my office.'

'Certainly sir,' answered Scudamore. Knowing the inspector's penchant for investigation he was surprised that the inspector had delegated this task.

Chard caught the quizzical expression on the constable's face.

'I must be seen to be prioritising "the case of the men on the bench" Constable,' he explained.

Scudamore acknowledged his superior's position by nodding sympathetically.

***

The very cold weather didn't look like it was going to last. Although some ice still remained on the roads, the thaw had already set in after only a day. Water dripped constantly from cracked gutters and there was the occasional cry of consternation from passers-by, as slurries of melting snow slid from roofs onto pavements.

Chard was not entirely happy with the superintendent's instructions. The inspector had been to the Butchers Arms to see what progress was being made. The landlord who had given Constable Matthews such a difficult time had thought twice about doing the same with the redoubtable Sergeant Morris, and everything was in hand.

That said, Chard was of the opinion that little would be achieved. Some of the casks used on the Saturday afternoon would have been drank dry. Also, there had been no other cases of illness reported. The landlord wasn't sure who had served Clark and Davies, but if it was poison, what would be the motive? Even if there was a motive against either victim, why deliberately target both men? It just wasn't credible. Nevertheless, taking the samples would at least

demonstrate to the superintendent that he was at least doing something about the case.

As Chard walked into Market Street, he could hear a commotion from up ahead, where a small crowd was gathered outside the Silver Teapot.

'What is going on here?' demanded Chard of a spotty-faced young constable who was failing to move on the crowd.

'That's what we want to know,' spoke up a thick-set elderly man, his jaw thrust forward determinedly. 'He won't let us in.'

'*Beth sy'n bod?*' added a small elfin-faced woman, warmly clad in a thick coat.

Chard smiled reassuringly at the woman, not understanding what she had asked, but assuming that she wanted to know what was going on. Raising his arms in a placatory manner, and aware of the air of authority of his uniform, the inspector addressed the small gathering.

'There is nothing to be alarmed about. We are just having a discussion with the proprietor, who I am sure is being most helpful. Please do move along.'

The young constable audibly breathed a sigh of relief, as the crowd started to move on.

'Just a moment Inspector,' called out one man in a long brown coat and dented hat. He held a notebook in one hand and a pencil in the other.

'We've had reports of there being an outbreak of a strange disease in the town and that a man has died. Can you confirm or deny the rumour?'

Oh God! thought Chard. The bloody press has got hold of it.

'Well Inspector?'

Chard could see the crowd starting to reform. 'No comment,' he stated loudly before patting the constable on the shoulder and disappearing into the tearoom.

Inside the premises the inspector found Sergeant Jackson standing over a seated proprietor, questioning him in an overly aggressive manner, whilst a handful of worried staff stood at the back of the room.

'Sergeant, what do you have to report?'

Jackson turned to his inspector and grunted. 'Mr Boucher here reckons that the men had a cup of tea and some cake, then left.'

'Are the same staff here today?'

'Most of them, but not all.'

Chard addressed the proprietor, a slim man of neat appearance who looked very intimidated by Sergeant Jackson.

'Mr. Boucher, do you remember me from Saturday afternoon?'

'No Inspector, it was very busy.'

'Perhaps it was because I was not in uniform. Do you remember anyone else?

'There were a couple of clergymen, and a noisy family, but it was just so hectic,' apologised the proprietor.'

'Why did you remember Mr Clark and Mr Davies having tea and cake?'

'Only because Mr Clark is a regular patron.'

'I see, well I suppose if that is all you can remember....'

'Wait a moment Inspector, I do remember something else. One of the waitresses complained that two men were rather abrupt with her when they placed their order. Two big men in tweed suits. I was going to have a word with them when I had time, but they didn't stay long.'

Chard scratched his sideburns in thought, 'I think I remember them myself. I believe they left just after Clark and Davies.' The inspector paused for a moment before changing tack. 'I assume all of the cake eaten by Clark and Davies was finished by the end of the day, or thrown away.'

'Correct Inspector. All of our food is fresh.'

'Similarly, I assume that the teapot and crockery have all been washed.'

'Of course.'

'What is your procedure for serving, say a pot of tea? For example, where is it made?'

The proprietor gave an impatient sigh before explaining.

'The order goes into the kitchen. Each order is done in turn. The pot is prepared in the kitchen. It is put on a tray with a jug of milk, a jug of hot water and a sugar bowl, then placed on the counter. When the waitress sees it, it is taken from the counter to the table.'

'So, when it is on the counter the tray can be unattended?'

'Only for a short while.'

'Do you know who served Mr. Clark and Mr. Davies?'

'I am afraid not.'

Chard sighed with frustration. 'Sergeant Jackson here will inter-view the staff for any more information, and we will need the names and addresses of any of the Saturday staff that aren't here today. In the meantime, I am afraid that I have orders to ensure that your premises must remain closed for forty-eight hours.'

'But that is intolerable…'

'I am sorry, but those are my instructions. A public health order from the council is on its way. You can either close voluntarily for a couple of days or I can pin a Public Health Notice to the front of your premises. Your choice, but I know what I would do.'

Chard left the premises in the hands of Sergeant Jackson and went out into the cold to find that the small crowd was still there.

He whispered to the constable that he would send someone to assist him, before addressing the onlookers.

'There is nothing the matter. You are just wasting your time here. The proprietor has had something to deal with at home and he is closing the tearoom for a couple of days. Move along now please, you are blocking the pavement.'

Just as Chard finished speaking, Constable Davies came hurrying up. It wasn't a sight he wanted to see, because whenever the overweight Davies rushed anywhere his face turned bright red and the inspector feared a heart attack.

'Ah, Constable Davies. Good timing, we were just helping these people to move along. Slow down though and catch your breath.'

It took a few moments for Davies to recover from his exertions and speak coherently to his superior.

'We've found someone who saw Clark and Davies on Saturday afternoon. They were taking a drink from the fountain in Penuel Square.'

'Damn!' exclaimed Chard. 'Very well, I know the superintendent would want us to take a belt and braces approach. Cordon it off and take samples from the fountain.'

'What's that? Are you shutting down the fountain?' interrupted

the reporter who was with the small number of people still loitering around the front door of the tearoom.

'It's the typhoid!' screamed an old woman who hurried away with the news.

'No, it's not the typhoid!' Chard shouted after her. 'It's not the typhoid,' he repeated to the reporter whilst wagging his finger aggressively. 'What is it then?' asked the reporter.

'I have no idea,' snapped Chard angrily.

'Thank you for the direct quote Inspector,' answered the reporter with a wink. Smiling, he put his notebook away and rushed off to see his editor.

***

Later that evening Chard's mind was in turmoil. He had just had the pleasure of spending an evening at the Clarence Theatre in the company of Alice, who took his arm as they left the auditorium. But he couldn't help but reflect on earlier events. Still feeling discomfited by the reporter at the tearoom, Chard had returned to the station with the intention of reading the notes from the Cilfynydd murder case. However, it was not to be. A very displeased Superintendent Jones had marched into his office and demanded to know the reason for the pandemonium outside. Putting on his cap, Chard had rushed into the station yard to discover what had irked his superior. The reason was self-evident. Samples taken from eight opened beer casks and each of the four bowls from the drinking fountain had to be tested. Chard thought it very unlikely that any of the samples would prove toxic or disease carrying. Unfortunately, Sergeant Humphreys had used his initiative and instructed his constables to round up a dozen stray dogs, on which to test the samples. The situation had not been helped by Constable Jenkins and Constable Temple having fetched in two particularly large and aggressive mongrels that had no intention of co-operating. Three smaller dogs proved adept at nipping the ankles of their handlers and the overall canine frenzy had caught on amongst the rest.

'Thomas, are you alright? You are frowning.'

Chard smiled at his companion.

'I am sorry Alice; I was deep in thought.'

'You did like the show, didn't you?'

In truth *The Bells of Haslemere* was not really a musical production, to his taste, but to please Alice he nodded enthusiastically.

'It was lovely, Alice. Really uplifting.'

'I suppose you must be worried about this business with the men that were taken ill.'

'Yes, I am,' confessed Chard as they walked down the theatre's staircase to the foyer. 'The papers will have a lot to say about it in the morning,' he added.

'People are already talking about the fountain being closed down. Then there's rumours about the Silver Teapot, and the Butcher's Arms.'

'We've taken steps to test the water from the fountain and the beer from the pub. We will know in the next twenty-four hours if we can give the all clear.'

'How did you test it? I thought you would ask Doctor Matthews to assist you.'

'We have kept small samples for the doctor, in case we need to define a specific substance. However, the first thing was to test whether the samples were toxic or not. So, after several bitten constables, we tested the samples on stray dogs.'

Alice looked shocked. 'That is so cruel!'

Chard held his hands up in supplication. 'It was genuinely not my idea, but it is a quick way of finding out if the samples are toxic. If nothing happens to the animals by tomorrow night, we can say that the water and the beer are safe. Frankly, I am sure that will be the case. In the meantime, the dogs are chained up in the yard.'

'I still think it's cruel,' pouted Alice.

Chard gave an apologetic shrug and felt a little embarrassed. The couple were now at the theatre entrance, where a number of people were waiting for their carriages to arrive. As Chard and Alice politely made their way through to the street, the inspector overheard a number of comments that gave a degree of concern.

'I heard there's been two cases of typhoid,' commented a large lady of mature years.

'Nonsense, I've heard it was a case of poison,' responded her companion.

'It's the Germans or the Russkis poisoning the water supply,' replied the man next to him.

'Not the Germans surely? They are our cousins,' retorted a lady who had heard the comment.

'Socialists, definitely socialists. They are to blame. Spreading disease everywhere,' came an authoritative statement from a man in formal coat and top hat.

'I say it's the Jews. Can't trust them,' muttered an old woman.

'It isn't poison, it's a plague from the Almighty sent amongst us for our wicked ways and the worship of the demon drink,' said a vicar.

'Let's get out of here,' grunted Chard, taking Alice by the arm.

***

It was only a ten-minute walk back to Doctor Matthews' house, yet it took much longer as Chard and Alice dawdled, lost in gentle conversation. The evening was milder than expected and there was little trace of ice remaining from earlier in the day. Eventually, despite their deliberate slow progress, they reached their destination and Chard saw his companion to the door.

'Perhaps one evening you would allow me to cook you a meal,' suggested Alice.

'You mean at my house?'

'No, of course not. That wouldn't be proper. However…' Alice hesitated before continuing, '…if you were to come around when Doctor Matthews is next out of town….'

'I don't think the good doctor would approve,' said Chard doubtfully.

'Then we won't tell him,' laughed Alice mischievously. 'Good night *cariad*,' she added, giving the inspector a kiss on the cheek.

Chard watched Alice enter the house and close the door. Despite his age and experience of several love affairs, he suddenly felt like a youth who had just walked out with a sweetheart for the first time. He gave a happy sigh and set off for home, content that whatever the morning would bring, he would be more than ready for it.

FOURTEEN

'I received your message in the middle of important correspondence. What on earth is so pressing?' demanded Ernest Wilkinson, taking a seat at the table of Hector Bowen.

Bowen smiled wolfishly. 'Glad you came Ernest. Nice restaurant, don't you think?'

'Good God man, are you eating steak at this time of day? It's only mid-morning,' said Wilkinson with a disgusted expression.

'I need my sustenance,' responded Bowen taking a mouthful of rare steak, the bloody juices from which dripped onto his shirt front.

'Never mind that. What do you want to tell me that is so important?'

Bowen continued to chew his steak as he talked. 'Have you seen this morning's paper?'

'Not yet. Why?'

Bowen threw a folded newspaper onto the table. 'Take a look at this,' he said triumphantly pointing at a headline.

Wilkinson adjusted his monocle and started to read. As he did so, Bowen chewed away, looking extremely pleased with himself.

'My word!' exclaimed Wilkinson when he had finished reading. 'Jeremiah Davies is dead. He possibly caught an unknown disease, but there is some speculation that it might be poison. The police inspector in charge is quoted as saying that he has no idea.'

'No idea my arse,' contradicted Bowen. 'I shall march into this afternoon's board meeting and demand action against the Barry Railway Company.'

'You are accusing them of murder?'

'Precisely, and when Armstrong refuses to do anything about it, I will show him up for the weak leader that he undoubtedly is.'

'I see. Then there will be one more chance to bring him down,' smiled Wilkinson.

'Exactly! We have him, I tell you. We have him!'

***

Chard took a quick glance to ensure that no-one was looking, then kicked his waste paper basket across the floor of his office.

The morning had not gone well, and his light-hearted feeling from the night before had dissipated under the steely glare of Superintendent Jones. Somebody, probably Jackson, had left a copy of the morning paper on his desk with Chard's quote highlighted.

'How could you possibly have thought it was a good idea to tell the public that you, and by intimation, we, have no idea what afflicted the two victims? Well, man?'

The words still rang in the inspector's ears. He had no defence and had to stand there and take the dressing down. At least it was in the privacy of the Superintendent's office, which was some comfort. Despite his sense of injustice, Chard could understand the superintendent's frustration. The Chairman of the Council had asked to be briefed and now the Member of Parliament was also getting involved.

Yet, at the moment there was little that could be done. If none of the dogs in the yard showed any ill effects by the end of the day, and no people were recorded as falling mysteriously ill, then disease could be ruled out. However, that would then mean poison, which presented its own set of problems. So far, Doctor Matthews had not identified a poison. Then there was the question of how it would have been administered. The fact that the two men had not long met indicated that any poison would have been taken that afternoon. The most puzzling thing of all was the motive. If the two men had only just met, then what did they have in common that would make someone want to poison them both? If only Clark was able to tell them what had happened; yet the news from the infirmary was not good. The surviving victim was still stable but not showing any improvement. And there was the attempted burglary at the County Hotel. Was it just a coincidence that it was Jeremiah Davies's room that had been broken into?

'I don't like coincidences,' said Chard aloud to no-one in particular. He shook his head. The only thing he could do was to chase up Doctor Matthews, but before that…

'Constable Scudamore!' he called from the door of his office.

The ginger-haired constable came into the room, with a notebook and several sheets of paper.

'How far have you got?' asked the inspector.

'I have checked my notes from the time we arrived at the scene of the fire with the interviews carried out by Sergeant Jackson and his constable, as you instructed sir.'

'And….?'

'There are some discrepancies.'

Chard grunted. 'Those discrepancies being….'

'Mrs Griffiths…'

'The busybody,' interrupted Chard.

'Yes sir, that's right. She mentioned a number of individuals who she saw on the street around the time of the fire. From the interviews subsequently taken, virtually all have been identified bar one person who only she appears to have noticed.'

Chard raised an eyebrow.

'A scruffy man in a long coat,' continued Scudamore, reading from his notebook. 'There's something else as well,' he added. 'The list of people mentioned by Mrs Griffiths included an old man called Jones and a grocer called Phillips. Both of them are mentioned in statements given by other witnesses.'

'Yes, what is wrong about that?'

'The funny thing is that there doesn't seem to be a statement here from either of them. I don't think that they've been interviewed.'

'I see,' responded Chard pursing his lips.

'What about the interview with the widow?'

'I haven't got it yet sir, but you can ask Constable Morgan. He was with Sergeant Jackson at the time.'

Chard stroked his chin thoughtfully. 'Thank you, Constable, that will be all. Send Morgan in. I would like a word with him.'

It was a miserable looking Constable Morgan that came before the inspector a few minutes later.

'Anything wrong Constable? You've got a face like a month of wet Sundays.'

'No sir,' denied Morgan.

Chard paused, wondering if the constable would say anything further, but nothing came.

'Very well. Tell me how the interview went with Mrs Hughes.'

'According to Mrs Hughes, apart from Mr Dixon who lived next to the workshop, everybody got on well enough with her husband. Though some customers had got behind with their payments.'

'Different to what Mrs Evans told me. She said he was really unpopular. What about Mrs Hughes's relationship with her husband?'

'They seemed to have argued recently over money. There was a big age difference between them and Sergeant Jackson seemed to think that was relevant.'

'Do you think it is relevant?'

'No sir.'

'Why?'

'Her reaction to being questioned. There is no doubt in my mind that her grief is entirely genuine.'

'This recent arguing about money. I wonder if it is due to the late paying by customers or some other cause.' The inspector leant back in his chair, lost in thought whilst Morgan waited in the uneasy silence.

'Very well,' said the inspector suddenly, getting to his feet. 'I need you to find and interview a grocer called Phillips and an old miner called Jones.'

'There'll be a few of those, sir,' replied Morgan, raising his eyebrows.

Chard smiled. 'There will indeed, but this one was wandering about at the time the fire started. Get Constable Scudamore to fill you in on the details from the various interviews. They should give you enough to go on. Just make sure that you get over to Cilfynydd first thing in the morning.'

When Morgan left the room, the inspector pondered before deciding to disobey his superintendent. 'There is more to this short-age of money business. I need to interview the widow myself,' he muttered under his breath.

***

In the board room of the Taff Vale Railway, the atmosphere was tense. A flustered Benjamin Armstrong sat at the head of the table.

His factotum, Jennings, stood a few steps behind, looking calmly on.

'We must do something about this affront to the company,' demanded Hector Bowen.

'Why do you think this terrible business is an affront to ourselves?' responded Armstrong.

'Why do you think? Jeremiah Davies leaves the BRC and joins us. Then inside a fortnight he is dead. Poisoned by his former employers.'

'We don't know that. Neither do we know that the cause was poison,' snapped Armstrong.

'Codswallop! You are just too scared to admit it,' accused Bowen.

'I am nothing of the sort,' retorted the chairman.

'I am afraid that it is beginning to look that way,' added Ernest Wilkinson, in slow, measured tones.

At the chorus of agreement around the table Armstrong's face reddened with the realisation that he was losing control.

'We should denounce them in the papers!' shouted an elderly white-haired man seated next to Bowen.

'That would be libellous without proof. We cannot make such accusations at this stage. They would not stoop so low.'

'Ha! See! You are defensive of them. I thought as much. If you won't take immediate action, then perhaps we should have a show of no confidence in you,' barked Bowen.

The chairman began to flounder. He needed more time to gather his thoughts and defer this challenge to his authority.

Jennings bent forward and whispered in Armstrong's ear. The chairman nodded before addressing the Board.

'Very well, you demand action. Then perhaps it is you, Mr Bowen, that should take the next steps on my behalf. Those next steps are to go to Pontypridd and ascertain from the police if Mr Davies was indeed poisoned, and if so, who they suspect.'

'But the police have stated in the paper that they have no idea,' argued Bowen.

'My point exactly. If they don't know, then how can you know?' accused Armstrong pointedly.

Before Bowen could respond, Wilkinson stood up, polishing his monocle with a handkerchief as he did so.

'I agree with the chairman. Mr Bowen should look into the matter on our behalf.'

There were murmurs of agreement and as Wilkinson sat back down, he whispered into Bowen's ear. 'I am sure you can find something or other that points to the Barry Railway Company. If the Board sees Armstrong refusing to take firm action against the BRC one more time, then he'll be out.'

A smile spread slowly across Bowen's face as he addressed the room. 'Gentlemen, I am only too happy to agree.'

FIFTEEN

Inspector Chard set off for the mortuary with Constable Temple in attendance, feeling happier at having instructed Constable Morgan to make some progress in the Hughes murder case.

'Do you think the doctor will have news for us sir?' asked Temple, as they entered the workhouse yard.

'I doubt it Constable, otherwise he would have sent a message. You never know though. I want to see how Mr Clark is getting on anyway, so we will go there afterwards.'

Temple smiled at the thought of seeing Miss Roper again.

As they entered the mortuary, they heard the discordant sound of metal against metal as if someone was rummaging through a cutlery drawer.

'Ah, Inspector,' greeted Doctor Matthews on seeing them enter. 'Good timing. I was just sorting out some of my bits and pieces ready to wash them.'

Chard was pleased to see that there was no corpse on the slab, just a pile of tin dishes alongside a tangled heap of forceps, probes and other paraphernalia.

'I have mixed news,' announced the doctor, absent-mindedly tweaking the end of his thin waxed moustache.

'Then do not keep us in suspense, Doctor. What have you ascertained?'

'Having carried out all possible tests, I can confidently say that our poor victim did not die from any known disease.'

'Which means he was poisoned, I assume.'

'Correct. Unfortunately, I still cannot confirm what type of poison.'

'You do realise Doctor, that identifying it could be crucial to the case.'

'Indeed, I do. That is why I need to go to London for a couple of days to confer with a colleague. You see, I do have an inkling as

to what it might be, but if I am right, it is generally undetectable.'

'So, what do you think it is?'

'No, Inspector. I would rather be sure than send you on a wild goose-chase. Just have patience. Hopefully I will have an answer for you by the end of the week.'

'Very well. I will leave you to it then Doctor,' responded Chard more abruptly than he had intended.

Doctor Matthews shook his head as the policemen left the room, disappointed at his friend's impatience.

Crossing the yard and entering the infirmary, Temple was pleased that they did indeed run into pretty, auburn-haired Miss Roper.

'Good afternoon, Miss Roper,' greeted the inspector.

The young woman, who had been checking some notes pinned to a notice board, turned and gave a polite smile.

'Good afternoon Inspector. I assume you want to see Doctor Henderson?'

'Yes please,' responded Chard. He was glad to see her smile, but she still seemed a shadow of her former self.

'He is in his office. Mrs Clark is with him,' she warned.

'Thanks for letting me know. Come on Temple,' ordered Chard, seeing that his constable wanted to linger.

As they approached Doctor Henderson's office, the policemen could hear the doctor trying to reassure a worried Mrs Clark that her husband would pull through. With a degree of hesitancy, the inspector gave a gentle knock on the door. Silence fell within, and a moment later the door was pulled open. On seeing his visitors, Doctor Henderson gave a slightly relieved smile.

'Good afternoon Inspector. I have just been explaining to Mrs Clark that her husband is stable but cannot be moved at this stage.'

The plump little woman pushed past the corpulent doctor and stood in front of Chard; her eyes pitifully red from crying.

'Oh Inspector. The doctor won't tell me what is wrong with my poor Theodore, and won't let me take him home.'

Doctor Henderson interrupted to try and explain. 'For the sake of his health I cannot allow him to be moved. His breathing and heart rate have stabilised, but he is still barely conscious. He is out

of danger, but I do not want him to relapse. If there is more improvement by the end of the week, I will recommend that he is transferred to the hospital in Porth.'

Chard spoke to Mrs Clark who was still looking up into his eyes. 'I am sorry Mrs Clark, but we believe that your husband was poisoned.'

The distressed woman started to weep, then pulled a dainty cotton handkerchief from the sleeve of her dress, which she used to dab her eyes.

'Who could have done such a thing to my dear Theodore?'

'That is what I would like to ask you,' asked Chard kindly. Out of the corner of his eye he noticed that Temple had taken out his notebook.

'No-one. He is a lovely man.'

'Surely, being a magistrate, he must have made enemies.'

'Do you think so? No. I refuse to believe it.'

'Perhaps if he gave an unduly harsh sentence?'

Mrs Clark looked affronted. 'Never. If anything, he was too soft-hearted.'

'What about away from the courthouse? Has he had any disputes within his social circle?'

'Of course not! He is far too amiable. We have a close-knit circle of friends who we have known for years. Theodore has his own friends in the business community of course. He is well respected as a shrewd investor in local industry and regularly dines out with the social elite.'

Chard shrugged. 'It is possible that he was accidentally poisoned by someone who disliked his friend Jeremiah Davies, the man who died.'

'I never met him, and I wish my poor Theodore hadn't met him either,' responded Mrs Clark, starting to weep once more. 'Please catch whoever did this, Inspector.'

'I will,' promised Chard. 'Don't you worry about that.'

The two policemen left Mrs Clark to the care of Doctor Henderson and walked back through the ward of the infirmary. As they passed by an empty bed, they noticed May Roper standing with her back to them.

'Goodbye Miss Roper,' called out the inspector.

May appeared startled and hurriedly put something inside the bedside cabinet, before turning around.

'Goodbye Inspector Chard, and Constable...?'

'Temple Miss, John Temple,' responded the lanky blond policeman. 'Pleased to have made your acquaintance.'

Chard gave the constable a sharp nudge with his elbow. 'Time to go Constable. I am putting you in charge on giving the dogs a final check over. Then you can take them away and set them free.'

***

May Roper woke suddenly. It had been the same dream again. The terror had returned for the first time in weeks. She imagined she felt the searing pain as the knife entered her body, and the helplessness as her life ebbed away. Getting out of bed, the young woman walked towards the window and pulled the curtains back a fraction. There was enough moonlight to illuminate the small clock that she kept on the windowsill.

'It's not even midnight,' she sighed to herself.

'If only I hadn't left my tonic behind when the policemen startled me,' thought May, cursing her luck.

She considered getting back into bed but started to shake inside. Only a sip of her tonic could guarantee a gentle, dream-free slumber. May paced up and down, desperately trying to decide what to do. She needed to sleep and in just over seven hours she would have to be up and ready for work. Her heart beat faster. 'I need my tonic!' The words screamed inside her head.

There was only one thing that could be done. Her parents were asleep, and the infirmary was only a twenty-minute walk away. Fifteen if she hurried. She could be there and back in little more than half an hour if she was lucky.

Her mind made up, May slipped a dress over her nightgown. The thought of going outdoors with bare legs and corsetless, like some prostitute, worried her. She felt ashamed, but there was nothing else for it. Stepping as lightly as possible, May went out onto the landing, pleased to hear her father's loud snores coming from

her parents' bedroom. At the bottom of the stairs, she took her thick, warm coat from the hook by the front door, and stepped outside.

The air was cold, but far milder than it had been on recent nights, for which May was very grateful. Walking as fast as she could, the young woman thought pensively about what to do when she reached the workhouse gates.

In theory, there should be no problem entering the workhouse and getting to the infirmary. There would be a guard on the gate no doubt, but whoever it was would know her. Not that the workhouse was terribly secure in any case. The inmates had nowhere to go, otherwise they wouldn't be there. If they sneaked out and entered a pub, they would be immediately recognised as inmates by their drab workhouse-issue clothing. As for anyone breaking in, what would be the point? There was nothing of any value to steal that couldn't be taken from easier premises.

No, getting into the workhouse and indeed the infirmary would be straightforward. The problem would be when she got inside. The patients in the infirmary would be fast asleep, but Nurse Harris would be on duty overnight.

When May arrived, she was surprised to find that the little wicket gate built into the large main gate was open. She stepped cautiously inside and looked about, but there was no sign of the night guard. Grateful for the guard's absence, she made her way towards the infirmary.

Still unsure of what she intended to say to Nurse Harris, May opened the infirmary door. Most of the beds were occupied, but everyone was asleep. The ward was almost in darkness, a pair of gas lamps, one at each end of the room, were turned down very low. May stepped forward silently, expecting to see Nurse Harris at her desk in the corner. To her surprise she was not there, and May realised that she might not have to explain her presence.

She hurried silently to the cabinet next to the empty bed where she had left her tonic, opened it and grabbed the little bottle. Unable to help herself, she pulled out the stopper and took a little sip. Immediately, she felt her nerves start to calm.

'Now everything will be alright,' she told herself.

A sudden movement made May glance down at the adjacent

bed. Instead of an empty pillow, she looked into the eyes of a terrified Nurse Harris.

May recoiled in shock. The nurse was tied up and gagged.

'What on earth?' she exclaimed, her heart pounding.

Putting the tonic bottle into her pocket, May was just about to free the nurse when she heard a noise coming from the storeroom next to Doctor Henderson's office. To the nurse's dismay, she went forward to investigate. Treading softly, May crept towards the end of the ward.

The noise had stopped, but as she got closer, she heard frantic whispering. May cautiously poked her head around the door frame and peered inside. Dimly, she saw the shapes of two men searching for something. Things were scattered around the room; clearly, they hadn't found what they had come for.

The shock of seeing the intruders made her gasp audibly. The men turned and let out gasps of their own.

'What the f....?'

'Shit!'

May noticed that one of the men held something in his hand which he had been using to open a locked cupboard door. As he stepped towards her, she recognised that it was a knife.

'Now don't do anything silly Missy,' he said.

May froze, her eyes fixed on the knife. Then she screamed.

The scream was born from true terror, as she recalled the incident which had almost resulted in her death. Instantly, the patients in the ward began to wake.

'Shut up you bitch!' yelled one of the intruders. Without thinking, he hit her on the jaw and she fell to the ground.

Some of the patients were now awake and shouting. The more able were getting out of bed.

'Bollocks! Now you've done it. Run for it!'

Leaving the young woman prostrate on the floor, the intruders dashed out of the infirmary and disappeared into the night.

SIXTEEN

The following morning found Inspector Chard and Constable Temple once more at the infirmary.

'How did the intruders get in, Doctor?' asked the inspector.

Doctor Henderson looked embarrassed. 'Everyone knows that the guard on duty at the main gate likes a tipple. It appears that there was a knock on the wicket gate and when he opened it, he found a bottle of whisky stood there. It must have been drugged. He can't remember what happened next, but we found him sleeping in a coal store across the yard. He either forgot to close the wicket gate properly or the intruders climbed the wall.'

'Once they were inside the workhouse gates, how did they get inside the infirmary?'

'I am afraid that we don't bother to keep the infirmary locked. We've never thought it necessary,' explained the doctor. 'Poor Nurse Harris is quite a small lady and not exactly in her youth. They grabbed her from behind with a hand over her mouth and tied her up.'

'What were they looking for? Was anything taken?'

'That has been puzzling me,' admitted Doctor Henderson, furrowing his brow. 'Most of our medicines are freely obtainable elsewhere, apart from what is in the poisons cabinet.'

'Was that broken into?'

'No. So I don't know what else they would have been after. Nothing of value is left on the premises.'

'Was it just the one storeroom that they entered?'

'Thankfully yes. If they had gone into the one in which we have our Mr Clark, he might have had a relapse.'

'Perhaps that was who they were looking for?' suggested Constable Temple who had been busily making notes.

'Maybe Constable, but they were clearly searching for something as well.'

'It is fortunate that they were interrupted by Miss Roper,' pointed out Doctor Henderson.

'And what was she doing here in the middle of the night?'

The corpulent doctor looked pensive. Taking the inspector gently by the elbow, he pulled him aside, out of Constable Temple's hearing.

'This is just between you and I, Inspector. It must not go down in any official record or I am afraid that the governor of the workhouse will insist that she is dismissed.'

Chard was concerned. He liked May, and felt sorry for the ordeal that she had undergone the previous year. 'I cannot exclude the fact that she interrupted the intruders, Doctor.'

'I understand, but perhaps you needn't mention the reason why she was there at the time.'

'I can't promise, but just tell me the facts and I'll see what I can do.'

The doctor nodded and started to explain. 'After the intruders left, the patients untied Nurse Harris and then came to the aid of Miss Roper. She had been struck in the face and knocked unconscious.'

'Will she be alright?'

'Physically yes. Just bruising I am glad to say. Nurse Harris was confused to find her in the infirmary. There was no obvious reason for her to be here. Initially, Nurse Harris got two of the more able patients to lift Miss Roper on to a spare bed whilst someone fetched me from home. It became apparent that Miss Roper was bare-legged and not even wearing her corset, so clearly had come out in a rush. However, that wasn't the only thing. There was a bottle of laudanum on her person.'

'You surprise me Doctor. Surely she wouldn't risk losing her employment?'

'Of course, there's nothing wrong, or rather illegal, in taking laudanum. However, you are correct in your supposition that it would be a disciplinary matter liable to get her fired.' The doctor shrugged his shoulders. 'I have no doubt that she has become addicted. I questioned her thoroughly and she admitted that she had been taking it for some time. It calmed her and helped her to sleep

at night, but now she is dependent. I took her home myself as soon
as it was light and explained the situation to her parents. They were
naturally distraught, but we all agreed to keep it a secret until I can
wean her off the ghastly stuff.'

There was silence as Chard gave the matter some consideration,
whilst the doctor looked at him hopefully.

'Very well,' said Chard finally. 'We'll leave the reason for her
presence out of our notes, for now at least.' The inspector led the
doctor back towards Temple, who had been watching the two men
intently.

Indicating to Temple that he should resume taking notes, Chard
addressed the doctor once more. 'What did Miss Roper tell you
about what she saw?'

'Only that there were two men who evidently had been pulling
things about and trying to get into a cupboard.'

'Anything of value in the cupboards?'

'As I already told you, we keep nothing of any real value here.'

'Was Miss Roper able to describe the men?'

'She said they looked heavily built, wore jackets but no hats.
That's about it.'

'Did she say if she would be able to recognise the men again?'

'It apparently happened too quickly for her to take in the faces.'

'Not much to go on for us then. Very well, we'll take our leave of
you and get back to the station. Please give Miss Roper my best
wishes and I hope you are able to help with...' Chard paused, '...
her injuries.'

As they left the infirmary, the inspector commented to his constable. 'The two intruders could be the same men that broke into the
County Hotel, so we need to look into the background of Jeremiah
Davies. I will contact the Taff Vale Railway today and arrange to
visit their offices.'

***

Idris Morgan stood outside the grocer's shop in Cilfynydd and
waited. Through the shop window he could see the man that he
assumed to be Mr Phillips serving a customer whilst another two
shoppers waited their turn. Morgan stroked his mutton chop

whiskers as he perused the open boxes of produce displayed on a table outside the premises. The vegetables seemed to be of good quality, and the constable reflected that as the only shop of its kind in the village, it must be profitable.

It took only five minutes for the customers to leave. As Constable Morgan entered, a small bell at the top of the door announced his presence.

'Good morning. Mr. Phillips, I take it.'

'Yes, that's right Constable,' answered the man.

Idris took in the man's appearance. He was probably in his forties, of middling height, but obviously had had some form of injury as he stood slightly lop-sided. Tufts of hair ran either side of his otherwise bald head and he wore round wire spectacles that he took off and fiddled with nervously.

'I am hoping you can help me, Mr Phillips,' asked the constable, taking out his notebook.

'In what way?' asked the grocer, looking away and starting to dust the shop counter with a piece of cloth that he pulled from the pocket of his overall.

'It is to do with the fire that killed Mr Hughes.'

'I don't know anything about that, and I don't want to make a statement. That's what I told the last constable and that's what I'm telling you now,' responded Phillips, dusting furiously.

'The last constable?'

'Connelly, I think his name was, or some such. A bit wet behind the ears if you ask me. Looked too young to be a policeman.'

Jackson's new pet constable, thought Morgan. That explains a lot.

'Why don't you want to make a statement?' he demanded.

'I told you. I don't know anything, and I don't want to get involved,' answered the grocer, finally putting down the cloth.

'How well did you know Mr. Hughes?'

'Known him for years.'

'Did you get on?'

'He was obstinate, reckless and a damn fool.'

Morgan raised an eyebrow. 'Strong words there, Mr Phillips. Care to elaborate?'

'No. I've said enough and that's that.'

'Did you see anyone around Mr Hughes's workshop around the time the fire started? A stranger perhaps?'

'No, I didn't.'

'Not very talkative, are you?' said Morgan sarcastically. 'Do you know anyone that might have started the fire? Apart from yourself of course.'

Phillips straightened up and looked directly at the constable for the first time, alarm in his eyes. 'Me? Why should I be a suspect?'

'Well, we know you were out and about at the time. You were seen by a witness. Also, you hardly sound as if you liked the victim.'

'Me? No, we got on, Constable,' denied the grocer in a nervous voice. 'Best pals we were at one time. You want to look at some of his customers. Pressing them for payment he was, even the poorer ones. There was Mrs Griffiths, Mrs Evans and Mr Jones for a start. Then there was his neighbour. Always rowing they were,' he added with an emphatic point of the finger.

'Are you sure that you saw no stranger on the street that day. A scruffy looking man in a long coat perhaps?'

Phillips looked away and started to dust his perfectly clean counter once again. 'No. I can't remember who I saw. Leave me alone.'

Morgan stood silently for a few moments, watching the grocer closely before speaking once more. 'Very well. I will leave it for now, but don't be surprised if we call for you in the middle of the night and fetch you down the station for further questioning.'

Phillips did not look up from his pointless polishing as Constable Morgan opened the door and left.

***

It took Morgan twenty minutes to find the home of the Mr. Jones seen by the gossip Mrs. Griffiths on the afternoon of the fire. He had made several calls at houses of other men of the same name, before finally being directed to the right address. Morgan rapped hard on the door and then seemed to wait an eternity before it was opened.

'Yes?' queried the occupant as he opened the door.

Morgan gave a reassuring smile, tinged with sadness. He had seen too many men end up like Mr Jones, who stood, as best he could, with a hunched back, one hand on a crudely made walking stick. His rheumy eyes were set in a lined face that spoke of years of hardship, and premature old age. Looking perhaps seventy or eighty, he was more likely twenty years younger, thought the constable. The blueish tinge of parts of the man's skin, and the discolouration of a small scar on his cheek, where coal dust had long ago been rubbed into the cut to seal the wound, spoke of Mr Jones's past.

'Could I come in and have a word please, Mr Jones?' asked Morgan kindly.

The man nodded, and slowly turned to lead the policeman down the small hallway and into his living room.

It was a sparsely furnished room, with only a table, a wooden chest and two chairs placed close to the fireplace. There was a pervasive smell of decay, though whether it was due to lack of cleanliness or just conjured up by his imagination, Morgan could not tell.

Jones slowly lowered himself into one of the chairs and gestured for Morgan to take the other.

'How long did you work underground?' asked the constable.

'Forty… years,' answered Jones.

Morgan realised that his original supposition had been correct. Jones would probably have started in the pit between twelve and fourteen years of age so now he would only be in his fifties. Not old perhaps in age but old in body.

'My father did thirty in the Great Western Colliery.'

The old man nodded, realising that the constable's father would probably have been maimed or killed working at the pit. It was usually the only way to get out that early; the infirmary or the grave.

'I wonder if you can help me?' continued Morgan. 'It is about the recent fire that killed Mr Hughes. We think it was started deliberately.'

The sick man nodded, put a dirty handkerchief to his mouth and gave a sudden hacking cough.

'We know that you were on the street around the time that the fire started. Did you see anything unusual?'

'Your… sergeant… asked,' answered Jones. Each word was

laboured and Morgan knew that the man's lungs, coated with the coal dust of many years, must be burning as he spoke.

'I couldn't find notes of any statement by you.'

Jones coughed several times into the handkerchief and then spat into the fireplace. 'No... patience... that... man.'

Morgan gave an understanding smile but simmered within. Clearly Jackson had seen the ex-miner as an irrelevance.

'Did you see any strangers about around the time of the fire?'

'Someone... seen... before.' Jones became breathless and it took a minute or two before he could continue. 'Big... shabby... coat.'

'Take your time Mr Jones. There's no hurry.'

'Walked... into... shop... once.'

'You've seen this man in a shop?'

Jones nodded.

'A shop here in Cilfynydd?'

Another affirming nod. 'Phillips... the... grocer,' Jones wheezed.

'It's alright, no need to continue Mr Jones. We can leave it there for now,' suggested the constable, worried by the drawn, exhausted face of the ex-miner.

There was a waved arm in response, indicating that he wanted to continue. 'He... was... threatening... him....'

Morgan went to the man's aid as he went into a further series of hacking coughs before sitting back breathless. The constable found a dirty grey cushion and placed it behind the man's head, before patting him gently on the shoulder.

'That's all. Just rest now,' he added before heading back to the station with a look of grim determination.

***

Chard had tried to telephone the headquarters of the Taff Vale Railway several times but with no success. The promised efficiency of the new equipment was still just a promise, so the inspector resolved to send a telegram instead. He had just started to draft it when there was a polite knock on his office door.

'Sorry to bother you sir,' apologised Constable Jenkins, 'but there is a gentleman outside who insists on speaking to the senior officer, and the superintendent isn't here.'

'Tell him to go away and come back next week,' snapped Chard.

'Very well sir, but I don't think he'll go. He appears to be an important gentleman.'

Chard sighed. 'I'm very busy and I have to send this telegram to the Taff Vale Railway. Who is he anyway?'

'That's a coincidence sir. His name is Mr Bowen and that's who he says he represents.'

Chard's eyes lit up. 'Ah, that's different. Well go on then, Jenkins. Don't keep the man waiting. Send him in!'

The inspector's sudden good mood lasted up until the moment that Bowen entered the office. There was immediately something about the man that Chard didn't like, and the his first impressions were rarely wrong.

Hector Bowen had clearly dressed to make an impression. He wore an expensive overcoat with fur collar, a fashionable homburg and carried an ivory handled cane. Beneath the open coat could be seen a formal suit complete with waistcoat from which dangled a solid gold watch chain. Yet, despite the evident quality of dress, there was something that didn't look right. The man exuded an air of raw animalistic threat. It was if someone had taken a wild bear to be fitted out at Savile Row, thought Chard.

'I wanted to see the Superintendent, but I suppose you will have to do,' barked Bowen. The shaggy-haired businessman gave a smile that was intended to look affable, but failed.

'How can I help you, Mr Bowen? Please take a seat. I was just about to send a telegram to your company's offices.'

Bowen settled his powerful frame into the chair facing the inspector's desk and pointed a finger at Chard.

'Then I hope the telegram was to advise us that you have arrested a Barry Railway Company employee for this terrible act.'

'I would rather that you didn't point, Mr Bowen and no, it wasn't going to be for that reason. The telegram was going to ask for an interview with a senior representative of your company.'

'Well here I am. I am a member of the board of directors of the Taff Vale Railway, but you should be asking to talk to the Barry Railway Company. It was they who poisoned our Mr. Davies,' said Bowen definitively.

'How do you know that?'

'Isn't it obvious Inspector? Davies joined our company having left the BRC without warning. Their chairman, Thaddeus Cornwall, is a vindictive man and would never allow such a slight to go unpunished.'

Chard shook his head. 'I can see a former employer being annoyed, but murder? Don't you think that is a little extreme?'

'You clearly do not know anything about their vile business. Davies was a key man to them, and I tell you that they are to blame. We want and demand retribution.'

'I am sure that I will be talking with them soon,' placated Chard.

'*Non loqui sed facere* – Not talk but action,' blustered Bowen, trying to intimidate the inspector.

'*Non omnia possumus omnes* – We can't all of us do everything,' responded Chard, not the least impressed by Bowen's introduction of Latin. 'What was Davies doing in Pontypridd?'

'Keeping a low profile for fear of retribution by Cornwall,' answered Bowen.

Chard considered that perhaps there was something in the accusation after all.

'Perhaps we will know more when Davies's companion recovers enough to speak. However, I will bear in mind what you have said Mr Bowen, and I will investigate the possibility of the Barry Railway Company's involvement.'

Bowen gave a conciliatory grunt, then stood up to leave. 'Very well Inspector, I will take you at your word. In the meantime, I will make my own enquiries. If you need to speak to me, I will be staying at the New Inn.'

Chard watched his visitor leave and had the unshakeable feeling that the arrival of Bowen was bad news for everybody.

SEVENTEEN

Chard leaned back in his chair and considered the implications of the discussion with Bowen. There were too many complicated possibilities and he needed some space to think things through. Then again, he also needed to keep on top of the Cilfynydd investigation.

Chard went to find Sergeant Humphreys.

'Is Morgan back from Cilfynydd yet, Sergeant?'

'He's just got back and gone to the privy,' replied the sergeant with his disturbing toothless smile. 'Did you want to see him Inspector?'

'Yes, send him through to me when he returns.'

It wasn't more than a few minutes before Constable Morgan appeared at the doorway of the Inspector's office.

'Come in Constable and tell me how you got on.' Chard spoke in a gentle tone. He knew that he would have to tell Morgan about May but needed to have the constable's report of his investigations first.

'Well sir, I found out the reason for the missing statements,' answered Morgan with some hesitation in his voice. He felt anger at the failure of his fellow officers to do their job properly, but did not feel comfortable at the thought of reporting their shortcomings to the inspector.

'Well, out with it,' encouraged Chard.

'Phillips the shopkeeper had been unwilling to co-operate with Constable Connelly,' excused Morgan. 'He said he didn't see anything, but I feel certain that he is lying.'

'Then bring him in. A night in the cells might change his attitude.'

'I don't think so, sir. I think he is too frightened.'

'Frightened of what?'

'Retribution of some kind. I did however get some useful infor-

mation from the Mr Jones that we were looking for. It took a while to find him, but I tracked him down eventually. He must have been too ill for Sergeant Jackson to interview when he made his enquiries,' lied Morgan. 'Apparently there was a stranger in the village at the time of the fire, although Jones had seen him before. He had been threatening Phillips in his shop.'

'Did Jones know why he was threatening Phillips?' asked the inspector.

'No sir. It might be a coincidence but the other day, when I was on patrol, I came across another shop in Cilfynydd, an ironmongers. It looked to me as if the owner had been knocked around a bit. I tried to find out what had happened, but the man refused to tell me, so I let the matter go.'

'So, it is possible that we have someone charging protection money and making an example of those that don't pay up,' grimaced the inspector.

'My thoughts exactly sir. That's why I didn't go back and fetch Phillips in. I thought you might want to decide how best to proceed.'

'Well done, Constable. I don't want to scare away our potential killer. Was Jones able to give you a decent description of the man that threatened Phillips?'

Morgan shook his head.

'A pity, but never mind,' continued Chard, 'I'll give the matter some thought.'

The inspector gave the constable a concerned look. 'A word about your young lady, May.'

Morgan looked uncomfortable. 'It's alright sir. I explained that we hadn't been getting on. Good of you to be concerned, but there is no need. I intend calling on her tonight and breaking off our friendship.'

'You might wish to reconsider,' suggested Chard, kindly.

'I don't think so sir. As I explained the other day, she has had these strange moods recently that I can't fathom.'

Chard decided that it would be best to get to the point. 'I am afraid that there was an incident at the infirmary. Two men broke in during the night, and May received a blow to the jaw.'

The colour drained from Morgan's face. 'Is she alright?'

'Yes, the injury isn't serious, just bruising.'

Morgan gave a sigh of relief, then looked quizzical. 'Did you say during the night sir?'

Chard looked uneasy and wondered whether he should say anything further. 'May is being treated by Doctor Henderson for some kind of illness relating to her injuries last year. She left her medicine behind at the infirmary and had to go back and fetch it. In doing so, she interrupted the intruders,' lied the inspector.

'Medicine? She hasn't mentioned anything about this to me.'

'Perhaps she didn't want to worry you.'

'Thank you for telling me sir. I'll go and visit her straight from the station when my shift finishes.'

'The doctor suggests that she is left to herself for a couple of days. Perhaps leave it to the weekend?'

Morgan looked doubtful. 'Are you sure sir?'

'Yes, really. The doctor was most insistent.' Chard felt guilty with the deception, but the doctor had told him about May's addiction in confidence. Hopefully, by the weekend, Doctor Henderson would have had time to discuss the way forward with May and her parents. The inspector was relieved to see a nod of acceptance from his constable. 'Good. That's agreed then,' he continued. 'Give yourself an evening out at the pub tonight,' suggested Chard with a measured degree of levity. 'That's what I'll be doing.'

***

'Hello stranger,' teased Gwen as Chard entered the bar of the Ivor Arms. 'We haven't seen you for a while, I thought that you had forsaken us.'

'Never,' laughed the inspector, who despite the challenges of his investigations, was in a very happy mood. On returning from the police station, he had found a sealed note placed by Lucy on his dining table. Chard had opened the perfumed envelope and been delighted to see that it had been sent by Alice. He was invited to dine with her at Ezekiel's house on the following evening.

'I see that you've found a replacement barman,' joked Chard, inclining his head towards the counter where a young lad stood polishing some beer glasses.

'I wish I had. That boy is helping out washing the glasses and he's already broken three of them.' Gwen sighed, then nodded towards the far end of the room. 'Your drinking butties are stood over there as usual. I'll pop around the counter and serve you myself. We've got a new barrel on from the Captain's Brewery. It's quite a strong bitter, but I think you'll like it.'

'Then I'll have to give it a try, Gwen,' smiled Chard.

Chard walked across the room, hung his hat and coat on the wall hooks and went to join his friends.

'...And I say it's just a lot of toffs showing off...' argued Dic Jenkins.

'Well I would go and watch it if it was over here,' responded Will Horses.

'It is a good idea, but strictly speaking they should be doing it naked,' contributed Dai Books sagely.

Intrigued, Chard went nearer and leant his walking cane against the side of the bar.

'Riding a bike naked? That would chafe a bit,' grimaced Will.

'And what about naked tennis? You couldn't play properly with all your bits flopping about. *Duw* no,' shuddered Dic.

'What are you talking about?' interrupted the inspector.

'Oh, *shwmae* Mr Chard, we didn't notice you come in.'

'No Dic, I can see that you are all in deep discussion.'

'Of course, in ancient times the women did it naked as well,' continued Dai Books, not wanting to drop the conversation.

'Oi Dai! I don't know what you are talking about, but I don't want any filthy conversation here,' admonished Gwen, who had come to the counter with Chard's pint of bitter.

'I am just educating my butties, Gwen.'

'Yes, he's getting ready for his teaching job,' laughed Will.

'I've only put in for it and hopefully I won't get it,' snapped Dai.

'It's them Olympic Games see,' clarified Dic. 'In April it is, over in Greece.'

'Aye Gwen. They are even going to run from the town of Marathon to Athens and that's about twenty-five miles,' added Will.

'Why? Haven't they got any omnibuses?' asked the landlady.

'No, they are going to race twenty-five miles,' explained Will.

'Why would they do that?'

'Quite right,' agreed Dic. 'I mean, if you were being chased by a wild bear, or a lion…'

'Or a tiger,' contributed Dai.

'Yes, or a tiger as you say,' continued Dic, '…you would either be caught after half a mile or it would give up.'

'Daft foreign idea. It'll never catch on,' commented Gwen, shaking her head as she walked off to serve a new group of customers who had just come in.

'Of course, they got the idea for the games from us,' contributed Chard.

'What? Running twenty-five miles?' asked Will.

'No, I mean for the Olympic Games generally.' Chard took a sip of his beer and pulled a face. It was bitter beyond. Fine for some people's taste, but not his.

'I can assure you it was the Greeks,' corrected Dai Books.

'I mean the idea to revive the Olympic Games came from us. There is a small town in Shropshire called Much Wenlock which has had its own Olympic Games for many years. That chap de Coubertin was visiting England, saw these games and decided to try and copy them on a large scale.'

'Still just a load of nobs showing off…' argued Dic.

Chard laughed and settled himself down to enjoy the conversation, putting the unfinished beer to one side and ordering a glass of Jamesons instead.

It was a half hour later, after more humorous discussion, that he moved away from his friends and took a seat in a corner of the room, glass of whiskey in hand.

Now he felt in a suitable frame of mind to consider the complexities surrounding his investigations. The death of Davies was especially problematic. Firstly, the cause of death. The effect on the body had the hallmarks of poison, but there was no trace of any. So how would it be possible to make a case even if they knew the murderer? That at least solved the question as to why they used what they did. Stabbing someone in the back in a dark alley would be much simpler, but then it would mean the killer being at the scene at the time of the victim's demise. In Davies's case there was no-one

around when he and Clark succumbed to the poison.

The motive was now starting to take shape, assuming Bowen's accusation was correct, though it did seem a bit extreme. Could the Barry Railway Company be so vindictive? Yet if an expensive new poison had been used in the killing, perhaps by a professional assassin, then they would certainly have the money with which to pay for it. Was Clark an intended victim as well? It had crossed Chard's mind, so he had spoken with a clerk he knew at the courthouse. Apparently, it was true that he was a lenient magistrate, so any enemies would have come from his private life. Mrs Clark had denied that possibility, so Chard had asked the opinion of Superintendent Jones. He in turn had made enquiries amongst the higher social dignitaries of the town. By all accounts, the 'great and the good' considered him to be an extremely affable man. Yet, his friendship with Davies had put him in danger. Perhaps Davies had told him something that incriminated whoever was behind the murder?

Chard sipped his whiskey and gave a sigh as he thought on.

If the cause of death was poison, how was it administered? Chard remembered suddenly that some poisons are absorbed through the skin. He groaned at the added complication, but shook his head and continued with his original line of thought. If it was put into food or drink, then why poison both men? Was it deliberate or was it unavoidable? The men met at the Butchers Arms, went to a tearoom, then drank from a fountain. At the former they would have had separate drinks and at the latter there would have been more people poisoned. That left the tearoom and the shared teapot.

Further questioning by his constables had confirmed that neither the owner nor any of the staff on duty had any connection with Davies. So that left the customers. Luckily, the families had been traced and so had the elderly couple that had been present. All had been excluded from future inquiries. That left the two men of the cloth that had been seen arguing and the two men in tweed jackets. Could either or both pairs of men be the intruders at the County Hotel, and/or the culprits who broke into the infirmary?

Chard drummed his fingers on the table then decided that further thought on the case was not going to help him tonight. He comforted himself that at least there had been definite progress on

the Hughes killing. It seemed certain that there was some sort of protection racket in Cilfynydd. Tomorrow he would visit Mrs Hughes to progress the investigation in person, regardless of the superintendent's instructions. Then in the evening there would be dinner with Alice. With that thought, the inspector finished his drink and smiled.

***

Hector Bowen had visited the Taff Vale Railway station at Pontypridd several times previously but had never spent a night in the town. Nonetheless, as he left the New Inn and went into the night, the businessman knew exactly where he was going. Bowen had made some enquiries earlier in the day. It hadn't taken long to get the name of the man he wanted to see and where he could find him.

Gone was the expensive coat, cane and fashionable homburg hat, Bowen now wore a more casual jacket and trousers. As he walked up the street towards the Tumble, Bowen took out a flat cap and pulled it firmly down on his head. There was a slight chill in the air despite the improved weather and he missed the warmth of his coat, but he didn't have far to go.

The Half Moon stood on the junction known as the Tumble. The Tram Road ran to one side of it, whilst the road on the other side passed under the railway bridge and up the Graig hill. As Bowen entered, he inhaled the stench of cheap tobacco and long-spilled beer.

'*Shwmae*. What can I get you?' asked the barman, a skinny, bald-headed individual with several missing teeth. There were few patrons in the middle of the week, and he was clearly eager to secure some custom.

Bowen glanced around the room until his eyes settled on a man who sat alone at a table, staring into a glass of beer.

'Two whiskies,' he ordered.

The barman's eyes lit up and he turned towards the assortment of bottles that stood untidily on a shelf.

'None of your rotgut stuff mind,' warned Bowen; and the threat in his voice made the barman switch his attention to a different bottle than he had originally intended.

When the whiskies were poured, Bowen took a sip from one of the glasses and grunted approval before making payment. Taking the glasses, he walked to the table occupied by the lone drinker and sat down facing him.

The man looked up, annoyed at the unannounced intrusion into his thoughts. He was a tough looking individual, with a powerful frame, his hair close-cropped and a face only a mother could love. As he recognised the man before him, his expression registered shock, anger and confusion.

'O'Neill, I believe. Here, you look like you could do with this,' said Bowen as he proffered one of the glasses of whisky.

'I've been fired. I want nothing to do with the railway,' came the sharp reply, his broad Irish accent unmistakeable. When Bowen had, on rare occasions, visited the Pontypridd station, his ostentatious appearance and appalling manners had made him an easily recognisable figure to the Taff Vale Railway workers. Yet O'Neill remained confused at seeing this high-ranking railway official before him, clearly trying to keep a low profile.

'I heard there had been some misunderstanding. Nothing that can't be rectified,' replied Bowen. 'I assume that you wouldn't mind having your job back? Perhaps with a little extra money in your back pocket?'

O'Neill's expression changed to one of hope. 'I've got a family to feed. I need money Mr Bowen,' he explained with desperation in his voice. 'I didn't mean to hit the foreman. I just got angry.'

'So I understand. I was impressed that your fellow workers all stood behind you. You clearly were very popular with the rest of the men.'

'I get on, yes.'

'Well, I think that you are just the man I am looking for. I take it that you have no particular regard for the Barry Railway Company?'

'Load of bastards, if you don't mind me saying so.'

'Excellent, that's just what I wanted to hear.' There was a pause before Bowen put forward his proposition.

'You see O'Neill, there are those that would like to see our two companies develop a friendly relationship. Eventually we would work so closely together that a merger would be inevitable. If that were

to happen there would have to be job losses. You wouldn't be the only one losing your job, there would be many others. Now I don't want that.'

'Neither do I, Mr Bowen.'

'Good. Therefore, it is in our interest for us not to develop a friendly relationship and I think that this town is a good place to start. You may have heard about the two men taken ill in Ynysangharad Fields.'

'Of course, Mr Bowen.'

'Well the fellow who died had recently come to work for us and he was poisoned by the Barry Railway Company.'

'The bastards!'

Bowen smiled at the response. 'I need a head of station security. If you are interested, turn up at the station tomorrow morning at 9 a.m. and I will discuss things in more detail. I suggest that you might want to finish your drink and go home. You will need a clear head in the morning.'

'Yes sir, Mr Bowen.'

O'Neill downed his whisky and got to his feet.

Bowen smiled to himself as his new head of security rushed off to tell his wife the good news. The truth of the matter was that money could be made if the two rail companies were to merge, but not near as much as he personally could acquire if he became chairman of the TVR. That was the target and it depended on no merger. The prize was nearly in his grasp. 'Damn! I could do with a handful of Mrs Torres tonight,' he thought, 'but it will have to wait.'

EIGHTEEN

As Chard approached the police station the following morning, he was alerted to a commotion in the yard. He could hear the scuffle of running feet, shouts and curses, and assumed there was a particularly violent prisoner being fetched in. As he turned the corner, the inspector was greeted with an unexpected sight,

'Try that again. You're lucky they're holding me back,' yelled Constable Temple whose arms were being held by the weighty Constable Davies.

'I would if I could, you long streak of piss!' shouted back Constable Morgan, who in turn was being restrained by Constable Jenkins.

'Bollocks! Don't forget, I know what a coward you are.'

'Oi! Don't you call my cousin a coward or I'll lamp you one as well,' called out Constable Matthews who had just arrived on the scene.

Before Chard could bellow a command to restore order, he noticed Sergeant Morris come striding out of the station.

'What the fuck is going on?' he shouted as he approached, red-faced with anger.

The constables all stood stock still. To hear the sergeant swear was a rarity, and to see the huge officer approaching in anger was a sight to freeze the blood.

Morris could clearly see that Temple and Morgan had been fighting, even without the taller man's cut lip. Going up to the two protagonists, he grabbed each one by the neck, and then clashed their skulls together with an almighty crack before letting go. Both constables reeled away holding their ringing heads, but not daring to complain.

'I had enough of you two before Temple went away. It ends now! If there is any further disturbance of this kind, I will arrange a station boxing match, and each of you will fight Constable Jenkins.'

Jenkins stood back proudly, knowing that everyone was aware of

his prowess as the champion boxer of the constabulary.

Sergeant Morris turned away and observed his Inspector who had been watching the drama develop with interest.

'Sorry you had to see that sir,' said the sergeant hesitantly. 'I wasn't going to report the incident officially.'

'No, I understand Sergeant. I wouldn't want the Superintendent to hear about it either. We are short enough of officers. Having both men fired wouldn't help matters.'

Morris gave a grateful smile. 'Thank you for understanding sir.'

Chard acknowledged with a gentle nod. 'Once those two idiots have calmed down, have them sent to my office one at a time. I'll give them something to take their minds off their squabbling.'

***

It was sometime later, after Chard had received a long sermon from Superintendent Jones about the importance of solving the Davies killing quickly, that he was able to sit at his desk and reflect. It had been less than a week since Davies had died, but a fortnight to the day since Hughes had been killed, most horribly, in the fire. Despite having been ordered to concentrate his personal efforts on the Davies case, Chard could not accept that just because Hughes was of a lower class, the matter was less important. He glanced at the bag of items that still lay in the corner, went over and poured the pieces of glass and metal onto the carpet. They still smelled of smoke which triggered the unpleasant memory of the charred corpse. There were two similar portions of twisted, blackened metal and as he recognised what he was looking at, a smile came to his lips. Any further thoughts were interrupted by a knock on the office door.

'Sergeant Morris said that you wanted to see me sir,' said a dejected and somewhat nervous Constable Morgan.

'Yes. You do realise that if I was to take this morning's incident out of Sergeant Morris's hands and report it formally, then you would possibly be kicked out of the constabulary?'

Morgan nodded in response; eyes averted from the gaze of his superior.

'You clearly landed a blow on Temple. What set things off?' continued the inspector.

'Sinner went to May's house to give her some flowers.'

Chard's fingers drummed the desk as he considered what to say next. 'I see. So you were jealous. I thought you were breaking up with the young lady.'

'I was considering it sir, but that wasn't the point. Technically she is still mine.'

'She isn't your possession Morgan, like a piece of furniture,' admonished Chard.

'I was thinking of her best interests, sir. You told me that she wasn't well and not to visit her for a while. The only reason Sinner went there was to get my back up. He has no concern about her well-being.'

'I will speak to him about the matter, but in the meantime, I want no more incidents between the pair of you. If it happens again then it will be a formal case of misconduct. Do you understand?'

'Yes sir,' answered the constable, shaken by the severity in Chard's voice.

'Good. Now let us get on with more urgent business. Your sole concern, until I tell you otherwise, is to trace the two men in tweed jackets and the two clergymen who were in the tearoom on the day of Davies's demise. Do whatever is necessary. Now go and don't come back until you find something.'

With that curt dismissal ringing in his ears, Morgan left the office, only to be replaced a few minutes later by a shamefaced Constable Temple. The cut on his lip had stopped bleeding and was already starting to crust over.

'You wanted to see me sir?'

'I did indeed, Constable Temple. Do I strike you as someone who is inclined to sweep things under the carpet?'

Temple looked unsure as to how he should answer.

'I know I might sometimes give that impression,' continued Chard. 'However, that perception is very much in error. I might be inclined to treat things leniently every now and again as necessity demands, but I don't forget them.'

Temple gulped but otherwise remained silent.

'I don't take kindly to officers fighting with their colleagues, regardless of who caused it.'

'It was Morgan who struck me, sir.'

'Yes, and you assaulted his fist with your face.'

Temple resolved to make no further defence as the inspector clearly was having none of it.

'I am aware that you paid Miss Roper a visit, Constable. Do you have any serious intentions towards her?'

'Not really sir. It's just that she is an attractive young lady and...'

'Let me stop you right there, Constable. Let it be understood that I have an avuncular fondness for Miss Roper, and I do not want her affections played with. I don't care about your past history with Morgan, but I will not have Miss Roper used as a weapon in your feud.'

'If it helps sir, I didn't get past the front door. I just gave some flowers to her father who looked none too pleased.'

'Well, that's something at least. If I ever have to talk to you about this again, you will be for the high jump. Steer clear of Miss Roper. Is that understood?'

'Yes sir,' agreed the constable.

'Then we can move on and talk about something else.'

Temple looked relieved.

'I have a job for you. Morgan seems to have stumbled across something going on in Cilfynydd that may relate directly to the death of Hughes. Last Monday he came across a shopkeeper that had apparently been beaten up. It appears that someone has been extorting money from local businesses. Monday is possibly when they collect their money. Next week, I want you to go to Cilfynydd, out of uniform, try to spot the culprit and then follow them. Do nothing else. Morgan will give you the details of the businesses concerned. Go and ask him nicely. I will be watching,' warned Chard.

As the chastised Temple left the office, Chard kept looking until he saw the two constables conferring respectfully, if not amicably, then shook his head and went back to his desk.

***

Ben Gardner was in a rush. He was in danger of being late for his afternoon shift and for an engine driver of the Barry Railway Company, it would never do. The short cut from his house took him

down a narrow alley and he hurried headlong, thinking of nothing other than the trouble he could be in.

'Well, well, what do we have here?'

Ben came up short and looked up at the two men that were now blocking his path. He recognised both as being employees of the rival Taff Vale Railway.

'I'm in a rush,' explained Ben, assuming that the men would be sympathetic to a fellow railwayman, irrespective of employer.

'Not so fast,' disputed the bigger, rougher looking of the two. 'We want a word.'

'What about? I haven't got time to talk,' answered Ben nervously. He noticed that the second man was tapping a pickaxe handle against the palm of his hand.

'One of our men has been poisoned and I've been told it was done by one of your lot.' The strong Irish accent was heavy with threat.

'You mean the bloke that was found in the park? That was nothing to do with us.'

'We think it's time to pay the deed back,' came the response, ignoring the denial.

Without further warning the man with the axe handle prodded Ben in the chest, forcing him to take a step backwards. Then the Irishman made to grab the engine driver's right arm. Ben shook the attempt off, but before he could do anything else, his assailant thumped him hard in the stomach, causing him to double up. Still holding his stomach and gasping for breath, the BRC worker turned to run away. The second assailant was too quick, and the axe handle crashed down on the undefended man's upper back sending him heavily to the floor.

'Tell your mates that's just the beginning,' came the scornful warning from the man with the Irish accent. It was the last thing Ben heard before he lost consciousness.

***

It was mid-afternoon before Chard reached Cilfynydd, and when he arrived at the widow's door, he realised that his journey was might be wasted. Mrs Hughes worked and there was no guarantee that she

would be in. Even worse, he hadn't come in the police gig with a constable, or borrowed the Superintendent's horse, because he hadn't wanted his superior to question where he was going. Chard had taken a hansom cab and sent it away, but there was no omnibus due back to Pontypridd for another hour. So it was a relief that his knock was answered, and the door was opened by the sombrely dressed widow.

'Good day, Mrs Hughes. I am Inspector Chard; I wonder if I could have a word?'

'I don't think that I have the option to refuse, do I?' came the quietly spoken response. The woman turned and led Chard inside without any further discussion.

'I was afraid that you might have been at work,' said Chard pleasantly, hoping to start some kind of rapport.

They entered the sitting room and the widow gestured for the inspector to sit opposite herself, close to the fireplace.

'I have left my employment,' she answered sadly. 'Apparently having someone around the place who is unable to smile at the customers is bad for business. The neighbours have been kind and I will gain other employment somehow. If necessary, I will take in washing if that's the only work I can get.'

'I am terribly sorry to hear that,' responded Chard, genuinely moved by the poor widow's plight. 'Where were you employed? Perhaps I could have a word with them?'

'No. I would prefer that you did not. I don't want any trouble.'

'If you insist. I would like to know though, so that I don't give them any custom.'

The widow paused. 'The Tredegar Arms, but I would rather forget about working there. I have other things to consider now. At least permission has finally been given to bury my poor husband's body. The funeral is tomorrow morning and there is so much to do,' she explained as a tear started to form in the corner of her eye.

'I won't keep you long and as you can see, I haven't brought anyone with me, so this isn't a formal interview.'

'You know that I have already spoken to two policemen? I didn't find that a very pleasant experience. The sergeant in particular made me feel very uncomfortable.'

'I promise that I have no intention of upsetting you, Mrs Hughes, or would you prefer I called you Sarah?'

'Do not presume to be familiar with me, Inspector.'

'Sorry, I didn't mean to offend, I just wanted to put you at ease.'

'I would prefer that you cut to the chase,' she answered coldly.

'Very well. I want to ask a couple of questions regarding the workshop. Firstly, the lighting. Apparently, there were no internal gas fittings, so light must have come from an oil lamp.'

'Yes,' confirmed the widow. 'There was a large one. William didn't usually work very late but it gave enough light for him to work by.'

'Was there a smaller one as well?'

'No. Just the big one.'

'What about windows?' asked the inspector.

'There was one at the back and one at the side, but they were obviously not much use once the light faded.'

'That wasn't why I was asking, Mrs Hughes.'

The widow looked puzzled as the inspector continued. 'We have reason to believe that someone may have been extorting money from your husband, which is perhaps why he suddenly became short of money.'

'I know nothing of this,' she exclaimed.

'Are you sure that you haven't seen anyone unfamiliar around your husband with whom he seemed on bad terms?'

Mrs Hughes stared at Chard looking utterly confused. 'No Inspector, I've no idea what you are talking about.'

'It seems possible that your husband was made an example of, in order to scare other victims. Earlier today I examined some objects that I recovered from the scene of the fire. I identified the twisted remains of metal casings belonging to two oil lamps. If my assumptions are correct, the people who did this are extremely vicious. They must have tied up your husband, locked the door, then thrown a lit oil lamp through one of the windows.'

Mrs Hughes let out a sudden wail and started to weep uncontrollably. Unsure how to respond, Chard passed her a handkerchief from his pocket and tried to offer some comfort.

'I promise you. I will hunt down the culprits and they will hang;

I can assure you of that. It will be our priority,' he stated, aware that his superior would not agree.

Despite Chard's best efforts the weeping could not be abated, and he was glad to hear a knock on the door, which gave him an excuse to leave the room.

On opening the front door, the inspector found Mrs Evans on the doorstep, who expressed shock at seeing him.

'What on earth?' she exclaimed. Before she could continue, the sound of the widow's weeping came to her ears.

'What have you been doing to the poor thing? Let me in at once! At once I say!'

Chard was thrown back against the wall as the angry woman brushed past. Once further down the hall she turned and shouted '*Ewch!*'

The inspector didn't need to speak Welsh in order to understand that he was no longer welcome. Making a hasty exit, Chard went out into the street and rather than wait for an omnibus, decided to exercise himself by the long walk back to the station.

NINETEEN

It was a cool, pleasant evening and the light had not entirely faded, yet Chard felt a nervous tremor run through his body. The inspector straightened his tie as he waited for the door to be answered. He was dressed in his best suit and had trimmed his moustache and sideburns so short that they were barely visible. Tapping the end of his cane impatiently against the doorstep, Chard wondered why he was so on edge. All he was doing was having a meal with a friend, he lied to himself.

Finally, Alice opened the door. She smiled, and Chard could not help but smile back. Alice wore a high-necked burgundy dress with black beading and a beautiful silver and turquoise brooch. Her brown hair was neatly arranged, and he could smell the delicate fragrance of the bergamot perfume that she wore.

'Do come in Thomas, it must be a bit chilly out there.'

'It's surprisingly agreeable,' answered the inspector as Alice took his hat, coat and cane.

'Please go through to the dining room whilst I hang these things up.'

As Chard entered, he felt the warmth from the fireplace and could smell a wonderful aroma from the kitchen beyond.

'I was concerned that you weren't going to come and then all my food would go to waste,' teased Alice as she returned.

'What could possibly make you think that I might not come?' replied Chard with a playful smile.

'Because you are worried about eating at your friend's table, with his housekeeper, without his knowledge.'

'I have to confess that there is a degree of truth in that. I do feel rather guilty.'

'We all have to be naughty now and again,' laughed Alice, wagging her finger playfully. 'Make yourself comfortable whilst I check on things in the kitchen. Would you like a glass of sherry?'

Chard accepted the offer and sipped the small glass of amontillado until Alice returned with two bowls of hot soup. 'It's cream of leek,' she announced. 'Doctor Matthews says there's a fancy French name for it, but I was taught the recipe by my mother and she never went anywhere near France.'

Chard took a mouthful and caught Alice's slight scowl as he added a little more pepper from the condiments on the table.

'It's lovely, but I tend to like more pepper than most people,' he explained before quickly changing the subject. 'May I say how very beautiful you look tonight?'

'Thank you. May I return the compliment by saying how handsome you look now that you've trimmed your sideburns and moustache?'

'You may indeed, but I cannot vow to keep them like this.'

They both laughed and chatted idly as they ate, until Alice went to see to the main course.

As he waited, Chard's stomach rumbled in anticipation. His hopes were met, as Alice came through with the source of the wonderful meaty aromas that had continued to emanate from the kitchen.

'Game pie with carrots, sprouts, roast parsnips and gravy. The gravy has been heavily peppered.' She added pointedly.

Chard tucked into the meal with gusto, only to pause when he realised that Alice was staring at him.

'You will get indigestion if you carry on eating like that Thomas,' she scolded.

'Sorry. This is so delicious.'

'Well give yourself time to recover a little and let us talk for a moment,' suggested Alice. 'You've always avoided talking about your past and why you came here. When I was nursing you after your accident, you mentioned that you were orphaned when just a boy, but that's all I know.'

'There's not much to tell. My parents were killed in an accident, leaving me in the care of my mother's sister and her husband. My father had been a successful businessman and I was left a considerable sum, which was kept in trust. I attended Shrewsbury School before I went to study at Owen's College in Manchester.'

'I am impressed Thomas. You hadn't mentioned that before,' said Alice.

Chard grimaced. 'My time at Shrewsbury School was not a happy one. My allowance from the trust was not great and I was looked down on because my family was "trade". I also preferred to spend my free time with the local boys from the town, rather than my stuck-up classmates.'

'Was Manchester any better?' asked Alice.

'Thankfully yes. Owen's College became part of the new Victoria University during my time there. The teaching was very progressive and with one or two exceptions, I found my fellow students agreeable.'

'What happened afterwards?'

'By the time I left university I had received my full inheritance, which left me comfortable, but not rich. The police force in Manchester was having difficulty recruiting for their detective department and I joined it on a whim. During my time there, I was fortunate enough to be involved in a couple of important cases and I realised that the job suited me. A few years later, there was a vacancy for an inspector back in Shrewsbury and, thanks to the recommendation of my Chief Constable, they gave me the post. That's all there is to know,' he said with some finality, picking his cutlery up once more.

'You still haven't explained why you came here.'

'I'm afraid I don't really want to talk about it,' answered Chard.

'Why should I not be told?' persisted Alice.

'Because I haven't told anyone. At least, I haven't told them the truth. I gave an explanation to a friend last year, during my investigation into the Treforest murder case. It was not a lie as such, but it wasn't the actual reason why I left Shropshire. I felt guilty about the matter and I don't want to mislead you as well.'

'So don't mislead me. Tell me about it,' insisted Alice.

'Perhaps in time, but that is my last word on the subject,' responded Chard. Averting his eyes from Alice's gaze, he took another mouthful of game pie.

For a while the couple ate in silence. Then, feeling that she had offended her guest, Alice resumed the conversation on safer ground. 'Tell me about your investigations, Thomas.'

Chard visibly relaxed, glad that Alice was interested in his work. 'It's very mixed I'm afraid. There has been some progress with finding out who killed the poor soul in Cilfynydd, but we aren't progressing fast enough with the poisoning.'

'You are absolutely sure it was poison?'

'Yes, I'm confident of that, but I will know more when Doctor Matthews returns. I am also reasonably certain that the poisoning was carried out in the Silver Teapot on the day that we were there.'

Alice gave a shudder. 'Surely not?'

'I am afraid so. We are trying to trace the clergymen that were sat close to us. There were also two men in tweed jackets that we suspect may have been involved somehow. I don't suppose that you can remember anything about them? How they spoke, or if they had any distinguishing features?'

'No, I don't remember anything about them. It is just too terrible to think about. Let's change the subject.' added Alice hastily. 'What do you think about those International Socialists meeting in London?'

'I don't think the Superintendent is very happy about it,' answered Chard, picking up his knife and fork once more. 'He thinks that we are sitting on a powder keg as it is. The last thing he wants is any talk of social unrest.'

The couple continued with their meal whilst discussing the latest titbits of national news and local gossip. After they had finished a light pudding, Alice suggested that they retire to the sitting room.

Alice lit the fire, then sat on the sofa next to Chard and took his hand.

'Thomas, I want you to know that I have never looked at another man since I lost my dear husband. I didn't think I could ever feel anything in my heart for someone else. When you first came to this house, I don't believe that I liked you, but then when you were fetched here after your accident....'

Chard smiled. 'It was unexpected for me as well. I hadn't intended to kiss you. It just happened.

'Then let it just happen again...'

***

Hector Bowen turned up the collar of his coat, pulled down his cap and glanced around to check that he was not being followed. It had taken a tour of the more disreputable establishments in the town to find out the information he needed. With a feeling of anticipation, Bowen felt inside his coat pocket. His fingers rubbed against the two small bottles that had been sent to him that afternoon by special messenger. Turning into Gas Lane he looked towards the distant gas lamp, that lit part of the pathway. Unable to see anyone, he gave a grunt of disappointment. For a moment he considered turning back towards the town centre, but spat on the pavement and walked on. Suddenly, he noticed someone move from the shadows into the glare of a streetlamp. It was a figure that was undeniably female.

Increasing his step and biting his lower lip as he thought of his basest instincts, Bowen approached the girl.

'Hello my dear,' he greeted.

'Good evening sir,' answered the girl coyly. She was young, pretty and every bit as desirable as Bowen had been told.

'What is your name my pretty little thing?'

'Why it's Maisy sir, and what would yours be?' she replied.

'You can call me Ben,' he lied, thinking it amusing to use the Christian name of the Taff Vale Railway chairman.

Maisy stroked the shaggy hair that hung from beneath Bowen's cap. 'Well Ben, are you looking for some company?'

Bowen gave a guttural laugh. 'Are you willing for a shilling?'

'A shilling? What sort of girl do you think I am?' teased the young prostitute, who had looked beyond the rather unimpressive coat and cap. With a practised eye, Maisy had taken in the diamond studs in Bowen's collar. 'I think we might be talking ten shillings at least and perhaps double that, depending on your inclinations.'

Bowen started to salivate at the prospect and quickly nodded his agreement. 'Do you have a place?'

'For a fine gentleman like yourself, of course. I am sharing a place with two other girls.'

'I would rather we kept things private, no-one else around.'

'That is alright. They have been hired for the night by two of the town's councillors and won't be back until the morning. We shall be quite alone.'

Bowen gave a wicked smile and let himself be led to a small terraced house close to the river.

Once inside, and confident that they were alone, he buried his slavering mouth into the girl's neck and inhaled the heavy scent of her cheap perfume.

'Slow down Ben, we've got time,' laughed Maisy as she pushed him away.

'I've got a little something that will make us feel more relaxed and in the mood for what is to come.'

'I've got some cocaine if that's what you want. No charge, it's cheap enough,' offered Maisy.

'No thank you,' said Bowen. 'This is better. Look, one bottle for me and one for you. Watch while I drink mine.' Bowen checked which bottle was which, then undid the clip and drank one of them. He threw his coat off and stretched out his brawny arms. 'I feel invigorated already. Now it's your turn. Down in one mind!'

With some hesitation, Maisy took the other bottle and drank it back in one gulp. 'That tasted rather bitter,' she said before turning away and starting to remove her clothes. Having only removed her immediate outer garments, Maisy suddenly felt her legs collapse beneath her. She was aware of what happened next but was unable to move, and it was some nightmarish hours later before she lapsed into unconsciousness.

***

Chard lay naked beneath a single cotton sheet, in a room lit only by the moonlight that shone through a small gap in the curtains. The sheet felt cold against his skin and he tried to distract himself by thinking of other matters. He felt a mixture of emotions. Guilt that he was in the house of a friend and somehow betraying Doctor Matthews trust; anxiety that he would be seen in the morning by the scullery maid who would arrive at dawn; and eagerness as he awaited Alice's return to the room.

The housekeeper's room had no gaslight fitting and so, when Alice returned, she came carrying a small lamp. Chard felt his body tense as he saw her in the doorway, her petite frame covered only by a flimsy chemise. Alice approached the bed and turned out the lamp.

There was a rustle of cotton as she removed her clothing and for a moment the moonlight exposed Alice's naked silhouette. She pulled back the sheet of the single bed and Chard moved over to allow her in. Alice lay alongside him, her head on his chest and the warmth of her thigh resting against his own. She pulled the sheet back up and Chard felt it fall softly across his body. Alice tilted her head upwards and Chard moved awkwardly in the bed to kiss her tenderly on the lips. It was a long lingering kiss, and his senses became lost in the fragrance of her perfume, the taste of her lips and the warmth of her body. Gently, Chard kissed Alice's neck and he felt her body quiver. He tried to move in the bed once more in order to make more room, but Alice stopped him, and he lay back in his original position. Chard felt her knee move across his body, brushing against the evidence of his arousal. Then, he felt her warm body move position as she sat astride him. Chard took a sharp intake of breath as Alice's fingers reached for his manhood, clenching tightly. Then in a moment, they were as one. Alice's body shuddered, and Chard gasped aloud as their lovemaking gained pace, their passion all-consuming, until eventually, they fell asleep in each other's arms.

TWENTY

Chard was tired. He had awoken at the crack of dawn, kissed Alice gently on the cheek, dressed and left the house only moments before the scullery maid had turned the corner into the street. He arrived at his own front door at the same time as his own maid, Lucy. Ignoring her quizzical look, the inspector went to his room and lay on his bed fully clothed, falling into a deep slumber. As a result, he arrived late at the police station, much to the displeasure of Superintendent Jones; who summoned him at once to a meeting in his office with Colonel Grover from the local authority. It had been long and difficult, with the representative of Pontypridd Urban District Council demanding to know, in detail, what was being done to solve the outstanding cases. It was midday before Chard finally sat at his desk and read the hand-written note from Doctor Henderson. Cursing his luck at not having seen the note earlier, the inspector rushed to the infirmary where he found Henderson at his desk, completing paperwork.

The grey-haired doctor looked up and gave a sigh.

'I am sorry Inspector. I am afraid you are too late. Didn't you get my second note?'

'The only note I had said that you feared another poisoning had occurred.'

'I should have sent a more reliable messenger. I gave a second message to young Johnny, one of the workhouse inmates. If he has absconded for the day, I'll have him beaten on his return. I am afraid it was a false alarm. My fault. I should have waited until I was sure.'

'What happened?'

The doctor gave a rueful expression and indicated to an empty chair. 'Take a seat and I'll explain.'

Chard removed his cap and sat down, eager to hear the reason for the doctor's apparent error in judgement.

'Earlier this morning, before I arrived, a young woman was

brought to the infirmary by two of her friends. They were by all accounts ladies of low repute, if you take my meaning. A neighbour had driven them here in his cart, as the patient was comatose. Her companions had no idea what had happened to her, but they knew she had been in good health the previous day. On my arrival, the duty nurse told me that she had been unable to bring the patient around, so I scribbled a note to you, fearing that she may have been poisoned like Mr. Clark.'

'But that was not the case?' queried the inspector.

'No. I examined her fully with Nurse Harris present, whilst she was still in a stupor. Her vital functions appeared normal. No signs of damage to the digestive or respiratory systems. The pulse was very low, and the pupils were dilated. I believe that opiates had been involved.'

'So, no need for treatment then?'

'No, not as such,' replied the doctor hesitantly.

'From your demeanour there seems to be something that you are reluctant to mention.'

'Well, it's rather delicate. The young woman had suffered severe bruising and inflammation of a most intimate nature. I cannot say anything further, but I fear that she may have been drugged and then most viciously abused.'

'Then I will need to speak to her. I deplore the ill-use of women and if she has been abused it could happen to someone else.'

'I am afraid you're too late. She eventually came around about an hour ago, just as her friends returned to see how she was. They all left together despite my advice that the patient should stay a while longer.'

'How can I find her?'

'Her name is Maisy. That's all we have. We are so used to May being here and taking down all the details for our records that we simply forgot.'

'How is Miss Roper?' enquired Chard.

'I've visited her at home and discussed how we should proceed with her treatment. She will be returning to work on Monday so that I'll be able to keep an eye on her. I will administer prescribed doses of laudanum, reducing the amounts gradually over time. Eventually

she will be weaned off it and hopefully return to normal, though it won't be easy for her. I have explained my intention to her parents and told them that she will have to take "medication" for a while.'

'That's very commendable of you, Doctor. There are some who would just have dismissed her.'

'Commendable my foot! Have you seen all this paperwork I've been left with?' joked Henderson, pointing at the forms on his desk.

'I can see you've been busy.'

'Mostly the aged and infirm from the workhouse, but I've also treated one or two railwaymen who've had cuts and bruises. They wouldn't talk about the cause, but I assume there's been some brawling going on. I've heard rumours of trouble between the two railway companies.'

'Thanks for the warning. There's been bad blood between them for a while, so it's worth keeping an eye on it.'

Doctor Henderson smiled as he remembered the other matter that he needed to mention. 'There is some good news for you though, Inspector. Clark is showing signs of improvement.'

Chard's response was halted by the doctor holding up his hand. 'No. Before you say anything, he is not in a fit state to be questioned yet. Hopefully, soon though, and I also trust that it won't be too long before we can move him to the hospital in Porth.'

'That's excellent news, and with Doctor Matthews due back later today I should make progress on the investigation. Things are looking up.'

***

It wasn't until late in the evening that Chard received a knock on the door of his house. He opened it to find Doctor Matthews, looking extremely smug.

'I hope you don't mind me interrupting your evening, Thomas?'

'Not at all, I was only reading the newspaper. Do come in and I'll pour you a brandy.'

'No need Thomas, I won't stop long. I just wanted to give you a brief account of my trip to London and then I'll be going home. Talking of which, has there been any trouble around here recently?'

'How do you mean?'

'Well, I just bumped into one of your constables and he told me that there was some suspicious activity in my street early this morning. Apparently, there may have been an attempted illegal entry.'

Chard reddened. 'Which constable was that?'

'My namesake, Constable Matthews.'

'Ignore him Ezekiel, there have been no such reports. Now you were going to tell me about your trip to London?' prompted the inspector.

Chard led the doctor into the parlour and they sat by the crackling fire.

'You see, I had a suspicion that the poison might be aconite. Its use was favoured in ancient times because it leaves no obvious trace. However, it is one thing to suspect aconite poison and quite another to prove it in a court of law. Then I remembered an old friend, a Doctor Berry. A few years back he was an expert witness in a murder case at the Old Bailey involving poison. I wasn't sure if the poison used was aconite but as it transpired, my memory was correct.'

'I assume that your friend was able to tell you everything you needed to know?'

The doctor's nose started its customary twitch as he continued his account. 'Not quite. I did go to the Old Bailey to check the court papers and then I spoke to a Doctor Stevenson who was the other expert witness.'

'How easy is it to get hold of the poison?'

'It can be made by a chemist in a highly concentrated form, but it can also be made from a number of aconitum plants. The most common being wolfsbane, also known as monkshood.'

'Are you confident that you can determine the cause of death as aconite poisoning in respect of Davies?'

'Yes, Thomas. I know exactly what tests to perform in order to satisfy a court. Unfortunately, aconitine cannot be detected in the normal manner. I would have to copy Doctor Berry's methods exactly and then use case precedent,' he confirmed.

'You sound a little unsure,' commented Chard quizzically.

'I am. You see I am going to need Doctor Henderson's assistance. One person's evidence is not enough, but he might not agree to help.'

'Nonsense, of course he'll help. Why wouldn't he?'

'You'll find out in due course. I hope to get this sorted out on Monday, so I'll get off home now and I'll speak to Doctor Henderson over the weekend.'

'We need the answer now, Ezekiel,' objected Chard.

'I need time to set up the experiment and it can't be done any sooner. Trust me. I'll have the confirmation for you on Monday.'

Chard escorted his friend to the door but just as Doctor Matthews was leaving, he turned with an excited look in his eye.

'I nearly forgot to tell you about the most important aspect of the case at the Old Bailey.'

'Really Ezekiel? What was it?'

'The poison was in a slice of cake!'

TWENTY-ONE

The following night, a rowdy group of men left the Rose and Crown and marched down the Graig hill. Their leader, white-haired but ramrod-straight and hard as nails, clenched his fists and raised his right arm as he addressed his men.

'We'll teach them, lads. Let's kick their arses out of the town.'

A cheer went up as they proceeded towards the railway bridge that led to the town centre.

'They won't be in the Taff Vale or the Horse and Groom,' the leader announced as he pointed to two pubs on the right-hand side of the road. 'It's the Red Lion that we want.'

As the mob came close to the dimly lit railway bridge, they could just make out a similar sized group of around a dozen men emerging from the Red Lion. In front was a big man in a flat cap, who walked forward until he was standing, arms folded, in the middle of the road.

Both parties came to a halt under the bridge, blocking the roadway.

'We heard you were coming,' shouted the leader of the Taff Vale Railway men, in a strong Irish accent.

There was no immediate reply from the opposition as a train thundered over the bridge above.

The confrontation had not gone unobserved by the Saturday night patrons of the various pubs on the Tumble junction. People spilled onto the street to watch the entertainment, further blocking the progress of traffic going into and out of the town. A Salvation Army band outside the Clarence Hotel stopped playing, and the leader sent one of its younger members to alert the police.

Once the train had passed by, the leader of the Barry Railway workers stepped forward midway between both groups.

'If you knew we were coming, then you'll know why we are here,' he declared, spitting on the ground.

One of the Taff Vale men started to sidle across to the other pavement, taking out of his pocket a steam valve handle that he had improvised into a knuckle-duster. The atmosphere was tense, with just one thing necessary to ignite the conflict, and the movement of the man with the knuckle-duster was all it took. The Barry leader was distracted just for a moment as he took a sideways glance and in that split-second, O'Neill punched him full in the face. The man's head jerked back, but then he righted himself, rubbed his jaw and spoke with considerable menace.

'You'll have to do better than that *bach*,' he growled.

Annoyed by the cheap blow on their leader, one of the Barry men ran forward. He was met by a Taff Vale worker who kicked him in the shin with his heavy boot, sending him hopping back to the safety of his comrades. For a few moments there was a pause, as if no-one quite knew what to do next. Then slowly and silently, both groups started to spread across the road in a line, moving forward as they did so, until they were only an arm's length apart.

O'Neill pulled out a small wooden club from inside his jacket, but before he could use it, his white-haired opponent sent an iron-hard fist into his ribs. At the same time the Taff Vale worker with the knuckle-duster swung a punch at a Barry man and missed, receiving a cut to his cheek from a pocketknife for his pains. There was a sudden flailing of arms and feet as everyone else joined in.

***

Chard sipped his beer and grimaced. It was Saturday night in the Ivor Arms and he should be in good spirits. There had been progress on the poisoning of Davies with the promise of more to come on Monday. Constable Temple would be keeping watch in Cilfynydd, and hopefully would identify the perpetrators of Hughes's murder on the same day. Morgan might need a kick up the arse to trace the tearoom occupants, but at least he was trying his best. To cap it off there was the wonderful relationship with Alice, which should make him feel elated. The only thing nagging him was Doctor Matthews's comment the previous evening. Had there really been suspicious persons around the doctor's street on the morning that he had sneaked out of his friend's house? No. It was exactly the sort of thing

that Constable Billy Matthews would have made up as a joke. Not that he would have been deliberately malicious in doing so. He was just overly mischievous and totally unaware of the consequences of one of his stupid japes. Chard would normally be quite happy to announce Alice as his sweetheart; but to have slept with her in the home of his friend, without the doctor having an inkling of the relationship would be a scandal. Someone must have recognised him that morning. Not Billy Matthews, he hadn't been on an early shift; but maybe Sergeant Jackson, or more likely one of his new pet constables. Was he worrying unnecessarily? Perhaps there was nothing in it. The inspector sighed.

'Looking a bit thoughtful there Mr Chard,' came a familiar voice.

'Oh, *shwmae* Will, I was just thinking about things in general, nothing specific.'

'That's alright then. I thought you might be daydreaming about Alice?' replied Will, nudging him gently in the ribs.

Chard nearly dropped his drink. 'What do you mean?'

'Well, you're walking out with Alice Murray, aren't you? Or has it broken up?'

'W... w... what do you mean?' stammered the inspector.

'You and Alice, walking out, like I said.'

'How do you know?'

'I'm a cab driver remember. One of my butties was picking up a couple of customers outside the theatre the other night and saw the pair of you coming out together. Why? What's wrong?'

Chard breathed a sigh of relief that the information about their relationship hadn't come from someone seeing him leave the doctor's house early the previous morning. 'Nothing really, Will. It's just that I haven't told Doctor Matthews yet, and I've a feeling that he will be offended about me courting his housekeeper.'

'Don't worry Mr Chard, he won't hear about it from me. Good luck to the pair of you. I've always liked Alice.'

'You know her then?'

'Yes, we're about the same age and used to live in the same street. Alice Tudor she was then of course, before she was married. Always had a smile on her face. I felt so sorry for her when she had all that trouble at the railway.'

'What trouble was that?' asked Chard, raising an eyebrow.

'A load of nonsense. She worked for the Barry Railway Company and was accused of stealing. The truth, from her own lips, was that someone in authority tried interfering with her and she slapped him. Anyway, no charges were brought which proves her point, but she did lose her job.' Will hesitated and went quiet for a moment. 'Sorry, I shouldn't have mentioned it. I've had too much beer.' Will turned his head away and gave a belch. 'I wouldn't tell her that you know about it if I were you Mr Chard.'

***

Beneath the railway bridge all hell had broken loose. A Barry man aimed a sharpened screwdriver at the groin of an opponent who narrowly avoided its thrust. Two men, unarmed, took up the formal stance of bare-knuckle fighters and stood toe to toe, jabbing and weaving. Neither able to land a telling blow. O'Neill and his adversary grappled, neither man prepared to take a step backwards.

It was at that point that the first police officers arrived. Sergeant Humphreys led the way with four of his constables, all of whom had drawn their truncheons in readiness.

'Leave this to us Sergeant,' suggested Constable Scudamore, worried about the older man's safety. 'We'll make a start and the rest of the lads won't be far behind.'

'It has to be me that takes the lead. I am the only sergeant present,' answered Humphreys stoically.

Fortunately, being a Saturday night, the busiest time of the week for the station, there was a full complement of officers on duty. The sound of whistles summoning support was audible across the town and could even be heard faintly above the hubbub in the Ivor Arms.

***

'Sorry Will, I can hear whistles. There must be something going on,' said Chard, eager to suspend his conversation, lest it returned to the subject of his relationship with Alice.

'No, finish your pint Mr Chard. It can't be that important.'

'You never know, Will,' answered the inspector, picking up his hat and cane. 'They might need me.'

Without waiting for a response, the inspector waved to the landlady across the room and made for the door. Outside, he followed the direction of the whistles and ran towards the town centre.

***

The man armed with a knuckle-duster swung a kick at the Barry worker with the pocketknife, catching him in the thigh. O'Neill was struggling to contain his adversary who made a grab for his throat, narrowly missing. Overall, the Taff Vale fighters were losing ground.

Sergeant Humphreys stepped forward with Constable Jenkins, the champion boxer, close behind. He tapped one of the retreating Taff Vale men on the shoulder. Bigger than the sergeant, he carried a pickaxe handle and turned to face the policeman with defiance in his eyes.

'Put that thing down, you silly bugger,' commanded the sergeant through his missing front teeth. The man glanced at the face of Jenkins in the background and sheepishly dropped his weapon.

Then suddenly the first of the Barry men went down, having been grabbed by the neck and hurled onto the pavement, hitting his head on the flagstones. Nevertheless, it was the Taff Vale line that had broken, and it was a Barry man who came before Sergeant Humphreys asking him to keep the police back.

'It's a private matter Sergeant,' he slurred drunkenly. 'Give us a few more minutes and it'll be over.'

'I don't give a toss about you hurting each other, but the peace must be maintained,' the officer replied. 'And you are holding up the traffic,' the sergeant added as an afterthought.

Having seen the police, the Taff Vale men started to battle more ferociously. They wanted to finish having the upper hand. Indeed, moments later the fighter with the sharpened screwdriver was felled. Meanwhile, the man stood before Sergeant Humphreys continued to argue.

'Look. If you are going to break up the fight then stop them first,' he shouted, pointing at the Taff Vale fighters. The man was wild-eyed, devoid of reason and from the smell of alcohol on his breath, clearly drunk.

'We are,' answered the sergeant, as Constable Davies strode forward and hit the embattled O'Neill in the kidneys with his truncheon.

'Fuck you,' came the response, as without warning the drunk swung a punch that broke the sergeant's nose. Jenkins and Scudamore jumped on the sergeant's assailant, struggling despite their combined strength to keep the man under control. Then there was a scream which echoed off the tiled walls of the underpass, as the man with the screwdriver regained his feet and thrust it into the stomach of his opponent. By now more policemen were arriving, applying themselves to the fight with vigour. Seeing the inevitable, both groups of fighters started to drift away, fleeing up the Graig hill in an effort to evade arrest.

Chard arrived just as the last man disappeared into the night.

'What the hell is going on?' he demanded of Constable Davies.

'A big scrap between the railway workers sir. Apparently, the Barry men came to start trouble, but word had got out and the Taff Vale boys were ready for them.'

Chard gave a grunt. 'Trouble has been brewing for a while now. I've heard that there have been a few unreported incidents. Anyone for the cells?'

'Five arrests sir. One of them had a minor stab wound to the stomach and another a bad cut to the head. It could have been worse.'

'Very well, have the two injured taken under guard to the infirmary for patching up, then bring them to the cells. The other three can go straight to the station. I'll go ahead and speak to Sergeant Humphreys.'

'He's over by there sir, standing by the wall with Constable Scudamore.'

'What on earth is he doing here? He shouldn't be in a fight,' exclaimed Chard, with concern.

The inspector walked across to where Scudamore was assisting Sergeant Humphreys by holding a bloodied handkerchief to his nose.

'Good grief! What happened?' asked Chard.

'One of the brawlers threw a cheap punch at the sergeant sir.

I'm trying to straighten his nose,' explained Scudamore.

'Well don't. Get him up to the infirmary. They'll do a better job.'

'I'm alright sir,' argued Humphreys, speaking with some difficulty. 'I'll get back to the station and book the prisoners in.'

'No, you won't and that's an order,' replied Chard firmly.

Nodding his reluctant acceptance, Sergeant Humphreys allowed himself to be escorted away.

Interviewing the prisoners could wait until the morning, which would mean that Chard would have an excuse for not going to the St David's Day service at St Catherine's. The superintendent wanted all available men to parade outside the church, his inspector included. He would have to placate him by attending the afternoon service of hymns in Penuel Square.

'At least Doctor Matthews and Alice will be there,' he told himself, smiling at the thought of seeing his lover once more.

TWENTY-TWO

Pleased as he was to have missed the parade, Chard was in a foul mood. The two prisoners sent up to the infirmary had not returned. The nurse on duty had insisted that they be kept in overnight in order to be seen by Doctor Henderson in the morning. That meant yet another visit to the infirmary. In the meantime, he had spent over an hour interviewing the other three prisoners. Two of them, including an obstreperous Irishman, had been released on the basis that there was no witness to them having caused injury. The other prisoner would appear before the magistrates for assaulting Sergeant Humphreys. None of them had been prepared to admit the cause of the affray, and they had an arrogance that left the inspector in a considerable temper.

'I suppose we had better talk to the two prisoners at the infirmary,' he snapped at Constable Morgan, who had been taking notes during the interviews. 'I might as well move my bloody office there!'

When they arrived at the infirmary, they found Doctor Henderson in an equally bad mood.

'Please make more effort to keep this town law-abiding Inspector,' he immediately complained, without even a polite good morning. 'It comes to something when a man cannot enjoy a little bit of rest on his day off, and on our patron saint's day as well.'

'I didn't start the breach of the peace, Doctor,' retorted Chard defensively.

'I didn't say you did, but you should be ensuring that nobody wants to start an affray in the first place.'

'Tell me how to do that and you wouldn't need a police force in the first place,' argued Chard, sticking his thumbs in his belt and leaning forward aggressively.

'I am sure that the Doctor didn't really mean anything by it sir. None of us are happy at having to be working this morning,' interjected Constable Morgan, in an attempt to placate them both.

Chard and Henderson were silent, embarrassed at having to be calmed by the young constable. The inspector cleared his throat.

'Yes, of course. Sorry for my outburst Doctor.'

'No need. I hardly greeted you in an appropriate manner. I had an unexpected visit from Doctor Matthews yesterday which annoyed me, and then to be called in this morning...' he shrugged.

'I am surprised that Doctor Matthews would annoy you. May I ask what he did?'

The portly doctor absent-mindedly pulled on the end of his moustache as he decided whether to discuss the matter. 'It was most curious. He said that he wanted to make a wager. As you are aware, we often play chess together and I have to admit that he usually gets the upper hand.'

Chard nodded. 'I have occasionally seen the chessboard out in your office.'

'He said that he wanted to play a game there and then. If I was to win, he would treat me to dinner at the New Inn. On the other hand, if I were to lose, I would have to agree to help him with a medical experiment under his instruction, without complaint.'

'Did you play?'

'I did and I lost, but that is not what annoyed me. I was mortally offended that he felt he needed to go to the lengths of a wager to make me help him. Why wouldn't I help him?'

'What is the medical experiment?' asked Chard.

'He hasn't told me yet. I will find out tomorrow. Whatever he wants I will do, but I found his method of getting my agreement most unsatisfactory.'

The doctor shook his head in disappointment, then changed the subject.

'I suppose that you want to ask about the prisoners that I've just treated?'

Chard nodded.

'They did need my attention. I was a bit worried about the stomach wound on the one, but the gut wasn't pierced, and he'll be alright. The head wound on the other needed to be stitched, but it looked worse than it was. Your constables handcuffed them to their beds, so they are quite secure. May I suggest that you send a van and

a couple of officers up to take them away as soon as possible? You can interview them at your station which I would find preferable to their remaining here.'

'Certainly Doctor,' sighed Chard. 'I suppose that I've wasted my time walking up here. I only came in case they couldn't be moved.'

Henderson smiled benignly. 'Not entirely wasted, Inspector. I have looked in on our most important patient, Mr Clark. He is well enough to be transferred and I have sent a message to his wife. I am even happy for you to talk to the patient.'

'Excellent Doctor, then lead me to him.'

Henderson took the two policemen through to the small side room where Clark lay in his bed, slightly propped up by pillows. Although pale, he looked remarkably improved since Chard saw him last.

'Mr Clark, do you feel well enough to talk?'

'I do,' he answered, no louder than a whisper.

'Very well. I have a few questions. I will try and make them as clear as possible so that you can just nod or shake your head if necessary. Is that acceptable?'

Clark nodded.

'We understand that you met Mr Davies at the Butcher's Arms, then went to the Silver Teapot before going to Ynysangharad fields. Did you go anywhere else?'

Clark shook his head.

'Do you know of anyone who would wish you ill?'

Clark did not respond for a while, but then shook his head once more.

'Did anyone wish Mr Davies any harm?'

'The... railway....' came the whispered response. Clark's eyelids began to flutter.

'That's enough Inspector,' interjected Doctor Henderson.

'I must ask him one more thing!'

Chard turned his attention back to the patient. 'Did anything you ate or drank taste odd?'

Clark nodded and struggled to speak as he pointed to his mouth. '...bitter...' he gasped before passing out.

***

Penuel Square was a riot of colour as people came out in their Sunday best to sing hymns in celebration of St David's Day. As if blessed by the Almighty, the weather was almost warm and the sun shone out of a clear blue sky. Being a Sunday there was none of the riotous behaviour that might have been fuelled by alcohol, but there was plenty of jollity and merriment nonetheless.

Taking a sly swig from a silver hip flask, Hector Bowen was surprised to be tapped on the shoulder by the handle of a walking cane.

'Oh. It's you Ernest. What are you doing here?'

'I thought that you might need a hand from an ally to help ferment discord between ourselves and the BRC,' answered Wilkinson. He removed his monocle and started to polish it as he spoke. 'However, from what I have heard, you seem to have been managing quite well on your own. I understand there was a bit of a fracas last night.'

Bowen laughed. 'Yes, I believe that a stranger in town stirred up trouble in the Rose and Crown by firing up the Barry workers. Then that person left and tipped off the Taff Vale lads so that they were ready for them.'

'I wonder who that was?' queried Wilkinson, raising an eyebrow.

'Yes, I wonder,' laughed Bowen. 'It'll just take another incident or two, then we can have another go at removing Armstrong as chairman. At the next board meeting I'll point out that the BRC poisoned one of our own, then indulged in a full-scale attack on our men; and that the attack wouldn't have happened if Armstrong had been forceful in response to the death of Davies. He'll look weak and I will depose him. What do you think, eh?'

'I think that is a most agreeable plan, Hector. I can see that you have things all in hand, so I will leave you to it.'

Bowen took another swig from his flask as Wilkinson tipped his top hat and disappeared into the crowds.

***

Despite the disappointment of getting little information out of Clark earlier in the day, Chard was smiling happily. He had changed into

his best suit before going to Penuel Square. After a quick look around, he had spotted Alice standing near to Doctor Matthews. She wore a pale blue skirt with matching jacket and a striped blouse. Her hat was also a pale blue, contrasting with her dark hair.

'Thomas, over here!' waved Doctor Matthews on seeing his friend.

'Hello Ezekiel,' greeted Chard who then turned to Alice, 'and Mrs Murray of course.'

Alice almost giggled at the false formality, and feigned a little cough to hide her amusement.

'I've been up the infirmary this morning. Clark has improved and is going to be moved to the hospital. I did manage to get a few words with him, but nothing of consequence. Oh, except that when I asked him if there was something unusual about anything he ate or drank, he indicated that something tasted bitter.'

The doctor slapped his thigh in excitement. 'Yes, oh yes! I knew I was right and tomorrow I'll prove it.'

'With Doctor Henderson's help?'

'Yes, that will be necessary. He has agreed to help me.'

'So, I've heard. He was rather offended by the way you went about it. It was as if you thought that an ordinary request would be refused.'

'I am afraid that it might have been. What we need to do is quite unpleasant. Let the matter lie until tomorrow Thomas, and then you'll understand.'

The doctor glanced around, hoping to find an excuse to break away from the conversation.

'You must excuse me Thomas, but I see one of my private patients over there and I would like a word with him. I'll leave you in the company of Mrs Murray if I may?'

Chard nodded, and happily watched the doctor make his way through the crowd and out of sight.

'Well Mrs Murray, I hope you do not mind being in my company,' teased Chard.

'As long as you are not too forward Inspector Chard,' laughed Alice.

The couple stepped further into the crowd so that their bodies

were forced close together, allowing them to hold hands unobserved.

'How long are we going to keep up this pretence?' whispered Alice.

'Not for much longer. I will tell Doctor Matthews soon, because we've been seen out together by some of my acquaintances. Although the doctor doesn't mix in the same social circle, he is bound to find out. I just need to find the right time to mention it.'

'Do you think he'll be angry with you?'

'I think that is a possibility.'

'Perhaps he will dismiss me,' responded Alice, sounding worried.

'I am sure he won't. He will only blame me,' replied Chard, the words lacking conviction.

'Who told you that we had been seen?'

'Just someone I know. Will Owens, a hansom cab driver. He mentioned that you used to work for the railway before you were married.'

Alice's face reddened and she looked away. 'Never mention that again, Thomas.'

'I am sorry Alice. I didn't mean to upset you.'

'I am feeling a little unwell. You must excuse me. I'll send you a message when I am feeling more myself.' Alice gave Chard's hand a gentle squeeze before turning and pushing her way through the singing crowd.

Chard was bewildered by Alice's reaction, and was about to go after her, when he felt a tap on the shoulder. He turned and stepped back in alarm at the unedifying sight of Dic Jenkins, wearing his Sunday best. Instead of the usual long shabby coat and flat cap, he sported an ill-fitting black suit, a shirt that had once been white and a red bow tie. His bowler hat somehow made his drooping black moustache, bulbous nose and shifty eyes even more disconcerting than usual.

'Come on Mr Chard, join in,' insisted Dic, holding the inspector by the elbow. Chard looked back around for Alice but she had disappeared, so with a shrug he joined in the hymn. Once the singing had finished, Chard complimented Dic on the effort that he had put into his appearance.

'You are looking quite dapper today Dic.'

'Oh yes, mun. I know how to dress when I 'as to. Always got my best suit on for our patron saint's day. Pity it's on a Sunday this year though. Proper parched I am.'

'I admit I could do with a drink myself,' confided the inspector.

'Well, you are looking a bit out of sorts, if you don't mind me saying so Mr Chard. I suppose you've had a lot on your mind, with your investigations.'

Chard had actually been worrying about Alice's reaction, but felt happy to confirm Dic's assumption.

'Yes, Dic. Still working on a couple of cases.'

'The man Clark. Has he died yet?'

'No. In fact he seems to be getting better. They're sending him to the hospital to complete his recovery.'

'Pity,' grumbled Dic.

Chard looked at his acquaintance quizzically.

'Pity? Why do you say that?'

'Because he's an arsehole.'

'Dic, I'm surprised at you. The poor man has been poisoned. He is lucky to be alive.'

'And he's still an arsehole.'

'Then you're the only person to have that opinion of him.'

Dic looked sternly at the inspector. 'Really? Who have you asked?'

'His wife and everyone in his social circle.'

'Exactly. He is rich and his friends are all businessmen, mine owners and the like. They are bound to like him. You won't have asked any "normal" people.'

'If you are getting at the fact that he is a magistrate then I can assure you that it didn't escape our attention. We looked at anyone who might have a grudge about having been given a harsh sentence. Nothing came up. If anything, he was very lenient.'

'Exactly!'

'What do you mean? You aren't making sense Dic.'

'You know about the Albion Colliery disaster?'

'Yes, the year before I arrived.'

'Did you know about the inquiry?'

'I was told about it recently. Any charges against the Albion were minimal.'

'There you are then! The chairman of the inquiry who let them off virtually scot free was Clark. It was all over the papers. The government man sent to prosecute them was nearly tearing his hair out!'

'Are you sure?'

'Of course I'm sure. He is hated by everyone who lost someone in the disaster. All poor people of course. Clark hasn't dared go to Cilfynydd in person ever since. They'd lynch him.'

The implications hit the inspector straight away. Had the target of the poisoning been Clark, or Davies, or was he looking for someone who hated them both?

TWENTY-THREE

It was mid-morning and a steady drizzle fell on the village of Cilfynydd. Cursing the damp, Constable Temple waited patiently on a street corner. He had been there since arriving on the eight o'clock omnibus from Pontypridd. Despite his civilian clothes the constable felt conspicuous. It wasn't particularly the burn scars on his right cheek. It was more that in mining villages like this, everyone knew everyone. Nevertheless, if the man he was waiting for was an outsider also, he might be able to observe him without being detected.

Every now and then, a villager would pass on the street and give an odd glance in Temple's direction, but none actually approached him. It was with relief however, that the constable eventually noticed a likely suspect come into view and head for Mr Phillip's shop. The man wore a long shabby coat, riding boots and a wide-brimmed hat, his face obscured from view. Over his shoulder he carried a leather bag that appeared to be empty, its fastening strap flapping loose as he walked.

At the shop, the suspect waited for a short while until a customer exited, then went inside. Temple moved forward unobtrusively and took up position next to the shop door. Angry words could be heard inside and, guessing that the dispute would be keeping Phillips and his visitor fully occupied, Temple peered through the window.

There was no doubt as to the scene taking place. The suspected extortionist had Phillips by the throat with one hand, whilst snatching a handful of money off the counter with the other.

The constable ducked back. All he needed to do was to follow him to whichever part of Cilfynydd he was staying, then report back to the station. It couldn't be easier.

Only moments later the man came out, but he had further calls to make. Three more businesses received his unwelcome attention, and by now the leather bag that he carried over his shoulder was

full. Only then did he make his way to the main road and take a right turn. Temple kept the man in sight but stayed a good fifty yards behind, taking cover whenever he felt his quarry might turn around. Just as Temple watched the man reach the northern edge of the village, the constable gave a groan.

'Damn and blast! I thought he would be holed up in Cilfynydd itself.'

There, waiting with two saddled mountain ponies was an accomplice. The leather bag was tied to one of the saddles and both men mounted up, leaving Temple to throw his cap on the ground in sheer frustration.

***

Chard rubbed the side of his face as he entered the mortuary. He missed having his full sideburns, which he used to unconsciously scratch when deep in thought. The information from Dic Jenkins was causing him concern. Until now Davies had seemed to be the obvious target of the poisoning. Yet had things really changed? Both men had been poisoned after all. So, unless the killer was particularly callous, it was reasonable to assume that there was a link between the men that provided a motive.

'Out of my way Inspector,' barked a red-faced Doctor Henderson as he barged past Chard on his way out of the building.

The inspector was taken aback by Henderson's rudeness and turning on his heel, he pursued the portly doctor into the yard.

'Doctor Henderson wait a moment! What is the matter?'

'Don't ask me, ask that madman in there! He is an animal!'

'Who are you talking about? Not Doctor Matthews surely?'

'The man is despicable. No wonder he got my agreement through a wager. I would never have consented otherwise.'

'What are you talking about?'

'I do not wish to discuss it. Speak to him yourself. I certainly will not be conversing with the man for some time to come,' stated Henderson emphatically, before turning away to the infirmary.

Chard shrugged and returned to the mortuary. He pushed open the inner door and found Doctor Matthews standing over a table on which stood several glass vials. To the side was a metal tray on which

lay a number of dead white mice and a rack of glass test tubes.

'Hello, Thomas. Did you see Doctor Henderson on your way in?'

'I did indeed. What on earth did you do to upset him?'

Matthews waved his arm dismissively. 'It had to be done and he'll get over it. Never mind that, I can at last reveal my findings.'

'I take it that the mice had something to do with it.'

'Necessary casualties in the field of science, Thomas,' answered the doctor, his nose and thin waxed moustache twitching excitedly. Going to one of the vials he poured a very small amount of powder onto a spoon. 'This Thomas is our poison. I had it made up by a pharmacist in London. It is not as concentrated as it might be, but there is a reason for that.'

'What is it?' asked Chard, intrigued.

'Aconitine, as I suspected. When used as a poison it is generally undetectable in a corpse.'

'Then how do you know that is what killed Davies?'

'You will remember me telling you that the reason I went to London was because an old colleague had been an expert witness in a similar case?'

'Yes, I do,'.

'The case was successful and so I have followed the same procedures to the letter. If it convinced a jury at the Old Bailey, then that should be good enough for anyone.'

'What did it involve?'

Matthews raised a finger in the manner of a teacher addressing a pupil. 'First, I took six mice and split them into two groups. I then injected a tiny sample of the aconitine into the first three mice. Then I took a sample of the vomit I kept from the deceased Mr. Davies and injected it into the second group. The effect on each group was observed and found to be similar. Doctor Henderson and I dissected the poor creatures and examined their internal organs. Again, there were distinct similarities.'

'I see. Though why Doctor Henderson was so upset still escapes me. Is he inordinately fond of mice?'

'I haven't finished yet,' snapped Matthews impatiently. 'I said I had to follow the correct procedures exactly. That meant that both of us had to confirm that the taste was the same.'

'Sorry, I don't get you,' answered Chard, somewhat perplexed.

'I mean that as medical men, we had to confirm that the sample aconitine and the substance in the vomit had the same bitter taste.'

'Good Lord! You can't be serious!'

'It was essential to the case at the Old Bailey. There was no option. I took the tiniest possible sample of each.'

'But surely, apart from it being revolting, it must be incredibly dangerous.'

'As I said, only a very tiny amount was used. We had the taste on our tongues and then rinsed our mouths with water and spat it out. We might possibly vomit a bit in the next few hours, but that hopefully will be it. I shall join Doctor Henderson in the infirmary for the rest of the day to be on the safe side. He is currently briefing the nurses on what to do if we take a turn for the worse.'

Chard shook his head in disbelief. 'I think that was rather foolhardy, Ezekiel.'

'Those were the words used by Doctor Henderson, but in all fairness, he kept to the terms of the wager and went through with it.'

The inspector paused thoughtfully. 'You said that the taste was bitter. That was what Clark told me when I spoke to him.'

'Which is why, in the Old Bailey case, the poison had been put in a piece of sweet cake. It hid the bitterness.'

'You mentioned the last time we spoke that it can be made from plants. So the source may not be a chemist.'

Matthews nodded. 'It is found in nature, so anyone skilled with plants and herbs could produce it, but something produced by a chemist would be more reliable. Anyway, I think I had better get over to the infirmary now. Just in case,' he added with a wink.

Still shaking his head, Chard bade farewell to his friend and returned to the police station.

***

It was later in the afternoon that Chard was interrupted in his office by a disappointed looking Constable Temple.

The inspector glanced up from his paperwork. 'How did you get on Constable? I assume you didn't go to Cilfynydd in your uniform.'

'No sir. I only changed into uniform when I got back to the station,' confirmed Temple. 'As to my task, I had mixed fortunes.'

'In what way?'

'There is no doubt that extortion is taking place and I saw the culprit. Unfortunately, I couldn't see his face clearly.'

'I assume you followed him.'

'To the northern end of the village, sir. He had an accomplice waiting with a pair of ponies.'

'Damn! I should have thought of that. So, they got away?'

'I followed on foot for a while but then I lost them. However, I waited on the road to speak to passing travellers, to ask if anyone had seen the suspects. After not too long a wait, I spoke to a couple of gentlemen travelling in a shooting-brake that had come from Mountain Ash. Then just a few minutes later along came a wagon from Quakers Yard. Neither vehicle had passed the two men on ponies. That means they must have turned off the road and taken a track off to the east before Quakers Yard.'

Chard stroked his chin. 'Very well, in that case you can take some transport and spend the next few days trying to track the men down. Do not confront them, just locate them. Take someone with you....'

A knock on the door interrupted the conversation and Constable Morgan stood, waiting to be acknowledged.

'Ah, the very person,' said Chard. 'Temple, brief Constable Morgan and the two of you can work together.'

The constables gave each other an uneasy stare as Chard addressed Morgan. 'Well Constable Morgan, don't just stand there. What is it?'

Morgan averted his gaze from Temple and started to explain. 'You wanted to be told straight away if I managed to locate the men in the tearoom.'

'Yes, the priests or vicars.'

'I've had some success,' said Morgan with a triumphant smile. 'I had already tried our churches in the area, including the Catholic one, without success. Then I wondered if it would be worth asking at the chapels, because the ministers and vicars do tend to know each other. When I spoke to the minister from Sardis Chapel, I discovered that he had been in town on the day in question. He remembered

seeing, from a distance, someone he recognised. It was a vicar he had been introduced to at a religious seminar.'

'How do you know he is one of the men that we are trying to find?' asked Chard.

'The minister saw him in Market Street and then watched him go into the Silver Teapot in the company of another clergyman. The minister thought it was odd seeing him in Pontypridd. It was a Reverend James, the vicar of St. John's in Cardiff.'

'Excellent work. I will speak to the Superintendent to get clearance to go and interview him. Thank you both. That will be all.'

Chard missed the glare that passed between the constables and concentrated on ensuring that his uniform was immaculate before seeing his superior.

He had only just finished when Superintendent Jones burst into the room.

'Inspector Chard, we will be going to Cardiff first thing in the morning,' he bellowed.

Chard was flummoxed at his superior's apparent gift of premonition, but before he could make any comment the superintendent continued.

'I have had some impudent fellow come into my office and accuse us of interfering with justice.'

'Who might that be sir?'

'Name of Bowen. A director of the Taff Vale Railway. He has accused us of failing to prosecute the Barry Railway for poisoning their man Davies.'

'That is ridiculous sir.'

'Of course it is,' snapped Jones who was red-faced and extremely agitated.

'What is more, he heard that the other man, Clark, was moved out of the infirmary this morning and accused us of kidnapping him so that he doesn't reveal the truth.'

'That's preposterous!'

'I told him that Clark was probably being sent to the hospital and he said that he would be instructing some of his men to stand outside it.'

'Why?'

'To ensure that no-one from the rival company breaks in and silences Clark. He is insulting our integrity as a police force.'

'It seems to me that he is trying to defame the other company, and create as much publicity around it as possible,' suggested Chard.

'Well, I am not standing for it. I will not be insulted in my own office by such a blaggard. I am going to see the chairmen of both companies tomorrow and I want my senior deputy with me. Which means you. Out of courtesy I will clear the matter with the Cardiff Borough police force first.'

'Actually, the timing is convenient sir. As part of my enquiries I need to speak to a clergyman in Cardiff, so perhaps I can call at St John's church afterwards?'

'Certainly,' agreed the superintendent. 'The sooner this case is solved the better. It looks like tomorrow will be a busy day.'

***

May Roper was fighting her inner demons. She realised how lucky she was to have kept her position in the infirmary. Doctor Henderson had been so kind, and she would be forever grateful. Yet, now back in the doctor's office and having been allowed a small dose of her tonic, she felt tempted to break into the locked desk and take just a little more. The doctor had left early, having suffered a violent bout of sickness. Doctor Matthews had suffered the same symptoms, but after an hour they declared each other fit and well, before leaving the building.

The young clerk was trying the desk drawer, only to be thrown into a sudden fright by a knock on the office door.

'Good afternoon.'

May's heart started to pound as she turned to see a tall, well-dressed young man with an arrogant expression.

'Who are you?' she demanded.

'My name is Jennings. I assume you are Miss Roper. The nurse said that you would be here.'

'What do you want?' asked May, rather abruptly, for her heart was still beating rapidly.

'I am an employee of the Taff Vale Railway and a former colleague of Mr Davies who passed away.'

May started to regain her composure and she responded in a more measured manner. 'I am afraid that Mr Davies's body is in our mortuary and cannot be viewed. Arrangements have been made for the funeral director to take him tomorrow. I can pass on your name so that funeral arrangements can be communicated to you, if you wish.'

Jennings gave an insincere smile. 'No, that will not be necessary. You see, I have come about an associated matter and it is rather delicate.'

'Perhaps you had better discuss it with Doctor Henderson. I am afraid that he is not here right now.'

'I am aware of that. I watched him leave.'

'Then what is it that you want?'

Jennings repeated the insincere smile. 'Mr Davies was believed to have a piece of correspondence that did not belong to him. I just wondered if you might have seen it.'

Reaching into his pocket, Jennings fetched out a gold sovereign and placed it deliberately on the desk.

May glanced at the coin and then back at the visitor. 'I don't know anything about it.'

'Come now, you must have gone through his possessions when he came in here. A sovereign can buy you a lot of what you need.'

May looked bewildered.

'Miss Roper, I know the look. The redness around the eyes and the slightly nervous muscle spasms. Was that why you were trying to break into that drawer?'

'There were no items of correspondence in his possessions,' answered May, unable to deny the accusation.

'Are you sure?' snarled Jennings, curling his lip in anger.

'Yes, I'm sure. Of course I'm sure,' retorted May, regaining some courage. 'Now get out before I call the porters to throw you out.'

Jennings reddened, then turned and left without a word.

May was instantly aware that it would not be safe to mention what had just happened, in case her attempt to unlock the drawer came to light. Hugging herself tightly, she started to tremble and fell to her knees in tears.

TWENTY-FOUR

Chard was pleased when, on the following morning, he arrived with Superintendent Jones at the offices of the Barry Railway Company. There had been no hold ups on the journey, but conversation had been difficult. It wasn't that the superintendent was unpleasant, in fact he could be quite affable. It was more a lack of common interests, made worse by their differences in rank.

Chard had been well educated and although not rich, had sufficient wealth and status to feel comfortable in the higher levels of society. However, he had not lost 'the common touch', feeling equally at home with ordinary working people. Superintendent Jones though, felt that status was essential to maintaining the authority of the constabulary. Aware of the small number of officers under his command and the potential for civil unrest, topics such as the meeting of the International Socialists and Trade Unions Congress in London, were clearly not for discussion. The progress of the ongoing Mahdist war did keep conversation going for a little while, but the two men had lapsed into an awkward silence.

'Well, here we are, Inspector. I wonder what Mr Cornwall has got to say for himself,' commented Superintendent Jones, equally pleased to have reached their destination.

Arrangements for their visit had been made by telephone and the two officers were expected. They were greeted by a clerk and taken straight upstairs to the chairman's office, where Thaddeus Cornwall stood at his desk, ready to meet them.

'Good morning gentlemen. Please take a seat.' The chairman glanced at the clerk, 'Perkins! Fetch the brandy and three glasses.'

'Not for us, Mr Cornwall,' interrupted the Superintendent. 'We are on duty and I make no exceptions.'

Perkins hesitated in the doorway, unsure what to do.

'Don't just stand there Perkins. We don't want the brandy. Just get on with your work and stop dawdling.'

Cornwall turned his attention back to his visitors.

'Now how can I help you gentlemen?'

'You used to have an employee by the name of Jeremiah Davies,' stated the superintendent.

'That is correct.'

'Inspector Chard here is investigating the gentleman's recent death, and I would be obliged if you could assist him by answering some questions.'

'Of course,' agreed the chairman, not looking in any way perturbed.

'I believe he left the company unexpectedly,' stated Chard.

'Yes. He left us to join the Taff Vale Railway.'

'That must have made you rather angry.'

'People come and go all the time. It isn't unusual and no-one is irreplaceable.'

'Do you know if he had any enemies?'

'None whatsoever as far as I am aware. He didn't make friends easily, but then again he was not one to get into arguments.'

'You didn't seem surprised when the Superintendent mentioned that I was investigating his death.'

'The railways are a close community, Inspector. News travels fast. They say he was poisoned.'

'Indeed they do, and they are correct. Are you aware that accusations have been made claiming that your company is responsible?'

'I am aware of it,' admitted Cornwall, 'and it is complete nonsense.'

'You must understand our concerns, Mr Cornwall. A man has been poisoned who has no known enemies. The only thing that may have caused animosity is his sudden desertion from your company to that of your closest rival. Furthermore, despite your assertion that there was no animosity, other parties are openly accusing your company of involvement in the crime.'

'What about the other man that was with him? Why hasn't he told you what happened? I have a good mind to go to your infirmary and speak to him myself,' retorted Cornwall angrily.

'Mr Clark has been too ill to talk until very recently and he has not been able to help us He has been moved to the hospital in Porth.

I suggest that you leave Mr Clark alone, which is exactly what we will be telling the chairman of the Taff Vale Railway. Particularly as they are sending men to stand outside the hospital.'

Cornwall looked surprised. 'I wasn't aware of that. Where did you get that information?'

'From a man called Bowen,' interrupted the Superintendent.

Cornwall went silent and absent-mindedly drummed his fingers on the desk.

'Very well. I am sure you will get to the bottom of things and find that we had nothing to do with the death of Davies. Now if that is all?'

'Not quite,' replied the superintendent firmly. 'If there are two things about which I am most deeply concerned, they are mainte-nance of the peace and the care of my officers. On Saturday night there was a fracas caused by some of your workers attacking men from the Taff Vale Railway. I will not have such disturbances in my town. Do I make myself clear Mr Cornwall?' demanded Jones, raising his voice just a fraction.

Cornwall's cheeks reddened and he looked for a moment as if he was going to make a retort, but then thought better of it.

'Furthermore,' continued the superintendent, 'one of my sergeants was injured in the fight and I take any assaults on my officers very seriously. We have your man in custody and I can assure you that he is likely to receive a severe sentence.'

'Give the man's name to Perkins and he will be dismissed from the company this very day,' asserted Cornwall. 'Is there anything else?'

'That is all for the time being. The Inspector and I will take our leave. Good day.'

***

In a cab, on the way into the centre of Cardiff to visit the offices of the Taff Vale Railway, Chard reflected on their meeting with Cornwall.

'I am not sure that I've gained anything from it,' he confessed to the superintendent.

'Frankly Inspector, I think you should forget any involvement by

the company in the poisoning of Clark and Davies. It doesn't make sense. Murdering someone just because they have left your employment is rather extreme.'

'Yes sir, you are right, I acknowledge that point. I also realise that even if they did want to commit murder, then why not just slit his throat? Using poison is rather elaborate and can be indiscriminate.'

'As poor Mr Clark has found to his cost.'

'Unless Clark was the object of the poisoner,' added Chard. 'I have recently been informed that he was hated in some parts of the town.'

'Really? That surprises me. He is well thought of in social circles, as far as I am aware.'

'Not amongst the working classes of the town. They hold him responsible for the failure to prosecute the Albion Colliery Company after the disaster.'

'I remember that there was a little ill feeling at the time, but I assumed that was all over. He was just doing his job as he saw fit.'

'That isn't how the bereaved relatives saw it.'

'I don't know how you manage to find these things out Inspector. How am I to know what the lower social orders think?'

'I believe it is important to interact with them and understand their everyday lives. It is an invaluable aid to understanding the motives for criminal actions.'

'Part of your argument for a separate detective section I suppose,' sighed the superintendent. 'Well, perhaps you are right. The first thing though is to try and get an additional inspector, as I previously mentioned. The disappointing news, which I have been meaning to tell you, is that it will not be this year. The Chief Constable has reviewed our plans and the money for the post has been put to use elsewhere. However, it is just a postponement and things will change. I give you my word.'

Chard grimaced at the bad news, the ever-growing pile of paperwork back at the station heavy on his mind.

'Getting back to the murder, even if Clark was the target, the same question applies. Why use poison in such an indiscriminate way?' queried the superintendent.

'I agree sir. Clark could have been quietly knifed somewhere as

easily as Davies. Perhaps someone wanted both of them dead.'

Arriving at their destination, Superintendent Jones led the way into the Taff Vale Railway office building and gave their names to the clerk at the reception desk.

Instructed to proceed to the first floor up a grand oak staircase, Jones explained his intentions on the way.

'I am content that I have made my feelings clear to Cornwall, and that he will do what he can to prevent any further violence on the streets. Now I need to do the same with Mr Armstrong.'

'I felt that there was something that Cornwall wasn't telling us.'

'Don't overthink things, Inspector. This is just a matter of business rivalry, nothing more.'

At the first floor the officers were met by another clerk who took them to the chairman's office where, just like Cornwall, Mr Armstrong stood behind his desk, ready to greet them.

'Good morning,' please take a seat. 'Jennings, you may go.'

Chard assumed the chairman was speaking to the clerk that had fetched them in, but that subordinate had already left. He was speaking instead to a young man with an arrogant expression, standing quietly in a corner of the room.

Jennings gave the visitors a cursory nod of acknowledgement and left, closing the door gently behind.

'Good morning, Mr Armstrong. I am Superintendent Jones, and this is Inspector Chard.'

'How can I help you?' offered Armstrong.

Despite the similarity of the welcome, Chard was struck by the contrast in appearances between the two chairmen. Cornwall had been tall and imposing, whereas Armstrong was quite the opposite.

'We have come to discuss the recent outbreaks of violence that have taken place between your employees and those of the Barry Railway Company. However, my inspector wishes to ask you some questions regarding Mr Jeremiah Davies.'

'Yes, the poor fellow. Very dreadful.'

'I understand that he only came to work for you very recently. Is that correct?' asked Chard.

'Yes, Inspector. He was a very clever man and obtaining his services was quite a coup.'

'You must have offered him quite a good incentive I assume.'

'Yes, but that matter is confidential.'

'Is there any reason why someone from your company would want to harm him?'

Armstrong gave a nervous laugh. 'Of course not. What would be the point? We had only just hired him.'

'We understand that your company believes that he was poisoned by his former employers, the Barry Railway Company.'

'We most certainly do not! They are our rivals and my remit is to ensure that we fight them commercially but fairly; our company does not make false accusations.'

Superintendent Jones raised his eyebrows and then interjected.

'Mr Armstrong, I had a visit from a Mr Bowen who claimed to represent your company.'

The chairman rolled his eyes in exasperation. 'Ah, that explains your concerns, Superintendent. He is indeed one of our directors.'

'His manner was outrageously disrespectful, and he was insistent that we investigate your rivals.'

'I am afraid that our Mr Bowen is a loose cannon. He feels that I am not aggressive enough in my role as chairman and wants to take my place. I fear that he will seek any opportunity to stir up trouble. Unfortunately, I don't have the power to stop him from expressing his own opinion.'

'I suspect he may be the reason why there has been so much trouble in the town recently,' suggested Chard.

'I share my inspector's concerns,' added Jones. 'One of my sergeants was hurt during a disturbance on Saturday night and that is unacceptable. My men will treat any further outbreaks with the greatest severity.'

'I understand, but what can I do?' placated Armstrong. 'I cannot demand that our Mr Bowen returns to Cardiff. I can try and censure him, but many of the board of directors are on his side. By all means arrest any of our men that cause offences and lock them up. That will deter them.'

'That is all very well, but ideally we want to stop disturbances before they arise.'

Armstrong nodded. 'Yes, I can see that. Perhaps I can demon-

strate my willingness to co-operate as fully as possible. It has come to my attention this very morning that Mr Bowen has ordered some of our men to patrol the entrance to Porth Hospital. Apparently, the other gentleman that was taken ill is now a patient there. There is no practical reason for our men being outside. The only purpose is to fuel rumours against the Barry Railway Company. I am quite willing to send an official instruction to our workers advising them that unless they return to their station immediately, they will be fired. I will send Jennings to deliver the instruction in person this very hour. That will overrule anything that Bowen has told them.'

Jones and Chard glanced at each other.

'That would be most helpful,' said the superintendent.

'My pleasure,' replied a smiling Armstrong.

The meeting over, the policemen and headed back down the grand staircase.

'There's something that we're missing,' said Chard to himself as they walked into the fresh air.

TWENTY-FIVE

After a luncheon taken in one of Cardiff's many restaurants, Superintendent Jones returned to Pontypridd, leaving Chard to visit St John's Church. Situated in the heart of the town, the inspector had no difficulty in finding it. The door was open for parishioners to take silent prayer, but as he stepped inside, it appeared to Chard that the building was empty. He removed his cap and took in the carved ornamentation and stained-glass windows; the smell of polish and burnt wax heavy in the air.

The quiet was abruptly disturbed by a loud clatter, as a brass candlestick holder fell from a small table by the pulpit. As Chard glanced in the direction of the sound, he saw a head appear as a clergyman got slowly to his feet. The inspector walked forward, his footsteps echoing down the nave.

The vicar turned and looked in surprise at his uniformed visitor. 'You must excuse my clumsiness, it's a combination of old age and a gammy leg,' he explained.

Chard gave an understanding smile. 'No need to apologise vicar. Here, let me assist.'

The inspector picked up the fallen candlestick holder and replaced it on the table.

'Would I be addressing Reverend James?'

The clergyman, his hair a mass of tight grey curls framing a face that gave an impression of kindness and wisdom, gently nodded his head. 'I am indeed. I can see from your uniform that you are an inspector and not from this borough.'

'That is correct. My name is Chard and I wonder if you might be able to help me?'

'How exciting. I will certainly help you if I can. Shall we "take a pew" as they say?'

The two men sat side by side as the inspector explained the reason for his visit.

'I understand that you were in Pontypridd the Saturday before last. Is that correct?'

'Yes, I was. An old friend of mine from theological college has a Parish in the Rhondda. We decided to meet in Pontypridd for the afternoon.'

'Did you and your companion visit the Silver Teapot in Market Street?'

'Why, yes we did.'

'Did you recognise anyone you knew in the tearoom?'

The vicar stared at the inspector for a while before answering. 'No, however…' Reverend James paused before continuing. 'Am I right in thinking that you were there, Inspector, though not in uniform?'

'That is most observant of you. I recalled seeing two clergymen at a nearby table but could not for the life of me remember what either of you looked like.'

'I think I remember you because you came in whilst my friend and I were in the middle of a contentious discussion. You were looking for a seat and a lady got up to leave, but you persuaded her to stay. It just seemed a bit out of the ordinary, as if she was trying to avoid you. It distracted me from the thrust of my argument.'

'Sorry about that,' smiled Chard.

'No need. It was just a friendly debate. I soon got back on track and made my point convincingly. Now may I ask why my visit to the Silver Teapot is of interest?'

'Were you aware that two men were poisoned in Pontypridd on the same afternoon?'

'It was mentioned to me by a parishioner, just the other day. Why? Do you think I did it?'

'I doubt it very much. However, there is every likelihood that someone in the Silver Teapot was the guilty party. The two victims were present at the same time as we were. Do you recall seeing a large man sitting opposite a rather thin one?'

Reverend James looked shocked. 'You mean that was them? Yes, one of them was fat and the other skinny. They looked quite the odd pair.'

'Everybody has been traced and questioned except for the

occupants of two tables. Firstly, you and your friend. For all we knew, your attire might have been a disguise, so we needed to find you and initially just ask some basic questions.'

'Would you like my friend's details? I can write them down if you wish.'

'That would be helpful. The other thing that would be very useful depends on whether you can remember anything about the other customers that we want to trace. Do you recall two men in tweed jackets that were also sat nearby?'

The vicar gave a broad smile. 'Now there I believe I can help you.'

'You do recall them then?'

'Do you read, Inspector? Fiction, I mean.'

Chard was taken aback by the change in topic. 'Occasionally,' he responded.

'I often read. It takes me away from the difficult realities of life. It feeds my soul in some ways.'

'Yes, but if you don't mind…'

Reverend James ignored Chard's interruption and continued to speak. 'Do you like the writings of Mr Conan Doyle?'

'The chap that writes the detective stories. No, not much.'

'A pity. I rather like them. There is much to be said for exercising the powers of deduction.'

'Excuse me vicar, but what has this got to do with the tearoom?'

'Everything. The discussion that I was having with my friend, when you came in, was about the very subject. He was being very dismissive about Conan Doyle's writings and I was arguing my point. I set out to prove my case by taking the two men that you are interested in, as an example.'

'In what way?'

'By making a detailed observation of them, and using the very methods of deduction mentioned in Conan Doyle's stories.'

'I confess to being rather sceptical, but I am grateful for anything that might help my investigation,' responded Chard.

Reverend James gave a benign smile and continued his account. 'The tweed jackets that they wore were, despite one having a slight tear, of very good quality. They were of a type that cost a lot of money. Therefore, they were well paid. Yet, their hands were

calloused, a sign of working men. Their table manners were poor, and they looked as if they would have been more comfortable in a rougher establishment. They clearly did not want to be in the tearoom. So why were they there? I ascertained that they were in the employ of someone who could afford to pay them well for work that would be essentially manual. However, that employer was also telling them where they should eat. I put forward the theory that perhaps the owner of the Silver Teapot owed money. Possibly their creditor had sent the two men to spy on him or to threaten him later.'

'Would you be able to recognise them if you saw them again?'

'Both were thickset. One had a broken nose and a wart just below his right eye. The other had a wide gap between his two front teeth, a noticeable twitch under his left eye and a dimpled chin.'

Chard started to jot down the descriptions on a notepad.

'No need to make notes, Inspector. Just wait a little whilst I pop into the vestry.'

In fact, it was about fifteen minutes before the vicar returned during which time Chard was starting to feel concerned at his absence.

'Sorry for the delay, but I believe you will think it was worth the wait. The Good Lord has blessed me with one other skill.'

Chard took from the priest two perfect sketches of the men he was after, and smiled.

***

Hector Bowen cursed as he strode through Pontypridd dressed as inconspicuously as possible. It was late and there was a chill in the night air, prompting him to turn up the collar of his coat. Stopping for a moment, he glanced behind, having sensed that he was being followed. There were a few people out on the street but none nearby. He grunted in satisfaction and moved on, anger boiling from a bad day. He noticed the crumpled form of a man, down on his luck, sleeping in a doorway.

'You piece of dogshit,' Bowen snarled as he swung a boot into the prostrate form. Another kick and a stamp left the unfortunate vagrant groaning in pain. His tormentor turned and walked on; his anger not yet satiated.

'That fucking turd, Armstrong. How dare he override my orders. I'll break the bastard yet and his lapdog, Jennings,' he promised to himself. The instruction had come to the men outside Porth hospital late in the afternoon, and had been unequivocal. Despite his threats , none of the men could be coerced into maintaining their watch.

'I need that Torres slut to put me in good humour, but that will have to wait. Someone else will have to do. Something better than that last trollop though,' he thought.

Trying to avoid the brighter parts of the pavement close to the streetlamps, Bowen hurried to the Tumble junction and started down the Tram Road. There were several pubs on the road south out of town, close to the abattoir, and he was not familiar with any of them. The Boot Inn looked the most disreputable and for that reason, Bowen entered.

The smell inside was disgusting. A mixture of stale beer, cheap tobacco and body odour. Yet it was the atmosphere of filth and depravity that stirred the feeling in Bowen's loins. There were few customers, just a handful of men in soiled clothing, possibly having finished a late shift at the abattoir, and a shabbily dressed young woman who stood in a corner at the far end of the room.

Bowen pulled his cap down, hiding his face, and hid his voice by adopting a low guttural tone. 'Whisky,' he demanded, pointing at a bottle that at least bore a recognisable label. The squint-eyed little barman picked his teeth with a dirty fingernail, then poured a glass of the amber liquid for his unfamiliar customer.

Bowen paid and took his drink and moved away from the bar, back towards the door. He glanced across the room and could see that, as expected, the resident whore was staring in his direction. Removing a sovereign from his pocket he held it close to the nearest lamp, just for a moment. Then, sure that the glint of gold had been noted, Bowen downed his whisky and discreetly beckoned the girl with his finger. He turned, went into the night and waited for her to follow. She appeared shortly afterwards, having paused to cover her bare shoulders with a woollen shawl.

'Do you have a place?' Bowen asked, before she could speak. She wore no perfume and there was an earthy smell to her skin, which he inhaled as she moved closer.

'Upstairs in the pub. I have a room at the back. There is a rear entrance if you're interested.' She giggled; the stench of cheap gin heavy on her breath.

'We won't be interrupted?'

'No. Only I have a key to the back door, and I can lock the inner door so nobody from the pub can come in.'

'Then lead the way,' smiled Bowen slapping her on the buttock.

'My name is Marian by the way. What's yours?'

'Never you mind. Perhaps I'll tell you later.'

The girl led the way around the back of the pub and up a rickety external staircase. Bowen looked at her as she fumbled with the lock. Not up to the standard of Mrs Torres, but he could sense a certain vulnerability. No doubt she had experienced a hard life until now. No-one would willingly trade their body in such a low establishment without a background of abuse and neglect. Suffering would be a part of her life and no doubt she could take a lot of punishment. 'We'll see,' muttered Bowen as he felt for the two small vials in his pocket.

'Did you say something mister?'

'Nothing important.'

Marian lit a lamp and threw off the shawl. The room smelled of damp and in the flickering light Bowen could see it was sparsely furnished. There was just a small table with two chairs, a wooden chest and an unmade bed against the far wall.

'Take your coat off. Now do you want a *cwtch* first, or do you want to get down to things straight away?' asked the girl.

Bowen removed his cap and coat and stood there with two glass vials in his hand. He checked which one contained the stimulant solution, opened it and swallowed the contents.

Through a gin-addled haze Marian took her first proper look at her customer and gave an involuntary shudder. There had been worse looking customers, but this one seemed to give off a sense of raw savagery.

'Take this. You'll like it,' he demanded, offering the second vial.

'No, I don't think I want to.'

Bowen threw the sovereign on the bed. 'That's more than you'll earn in a week.'

She knew that was right and her hand grabbed greedily for the coin.

'Now you will need to show that you are worth it. So, drink!' urged Bowen. 'Then perhaps we will talk for a while. No need to be afraid.'

Marian drank from the vial and then sat on the edge of the bed. She listened as Bowen unleashed a torrent of perverted filth, describing practices that even as an experienced whore, she had never encountered. Suddenly, Marian found that her limbs would not respond. As a gag was forced into her mouth she tried to scream, but no sound came forth.

TWENTY-SIX

Getting in had been easy. Unlike the infirmary, which had a watchman on the gates of the workhouse, hospitals had no fear of intruders. Porth Hospital was well staffed inside though, even at night.

'I don't like this. There are too many people around,' complained one of the two men dressed in the long grey coats of hospital porters.

'Shut up, Cotter. There's no option. We've been ordered. The job's got to be done tonight.'

'But we can't even cover our faces.'

'Of course we can't. Porters don't wear hats, let alone masks. Quiet now while I look around the corner.'

The intruders had reached the end of a corridor with options to the left and right. It was dimly lit by the occasional wall lamp and all was quiet. One of them peered around to see if all was clear.

'Get back Cotter!' he whispered.

'What is it Sykes?'

'Nurse coming down the corridor,' he warned.

Both men stayed still and listened carefully as the sound of footsteps on the woodblock floor came nearer. They stopped, followed by the sound of a door opening and then closing.

'Quick! Follow me!' urged Sykes who, after a glance in both directions, turned right past the very door that the nurse had gone through.

'Walk softly, but don't duck down like that. Keep upright. If someone does spot us then we've got a chance of talking our way through.'

They had just walked past another door when it opened, and another nurse walked into the corridor.

'You there. Porters! Where are you going?'

Sykes turned with his head slightly bowed and spoke as humbly as he could manage.

'I am sorry Nurse. We're both new and it's our first night shift. I am afraid we have managed to get lost.'

The nurse looked curiously at the two men; one with a broken nose and the other who seemed to have a nervous twitch under his eye. 'Very well. Where are you supposed to be?'

'We were told to go to Ward Two. Apparently someone has passed away, and we've been told to take them to the mortuary.'

The nurse looked puzzled, as normally word would have been passed around by her superior, Sister Evans. 'You're headed in the right direction. Take the next left and then it's the second door on the right,'

'Thank you, Nurse,' replied Sykes, nodding deferentially as he backed away.

The nurse watched the two men go, and thought for a moment, before going down the corridor in the opposite direction until she found a young student nurse.

'Nurse White, I want you to go to the porters' room. There'll undoubtedly be two or three of them there having a smoke, waiting for work. Ask them if anyone new is on the shift tonight. If the answer is no, then tell them to go to Ward Two immediately.'

'Yes, Nurse Randall,' she replied obediently, before setting off in a quick walk; knowing that to run in the hospital corridor would earn an immediate reprimand.

Nurse Randall watched the messenger go, then turned on her heel, to follow the two suspicious porters.

Sykes and Cotter had found Ward Two easily from the directions, the only difficulty facing them being the ward nurse, at her small desk just inside the doorway. The lamp on her desk gave the only light in the ward of sleeping patients. She turned and stood on hearing the two men enter.

'Sorry to disturb you, Nurse,' whispered Sykes so as not to wake any patients. 'We've been told to move one of the beds. A Mr Clark is being moved to Ward Three. Could you point him out?'

'He's the one at the far end on the right, but why is he being moved in the middle of the night? I haven't been told about it.'

As the nurse spoke, Cotter moved silently behind her and dabbed

a handkerchief with a small bottle of chloroform. Without warning, he clasped the handkerchief over her mouth and wrapped his other arm around. Sykes then grabbed her legs and the two men carried her into a dark corner, by which time the chloroform had taken effect.

'Let's pull a curtain around Clark's bed and get to work. Hopefully we can be out of here in a few minutes,' asserted Sykes.

It was perhaps a minute later that Nurse Randall arrived. Walking confidently into the ward, but conscious of not wanting to wake the patients, she looked for the ward nurse. Surprised at seeing her absent, she frowned and peered into the darkness. At the end of the ward there seemed to be some movement. Walking hesitantly forward, she could just make out that a curtain had been pulled around one of the beds at the end of the room. As she got close, Nurse Randall could make out whispered voices. Steeling herself, the nurse pulled back the curtain, saw a flash of steel and screamed.

***

'*Iesu Mawr*! Open this door, you daft bitch!' yelled the landlord of the Boot Inn. He had helped himself to his own dubious supply of spirits after the last customer had left, and awoken sometime later. Despite the alcohol consumed he knew what he wanted, a damn good shag. 'Marian!' he yelled as he hammered on the internal door to her room. 'You owe me for your gin and I'm giving you the chance to pay it off. Let me in.'

There was no reply.

'If you don't let me in, I'll break the bloody door down and then you'll have to pay for it,' he threatened.

Still no reply.

The landlord staggered drunkenly back down the stairs and into the bar, where he picked up the heavy wooden mallet used for tapping the barrels. 'Right, you asked for it,' he proclaimed to the empty room. Barely managing to climb back up the stairs, the landlord leaned against Marian's door. Aiming at the lock he swung the mallet as hard as he could. The blow missed the lock itself, but it was good enough to shatter the rotting wood of the adjoining door frame. Losing his balance, the landlord fell against the door and it

swung open, causing him to fall on the floor. Struggling to his knees and then onto his feet, he saw Marian lying naked on the bed.

'Sleeping, are you? Well I'll wake you up,' he shouted, unbuttoning his trousers.

Losing his balance once more, the landlord's hand rested on Marian's leg to steady himself. It felt cold and something made him withdraw it quickly.

'Marian? Marian *cariad*? Are you alright love?' he asked, concerned despite his drunkenness.

He looked at her staring eyes; then the shock hit him, and he began to cry.

***

Nurse Randall's terrified scream woke the whole ward.

'Shit! Put that blade away! Let's run for it!' shouted Cotter.

The two startled intruders pushed past Nurse Randall and ran down the ward, aware that the patients were stirring; and that one or two of the more able were already getting out of bed. At that moment, three porters summoned by the student nurse rushed in. Alerted by Nurse Randall's scream, they were already on their guard as Sykes and Cotter hurtled towards them. Sykes came up short as one of the porters blocked his path. Cotter tried to run around another of the porters, but was grabbed around the waist by the third man. Sykes caught his opponent with a kick, but the porter just backed off, still barring the way to the door. Then Sykes felt a grab at his collar as a patient tried to help. The attempt was easily shrugged off, but in the moment of distraction, the porter saw his chance and threw himself head first at Sykes's face. The intruder went down in a heap. Cotter was unable to free himself from the two other porters. Securely held and seeing his partner-in-crime motionless on the ground, Cotter ceased to struggle.

***

The following morning proved to be yet another busy one for Inspector Chard. On arriving at the station, he was informed of the discovery of a body and set off immediately for the Boot Inn. Constable Billy Matthews, devoid of his usual humour, was already

at the scene, and with some sensitivity had covered the corpse's nakedness with a dirty sheet from the bed.

Chard pulled back the covering to reveal the dead woman's face. The eyes bulged and there was a sodden rag in her mouth.

'Looks like she choked on her own vomit sir, after she'd been gagged. I've interviewed the landlord, though he is barely sober. Apparently, she followed a stranger outside late last night. Nobody took much notice of him so there's no useful description. You may wish to pull the sheet back further, if you don't mind me saying so. There's a lot of bruising.'

Chard did as the constable suggested, then with a grunt of distaste he pulled the sheet back up. 'Have the poor soul sent to the mortuary and send for Dr Matthews to meet me there.'

Walking outside, Chard shivered and took a few deep breaths. Unlike some colleagues, he could never remain fully detached from a murder scene. He really wanted a stiff drink, but it would have to wait.

Back at the station, there was at least some good news as Super-intendent Jones greeted his arrival.

'I bring good tidings Inspector. G Division have two men in custody, and I think they are the suspects that you've been looking for.'

'Really sir? The men from the tearoom? How did they catch them?'

'Hospital staff apprehended them in the middle of the night. They were at Clark's bedside, holding a knife. Fortunately, G Division knew of our interest in Clark, so they sent a message this morning. The prisoners will be transferred here this afternoon.'

'Thank goodness for that sir. It's about time I had some good luck.'

The superintendent looked with some concern at his inspector. 'Where have you been? You look rather pale.'

'Another dead body I'm afraid.'

'Not another poisoning?'

'Not likely, but it appears to be a nasty case nonetheless.'

'Then you have three cases to solve. I feel guilty at not being able to bring in another inspector to support you. There is nothing for it, I will have to lend a hand myself.'

'There's no need, really sir. I can manage, and at last there's some progress now that we've got those two suspects in the poisoning case. In addition, we also have suspects for the Cilfynydd murder. I've got Morgan and Temple searching for them as we speak.'

'If you insist, Chard. Though I will intercede if I think it necessary. I was a decent inspector myself you know, before attaining my present rank.'

'I am sure you were sir,' replied Chard quickly.

Superintendent Jones nodded in a manner that suggested he was satisfied with Chard's response. 'Then I'll leave you to it. Crack on, Chard. Crack on.'

***

It was close to midday when the inspector arrived at the mortuary. He found Doctor Matthews, sleeves rolled up and wearing a stained white apron, standing over the cadaver. On noticing Chard enter, the doctor pulled a sheet over the corpse as far as the neck.

'I appreciate the thought, Ezekiel.'

'I didn't do it for your benefit, Thomas. Just a matter of dignity in death. I normally wouldn't bother but the poor woman has such bruising of an intimate nature. It just doesn't seem proper to expose her unless absolutely necessary.'

'You have a cause of death?'

'Choked on her own vomit. The gag was shoved down too far for her to get it out. Her hands weren't tied. At least there aren't any marks to suggest it. She had imbibed a considerable amount of alcohol, which may explain her inability to remove the gag and possibly the vomit. However, there are signs that indicate the use of opiates.'

Chard rubbed his chin in thought. 'Doctor Henderson had a similar case fetched in recently. A local dollymop who had been drugged and suffered bruising to her intimate parts. Fortunately, she survived the ordeal. Perhaps you can compare notes.'

'I am not sure if he is speaking to me,' replied Doctor Matthews, 'but I suppose on a matter of such importance he might come around.'

'I'll leave you to it then. I have more suspects to interview.'

***

Progress had already been made even before the two prisoners had arrived at Pontypridd police station. Before going to the mortuary Chard had given the sketch provided by Reverend James to one of the constables, who then took it around the town's hotels and inns. By the time he arrived back from the mortuary, their identities had been discovered.

'Let's make a start then Constable,' commented Chard to Constable Scudamore as he opened the door of the interview room. Inside, one of the prisoners sat next to a bare wooden table looking unconcerned.

'You seem very calm considering what's in store for you,' remarked the inspector, taking a seat opposite the felon.

'I'm not saying anything. There'll be a solicitor sent here for me as soon as word gets out.'

'Oh? So that means that you are working for someone. Who might that be?'

'I'm not saying anything.'

'I understand that you've refused to give your name…. Mr Francis Sykes.'

'How did you know?' asked the prisoner, losing some of his composure.

'Why have you been trying to kill Mr Clark?'

'I haven't. I'm saying nothing!'

'You were present when he was poisoned weren't you?'

No reply came. In fact, despite a torrent of questions, Sykes refused to say a word.

Scudamore leant across to his inspector and whispered. 'If you might want to leave the room and send in Constable Jenkins sir? Perhaps if you return in five minutes the prisoner might be more amicable.'

Chard gave the suggestion some consideration, but then shook his head.

'No. Get him out and fetch the other man in. Let us see if he's got the same bravado. Don't allow the prisoners to talk to each other. Keep them in separate cells from now on.'

Unlike Sykes, the other prisoner looked ill at ease. Chard rose

from his chair and walked slowly around the table until he was directly behind him. Cotter's eyes followed the inspector until, with head turned he was looking back up into Chard's face.

'Well then, Mr Jonathan Cotter. What have you got to tell me?'

'How did you know my name?'

'Sykes told me,' lied Chard.

'He said we shouldn't talk.'

'That's because he didn't want you to know that he was going to put the blame on you. He said that it was your plan to murder Clark. You failed in your attempt to poison him, so you went to the hospital to finish him off.'

'No! That's a lie!' shouted Cotter.

Chard ignored the denial.

'We know that you were present when Clark and Jeremiah Davies were poisoned. I suspect, when we search your accommodation, that we will find a jacket with a missing button. We can compare that with the button and threads left after a break-in at Davies's hotel room. You and Sykes were probably responsible for the break-in at the infirmary as well, though nothing was stolen. You will be charged with assault, the attempted murder of Clark and the murder of Davies.'

'Sykes didn't tell you anything after all, did he? He can't have done. Why would he say that I wanted to murder Clark when he knows damn well that neither of us meant him harm? We didn't know what would happen to him, nor Davies for that matter. You might have us down for assault but you're not pinning a murder on us.'

'One of you was clearly holding a knife over Clark. You must have been about to kill him.'

'Sykes had the knife to break into the bedside cupboard where his things were stored.'

'What were you looking for?'

'I've said enough.'

'You haven't convinced me. Who are you working for?'

'If I tell you that I'll be found dead before my trial. A solicitor will be sent to defend us, and I'll take my chances in court.'

Despite further pressure on him to talk, Cotter remained silent, and eventually Chard had him escorted back to the cells.

***

It was busy in the bar of the Ivor Arms for a weekday evening. At the far end of the room a sad looking Dai Books was being made to celebrate his good fortune by Will Horses and Dic Jenkins.

'You see, we knew you would get the job,' proclaimed Dic.

'I know I should be grateful, but if only there had been a vacancy at the Free Library instead,' responded Dai miserably.

'Never mind about that, *bach*. The new school will be a great success. Just think of all the great scholars it will produce,' said Will, full of encouragement.

'But I hate children,' moaned Dai.

'There you are, perfect qualifications for a teacher. You don't want to mollycoddle them.'

Tempted as he was to join in the good-humoured discussion, Chard sat alone at a table. He glanced once more at the note in his hand and managed a smile. It had been pushed through his front door earlier in the day. In it, Alice apologised for getting upset and vowed her undying affection. She would see him at church on the following Sunday, when they would discuss how to tell Doctor Matthews about their relationship.

The smile on Chard's face did not last long, as his thoughts returned to the prisoners he had interrogated earlier. There were things that bothered him. Firstly, there was the timing of the break-in at the hospital. Was it a coincidence that it happened the very night after the cordon of Taff Vale Railway men had been withdrawn? Secondly, who were Sykes and Cotter working for? Thirdly, what was it that they were after? Then finally, did they carry out the poisoning?

Chard mulled through the problems one by one. He didn't believe in coincidences, so someone must have told Sykes and Cotter that the hospital would be unguarded. That meant that it was likely that they were working on behalf of someone at the Taff Vale Railway. What they were after remained a mystery. However, it was the final question that was the most troubling. Did they really kill Davies? Unfortunately, he instinctively believed Cotter. If he and Sykes were desperate to find something, then it wouldn't have been in their interest to kill Davies or Clark until it was found. So, what

were the options? The only sweet thing eaten to mask the taste of the poison was the cake in the tearoom. The clergymen had been traced and now so had Sykes and Cotter. The other customers had previously been found and their backgrounds checked; none of them having any connection with the railways or the Albion disaster. That left the staff and only one had any possible motive. The following day he would have to speak once more with Mrs Evans. There was of course one more possibility that nagged at the inspector's mind, but it was too terrible to contemplate.

Gwen the landlady looked with surprise when Chard finished his first pint of the evening, got up from his table and left without having spoken to a soul.

TWENTY-SEVEN

'This is the third morning we've been tramping about this hillside,' moaned Constable Morgan.

'We spent Tuesday on the gig covering the larger tracks, this is only our second day on foot. It won't take much longer. We'll either find what we're after this morning, or we'll have to accept that they are hiding out in one of the places that we looked at yesterday,' replied Constable Temple

The hillside was sparsely populated with the occasional farm and a small number of remote cottages, some of which had long been abandoned. The farms had been easy to reach in their gig, as they were at the end of steep, but accessible, tracks. Yet, even they were time consuming, as the two policemen had needed to move carefully; remaining concealed during their observations. As for the cottages; they in the main had no paths suitable for the gig and so they had to leave the vehicle, tying the horse to the nearest tree or fencepost. Dressed in drab civilian clothes, Morgan and Temple had spent the previous day following the occasional pony track, observing possible hide-outs from behind hedges and dry-stone walls.

'If you hadn't have lost them on Monday....'

'*Caewch!*' snapped Temple angrily. 'I thought the suspect would be holed up in Cilfynydd, or at worse, going back into Ponty. If that had been the case I could have hopped on an omnibus and kept up.'

Morgan was about to continue the argument when he noticed smoke in the distance.

'Hold on, Sinner. We might be in luck. Let's head over there!'

Morgan indicated a ridge off to their right, and led the way up the steep incline, with Temple following close behind. Just over the ridge, they could see an old stone-built cottage surrounded by a dry-stone wall. It looked abandoned, except for the column of smoke rising from its chimney.

'Let's get closer, behind the wall. Follow me!' said Temple, setting off before Morgan could reply. Keeping low, they reached the cover of the stone wall. Cautiously, Morgan peered over, then ducked down as the rickety door of the cottage creaked open.

'Someone's coming out,' he whispered.

'I'll take a look,' said Temple.

Slowly, Temple raised his head until he could peek over the wall and observe the occupant of the cottage. Almost immediately, he ducked back down again.

'That's the man I followed on Monday. He's taking a piss against a bush. I got a quick look at his face. I think I know him.'

'How?'

'From when I worked in Merthyr. If it's who I think it is, he's a dangerous one. Jack Rankin is his name. He was wanted on suspicion of murdering a shopkeeper.'

'Any sign of his accomplice?'

'No. But if I'm right, the other man will be his older brother.'

'Let's get back to the station then.'

Temple shook his head. 'Can you imagine the trouble we'll be in if it turns out that I'm wrong? No, I need to be certain.'

The door of the cottage was heard to creak again. Morgan cautiously put his head above the wall. 'He's gone inside.'

'Good! Wait here!' said Temple as he set off in a crouched movement along the length of the wall, before climbing over it.

Morgan, his face a mask of annoyance at his colleague's impetuosity, could only watch as Temple crept towards the cottage and ducked below the level of the window.

The lanky, blond-haired constable turned and gave a thumbs-up sign to Morgan, before slowly peering inside the cottage.

The room was virtually bare, with an earthen floor and a couple of wooden boxes serving as benches. There was a fire in the hearth with a metal pan resting on it. The bacon within spattered fat into the grate as it sizzled, watched eagerly by the cottage's occupant.

Temple smiled. He had been right; it was the man wanted further up the valley in Merthyr. Now he could back off and return to the station with Morgan. Then the smile froze on his face, as he felt something sharp touch the nape of his neck.

'What do we have here then?' growled a voice heavy with menace.

Temple stood up very slowly, the pressure of what was undoubtedly a knife pricking his skin.

'That's it. Nice and slow and don't turn around. Walk towards the door and ease it open.'

Morgan watched from behind the wall, unable to do anything. The suspect's accomplice had come around the corner from the back of the cottage without warning. Before the constable could shout out, the villain's knife was already in his hand. He had been so close to Temple, that any alert would probably end in his colleague being killed.

As Morgan wondered what to do, Temple was led into the cottage.

'Look what I've found, Jack.'

The man by the fireplace turned. He had lank, greasy black hair and a hooked nose and he spoke, like his brother, with an accent that suggested they originally came from the north of England.

'Where did you find him?'

'Looking through the window.'

The younger Rankin left the fireplace and came across to stare Temple in the face.

'Now then lad. What would you be doing spying on us?'

'I'm just hungry mister. I saw the smoke and wondered if you had any spare food,' lied Temple.

Rankin looked him up and down. 'Bollocks! You are a lanky bastard, but you look fed enough to me.'

'No mister, honest!'

Jack Rankin ignored Temple and addressed his brother. 'Ted, are you sure he was on his own?'

'I think so Jack, why?'

'Because I recognise this lying turd. I remember the peelers from Merthyr, and this is one of them. See that burn scar on his cheek? You won't find many lanky, blond-haired lads with a mark like that. With him being out of uniform it must mean that the police are looking for us.'

Jack Rankin reached into his pocket and pulled out a pistol. It

was clearly a roughly made, single shot weapon, but deadly enough at close range.

'Now then Constable, I assume you aren't on your own.'

Temple straightened his posture and sneered at his captor. 'You're right, but he'll have gone for help by now. Knowing him, he will have run for it as soon as he saw me get into trouble. We'll have men here in the hour.'

Rankin spoke sharply to his brother. 'We'll have to cut and run. Have the gun whilst I take care of him.'

Ted took the gun but held the knife steady at Temple's neck whilst Jack Rankin came and twisted Temple's arm behind his back. Then, kicking the constable's legs from under him, he used his other arm to drag the constable towards the fire.

'Keep the gun on him Ted. He can either take a shot in the head or just lose his sight. Either way his face is going in the fire.'

Temple started to struggle and curse, terrified of the flames, but could not free himself. He was on the point of begging to be shot rather than blinded when there was an almighty crash, and the door of the cottage flew open.

In the doorway stood Constable Morgan, holding in his hand a length of metal rod he had scavenged from a rusted sheep trough.

Ted Rankin turned and pointed his gun at Morgan whilst glancing back towards his brother for instruction.

'If he takes a step closer, shoot him,' ordered Jack.

'I'm warning you. Let Constable Temple go.'

'You should have run. We can kill both of you now and take our time getting away,' snapped the elder brother.

Morgan looked into Ted's eyes. 'You haven't got the nerve for it. Put the pistol down.'

'Step back!' shouted Ted.

Ignoring the warning, Morgan walked forward, just as Ted pulled the trigger.

There was an enormous bang and a cloud of black smoke as the barrel of the crudely made weapon exploded. Ted was dazed and thrown into confusion by the unexpected mishap, but he still held the knife in his other hand.

His heart thumping loudly, Morgan fetched the metal rod down

hard and Ted howled with pain as the implement hit his hand, sending the knife to the floor.

Though not able to see what was happening, Temple could feel the heat from the fire on his cheek as his captor held him firmly. Jack Rankin was unsure what to do. He could only watch with alarm as his brother backed away from Morgan, yet he daren't release Temple in order to help.

Morgan aimed a kick at Ted's stomach forcing him to fall back further, then swung the rod into his body which stung the man with pain. Ted tried to grab Morgan and wrestle him to the ground, but the constable broke free easily. They circled each other warily. Throwing the metal rod at his opponent's face to distract him, Morgan stepped forward with a terrific punch to the stomach that floored Ted, leaving him groaning on the ground.

Jack Rankin rammed Temple's head hard against the fire grate, then leapt up at Constable Morgan. The policeman neatly dodged the grasping hands of the villain and grabbed his arm. But Rankin was an experienced brawler and not amenable to being subdued. Temple started to clear his head and slowly got to his feet. He was just about to come to his fellow officer's aid when Morgan twisted Jack's arm behind his back and then rammed him face first into the wall. The policeman watched his opponent slide unconscious to the floor before turning to Temple with a triumphant grin.

'Don't just stand there, Sinner. Find something to tie them up with before they recover.'

Soon, both felons were securely bound with a combination of leather belts and strips of material.

'You go and report to the station. I'll stay and guard them,' offered Morgan.

'Yes, will do,' agreed Temple, 'and thanks. That was very brave to take them both on.'

Morgan looked at the ground, clearly ill at ease. 'No need to say thanks. I owed it to you. It was my fault when we worked together before. I caused you to have that burn on your face. I lost my nerve. I'm sorry, I was a coward.'

'Well you aren't now. You saved my bacon today, so let's call it quits.'

***

Chard's original plans for the day were not working out. Having resolved to interview Mrs Evans about the poisoning of Clark and Davies, he had travelled to Cilfynydd to find that she was not at home. Annoyingly, she was at work in the Silver Teapot, only a short distance from the police station. Returning to Ponty, the inspector went to the tearoom and asked her to come to the station during her break. Consequently, it wasn't until after the tearoom's midday rush that Mrs Evans arrived at Chard's office.

'*Prynhawn da*, Inspector.'

'Good afternoon to you as well, Mrs Evans. As you are aware, I do not speak Welsh other than the odd word, so we will have to have this talk in English. Please take a seat. Constable Scudamore here will take notes whilst I ask you a few questions.'

'Very well. May I ask what all this is about? There appeared to be a deal of commotion going on as I came into the station.'

'That is due to another matter. The murder of Mr Hughes in fact. We've apprehended the men responsible. You can pass on the good news when you get back to Cilfynydd.'

Mrs Evans showed little emotion, much to Chard's surprise. 'Then why am I here?'

'It is with regard to the poisoning of Mr Davies and Mr Clark, the two men found in Ynysangharad Fields.'

'What of it?'

'We believe that the poisoning happened at your place of work.'

Mrs Evans was silent but gave Chard a frosty stare as he continued.

'It is a matter of procedure that when a crime is committed, we consider the factors of means, motive and opportunity. Everyone in the tearoom could have had the opportunity.'

'Why do you think the men were poisoned there?'

'A similar case occurred in London. The poison used was bitter, so it was introduced into a slice of cake. The sweetness of the cake hid the taste.'

'Go on. I will have my say later,' commented Mrs Evans with a sour expression on her face.

'Do you know what aconitine is?' continued Chard.

'I have never heard of it.'

'Come now, I understand that you have a way with herbs and remedies. Have you heard of wolfsbane?'

'Yes, of course. It is a very dangerous plant.'

'Do you have access to such a plant?'

'Yes, I do,' admitted Mrs Evans frostily. 'So do many others. It isn't that difficult to get hold of, if you know where to look.'

'Mrs Evans, you can see that you had the opportunity to poison the men and with your knowledge of plants you also had the means. I put it to you that you also had the motive. I am aware that Mr Clark was hated by the people that lost loved ones in the Albion disaster. You must have hated him also. We've checked everyone else present in the tearoom when Clark and Davies were there. None of them had any connection with the Albion disaster, or indeed with Mr Davies. Only you had a motive.'

Mrs Evans gave Chard a withering look and her eyes were ablaze as she responded to the accusation. She did not raise her voice, it wasn't necessary. The ferocity of tone was enough.

'I did hate Clark and I wanted to spit in his food, but why would I poison his companion? If there was any risk to someone else, I would not dare to do it. I would not want the death of an innocent man on my conscience. For that matter how sure are you that the poison was in the cake, or that it happened in the Silver Teapot at all? Most of the women in our village know a thing or two about plants, even some of the men come to that. I came into work on the same omnibus as Mrs Griffiths and Mr Dixon for that matter, so they were somewhere in the town. They might not have lost relatives, but you can guarantee that they lost friends.'

'I am satisfied that the poison must have been in the cake or the tea they drank.'

'Oh? So, you're not sure it was in the cake after all,' accused Mrs Evans. 'That means that you have no evidence. You can have all the means, motive and opportunity you like but it means damn all without proof. Now, unless you are going to charge me, I assume I am free to go,' she said, rising from her seat. It was clear from her tone that she considered it a statement rather than a question.

Chard grimaced; he could not object. She was right, there was no proof.

The inspector could only watch her bustle out of the room, and after dismissing Scudamore, he slumped in his chair. There was something that had to be done, but Chard had been ignoring it for some time as it had been too unpleasant to contemplate. He had to consider Alice.

Deciding that if he listed the facts it would help to clear his head and eliminate her from his enquiries, he started to write. Beneath her name he put, under a heading of 'motive', the loss of her husband and brother in the Albion disaster. Then he added the allegation, however false, that many years ago she had stolen from the railway company. Under 'opportunity' he noted her presence at the tearoom before he had arrived. After consideration, Chard wrote a final heading of 'means' with 'access to poisons?' and 'knowledge of herbs and plants?' beneath it. The inspector put his pen down and sat for half an hour just staring at the paper. He didn't believe the accusation of theft; and the 'means' comment was not convincing. Doctor Matthews was far too observant to notice any missing poisons from his supplies, and he didn't have aconitine until he conducted his recent test anyway. As for plants and herbs – she was an excellent cook, but that was the extent of it. No. She was innocent.

Chard's contemplation was interrupted by a flurry of activity outside his room and a knock on the door.

'The prisoners have arrived sir,' announced Constable Scudamore.

'Good, put them in the cells. I'll be there to interview them directly.'

Chard glanced at the bag of detritus from the fire that still littered the floor of his office and gave a grunt of satisfaction. Feeling that he could at last get one of the murders finally solved, the inspector got up and left his office, leaving his papers on the desk.

TWENTY-EIGHT

Superintendent Jones was concerned. Only recently he had admonished Inspector Chard for spending too much time actively investigating, rather than supervising his subordinates. News had just come in that those responsible for the fire in Cilfynydd had been apprehended. That had come about from Chard stepping back and letting the constables get on with it, as instructed. However, the poisoning of Clark and Davies remained unsolved and the superintendent had noticed the growing strain on his inspector. Chard was clearly struggling with his duties and needed help.

Jones stroked his bushy moustache in thought. He felt guilty. After all, he had promised an additional inspector to relieve the burden, but had failed to get approval from the Chief Constable.

'There is only one thing for it. I shall have to lend a hand,' he muttered to himself as he strode purposefully out of his office.

'Sergeant Jackson. Have you seen the inspector?'

'He's gone to the cells to interview the two prisoners caught by Temple and Morgan, sir.'

The superintendent gave a grunt of disappointment, then headed for Chard's office. Noticing some papers on the inspector's desk, he picked them up and started to browse through them.

'It seems that Chard has made some progress after all,' he thought to himself.

Taking the top paper with him the superintendent left the room and spoke to Sergeant Jackson again.

'Sergeant, do you know who Alice Murray might be? It seems that the inspector has been building a promising case.'

Jackson grinned wolfishly. 'I understand she is the housekeeper of Dr Matthews, sir. I am not one to talk, but rumour has it that the inspector has been keeping a close eye on her.'

'I couldn't see any record of an interview with her amongst the papers. Do you know if she has been interviewed?'

'I don't think so sir. Perhaps it has been awkward for the inspector. Her being the Doctor's housekeeper and all that, if you get my drift.'

'Yes, I can see that. I am aware that the inspector and Doctor Matthews are friends, so it must be rather difficult. Perhaps it would help if I were to lend a hand.'

'I am sure it would sir. If you like I could accompany you and take notes,' offered the sergeant with an eager smile.

'Yes, I think that would be helpful. I am sure that Inspector Chard would appreciate it.'

'I am sure he would sir.'

***

Chard's temper was at boiling point. Having spent half an hour with the younger Rankin brother in his cell, all he had got was dumb insolence. Not a single word had been spoken by the prisoner, not even after Constable Jenkins had hit the man for spitting on the cell floor.

'Very well, Rankin. Be assured that I will see you hang,' snapped the inspector, storming out of the cell.

Turning to Constable Jenkins who had followed close on his heels, Chard ordered that the prisoners be given minimum food and water for the night.

'I'll leave talking to the other one until the morning. I trust he'll be more co-operative than his brother after a night in the cells. The main thing is that they've been caught. No doubt their extortion victims will be only too pleased to give evidence against them.'

'I am sure that the Superintendent is delighted with the arrests, sir,' suggested Jenkins.

'Yes, no doubt. I'll update him fully in the morning after I've finished my interrogation of the other prisoner. Now, I think it's time I moved on to the murder at the Boot Inn. If the Superintendent asks where I am, tell him that I have gone out to track down a witness.'

'Which witness might that be, if you don't mind me asking, sir?'

'Apparently another prostitute was attacked recently and was treated at the infirmary. I need to find her, because she may help determine whether or not her assailant is the murderer.'

'One of us could do that, sir.'

Chard shook his head. 'No-one in the town is going to give that information to a uniformed constable. I know one or two people who might help, but I need to go home and change out of uniform first. Besides which, I need some fresh air after having to spend time with Rankin.'

***

Superintendent Jones knocked on the door of Doctor Matthews' residence, which was answered by his housekeeper.

'Good afternoon, I take it that you might be Mrs Murray. Is the doctor at home?' asked the superintendent, towering over Alice.

'No, I am afraid he is out visiting a patient.'

'Not to worry. It is yourself that I wanted to see. I am Superintendent Jones and this is Sergeant Jackson. May we come in?'

Alice frowned, but then nodded her assent and took her visitors through to the parlour.

'Please take a seat. Can I offer you some refreshment?'

'That won't be necessary, Mrs Murray. Please sit with us. I have some questions to ask you.'

Alice sat down, a worried expression on her face.

'Let me come straight to the point. I want to ask you about the poisoning of Mr Clark and Mr Davies which occurred recently,' stated the superintendent bluntly.

Initially taken aback, Alice took a moment to compose herself before replying. 'I am only too pleased to help if I can. What do you want to know?'

'You were present in the tearooms on the day they were taking ill, were you not?'

'Yes, I was,' replied the housekeeper, disconcerted by the superintendent's stern expression and the unpleasant smirk on Sergeant Jackson's face.

'Do you assist Doctor Matthews in his medical work?' continued the superintendent.

'No, of course not,' replied Alice looking puzzled.

'In particular, do you order medicines on his behalf?'

'Doctor Matthews does that himself,' said Alice. 'Why do you ask?'

Superintendent Jones ignored the question. 'I assume that you know where the doctor keeps his medical supplies?'

'Yes, of course I do. They are in a cabinet in his room.'

Superintendent Jones's eyes lit up, until Alice added, 'Which is locked. Doctor Matthews keeps the key on his person at all times.'

The superintendent paused for a moment, unsure what to ask next, before engaging eye contact with Alice once again.

'Are you familiar with the use of plants and herbs, Mrs Murray?'

'Naturally. I prepare meals for Doctor Matthews and I wouldn't be much of a cook if I wasn't.'

'I want you to tell me if you held any animosity towards Mr Clark?'

'No. Why would I?'

Superintendent Jones saw the slight glance, away from his stare, that betrayed the lie.

'Because as you very well know, he did not prosecute the Albion Steam Coal Company for the disaster that killed your husband and brother.'

Alice remained silent, biting her lower lip.

'I think your silence speaks for itself,' the superintendent accused. 'What about Mr Davies? Did you also have a particular dislike for him?'

'I never knew him. Why should I dislike him?'

'You mean you never met him at all? Not even when you worked for the railway?'

The colour drained from Alice's face. 'What do you mean?' she asked, quietly.

'I believe you were once employed by one of the railway companies before you were married.'

Alice raised her hand to her mouth, wondering what the policeman would say next.

'I also understand that you were accused of theft,' continued the Superintendent as Sergeant Jackson gave a leery grin.

'That was a lie! No action was taken,' blurted the housekeeper, a tear in her eye. 'Where is this leading? What are you accusing me of?'

'Let me ask you this, Mrs Murray. Did you poison Mr Clark and Mr Davies in the Silver Teapot tearoom?'

Alice met the superintendent's gaze. 'No. I did not. Inspector Chard was at my table. I could not have done anything of the sort without him seeing me.'

The superintendent stroked his moustache and replied confidently. 'Yet, by the time Inspector Chard entered the tearoom, you were already there. No, Mrs Murray. You most certainly had the opportunity as well as the motive. We will not take you into custody yet, but you can be assured that we have not finished with you. Unless you wish to make things easier for yourself by confessing?'

As tears started to fall from her eyes, Alice implored her accuser. 'You must believe me. I could never do such a thing. Where did you find all these things out about me? This just isn't right? Ask Thomas, I mean Inspector Chard.'

'There really is no need, Mrs Murray. It was the inspector that provided the information. He wrote it all down for us.'

***

Chard had gone straight home and changed into a plain grey suit and matching bowler hat. As he left his front door, cane in hand, Chard considered calling on Alice but dismissed the idea. Doctor Matthews was due to travel away again soon, and then they could spend plenty of time together. In the meantime, they had arranged to meet at church on Sunday, and that wasn't too long to wait. With that happy thought in mind, the inspector set off for the railway station yard to try and find his friend, Will Horses. His hansom cab often waited there for fares, and it proved to be the case on this occasion. Chard crossed the Tumble junction as a horse drawn tram rumbled past, entered the station yard and greeted Will.

'Good afternoon, Will. How's business?'

'*Shwmae* Mr Chard. Fair to middling. Nothing too strenuous for Merlin, but enough fares to keep a roof over my head,' answered the cab driver, stroking his beloved horse.'

'I wondered if you might help me with something?'

'Go ahead, Mr Chard. I'll help if I can.'

'I am trying to trace a young prostitute called Maisy. Last year I came across a girl of that name working in the back of the Victoria. Do you know her?'

Will's expression changed. He looked away for a moment, and when he faced the inspector once more, he avoided direct eye contact.

'She isn't in any trouble Will. That I promise. You have my solemn word,' added the inspector.

Will paused, then nodded in acceptance. 'I do know her, not closely mind,' he emphasised. 'I helped her out a few weeks back when a drunk customer cut up rough. I had just dropped a fare off in the Fairfield area and was on my way back to the town centre when I noticed her having some trouble. I chased the drunk off and bought her a gin in the nearest pub. That was all.'

'Do you know where I might find her?'

'I don't know where she lives, but if she's working then Fairfield might be your best bet.'

Chard thanked his friend and set off for home, determined to find the girl later that evening.

***

Some hours later, Chard, feeling fully refreshed after a rest at home and a meal at the New Inn, set off on his search. Maisy wasn't hard to find. Fairfield was not an area often frequented by whores and, standing under a streetlamp, dressed inappropriately for common decency, she was rather obvious.

Chard approached her confidently, but with the brim of his bowler tilted forward.

'Fancy some company mister? If you've got anything troubling you, I'm willing to lend a hand,' offered Maisy with an obscene gesture.

When the inspector got within arms reach, he tilted back his hat.

'Oh bollocks! It's you!' exclaimed Maisy, turning to run.

Chard grabbed her by the arm. 'No need to run. You aren't in trouble, but I do need to talk to you.'

'Well I don't want to talk to you. You closed down our nice little business in the Victoria last year. Now I have to work on the street.'

'I'm surprised that you feel safe enough to be still out here. Was it you that had to be taken to the infirmary last week?'

'How did you know?'

'Not many street girls with the name Maisy in the town.'

The prostitute looked up at Chard defiantly. 'What do you want to talk to me about?'

'I want to know who hurt you.'

'I never saw him before and I never want to see him again!'

'What did he look like?'

'Look, I am not pressing charges. I hope the bastard dies of the pox, but I am not going in front of the magistrate. It'll be his word against mine and nobody will believe me.'

'Why do you say that?

'Because I'm a street girl and he's a toff. I'll be branded a liar and he's the sort of gent who'll have me cut up for my troubles.'

'A toff you say?'

'He dressed normal but he had diamond collar studs and there was those things he said.'

'What things?'

'My Mam was a good Catholic. Took me to church when I was little. The man that attacked me said something a couple of times. I don't know what it meant but the words sounded like what the priest would say in a foreign language.'

'Latin?' asked the inspector.

'Yes, that's it.'

'I don't suppose he gave you his name?' asked Chard.

'He said to call him Ben, but I could tell he was lying.'

'Let's get back to what he looked like.'

'Big and broad with shaggy hair. He made me drink some stuff from a bottle, then … things happened.' Maisy started to become distressed and attempted to run away, but Chard grabbed her arm once more.

'You must be able to remember more!'

'No, now let me go!' demanded Maisy.

The inspector held on for a moment but then relented and released the girl's arm.

'Very well Maisy, but I may need to speak with you again. Take some advice and try to get off the streets,' he called out as she disappeared into the night.

TWENTY-NINE

May Roper woke feeling better than she had in many weeks. Her addiction was by no means cured, but she felt that there was light at the end of the tunnel. The feeling of abject desperation after her unwelcome visitor at the start of the week had subsided. Instead, she was at least able to concentrate on her morning's work and no longer yearned for her next dose of laudanum. As May folded the clothes that lay before her, she gave a sigh. It was sad really. A distant relative of Mr Davies had finally come forward and the body had been taken away earlier in the week. His clothes however, stained from the circumstances of his death, were to be donated to charity. As she placed the dead man's jacket to one side, her fingertips felt a ridge beneath the material that suggested something had been left in an outside pocket. Frowning, she felt inside, but there was nothing. Indeed, she knew that all the pockets had been emptied some time ago. Puzzled, May gave the jacket further inspection. Inside the lining there was some poorly crafted stitching. Breaking it apart, she inserted her hand and after feeling around, discovered a folded piece of paper.

'What's this?' she murmured to herself.

May began to read. Its importance wasn't immediately clear, yet she realised that it must be the correspondence that the unpleasant man from the Taff Vale Railway had been looking for. She stared at the document for quite some time before folding it up and tucking it inside the sleeve of her blouse.

***

Inspector Chard sat at his desk reflecting on his conversation with Maisy. He wanted to believe that her abuser might have been Hector Bowen. In many ways he seemed to fit the bill, but there was no real proof. A large, shaggy haired man from out of town; able to afford diamond collar studs; a tendency to speak the occasional bit of

Latin; and of a violent nature. Yes, it could be him, though Maisy wouldn't testify to it even if he brought them face to face. Perhaps it wouldn't hurt to investigate the matter further.

Chard got up from his desk and glanced at the small sack of debris that still occupied a corner of the room. 'I must get one of the constables to get rid of that rubbish from the fire,' he thought, before setting his mind to a more pressing task.

Gesturing Constable Jenkins to follow him, the inspector headed for the cell containing the elder Rankin.

'I hope you've got more sense than your brother,' said Chard.

Ted Rankin grunted in reply.

'He's wanted on suspicion of murder in Merthyr. With what the pair of you have been up to down here, he'll hang for certain. No doubt so will you. What have you got to say for yourself?'

'I've done nothing. Just looked after my brother, that's all. Jack didn't murder anyone in Merthyr, it was a fair fight. He's always been a daft bugger, getting involved in scraps. We were just spending a few weeks getting enough money together to get Jack away. In another two weeks he would have been gone, far away from here and me with him.'

'You attacked my constables.'

'They weren't in uniform. We thought we were being set upon. No one should have been coming to the cottage. It must have been deserted for years.'

'I don't believe a word of it!' shouted Chard. 'You've terrorised individuals in that community!'

'Not me. Jack may have been a little heavy handed, but you can't hang him for it, nor me either.'

'What about William Hughes? He burned to death. If that isn't worth a hanging, I don't know what is.'

'You can't blame that on us.'

'Your brother was seen to throw a lit oil lamp through the side window of the workshop,' lied the inspector.

Ted Rankin went silent but after a moment or two, he responded defiantly.

'Jack said that he knocked on the workshop door and there was no answer. He'd gone with the oil lamp just to threaten to set the

place on fire. When he found no-one was there and he couldn't break through the lock, he just lit the lamp and threw it through the window.'

'That's a load of bull! You knocked Hughes unconscious, tied him up so that he couldn't escape, then burnt him alive,' accused Chard, angered by the prisoner's denial.

'Jack wouldn't have done that. He couldn't do such a thing!' exclaimed Rankin, clearly shaken.

'He could and he did. Your brother will hang and if I get my way, so will you,' snapped the inspector angrily, before leaving the prisoner to contemplate his fate.

***

'How are the prisoners that were caught breaking into the hospital?' Chard asked Sergeant Humphreys a little later.

Humphreys, his face still bruised from the blow received in the previous weekend's street brawl, gave his usual toothless grin.

'They're as cocky as ever, sir. Confident that some fancy solicitor is going to turn up and get them off.'

Chard grimaced. 'I'll believe that when I see it.'

Before he could make another comment, the inspector was surprised to see a familiar figure walk into the station.

'Miss Roper! What a pleasant surprise. I am afraid that Constable Morgan isn't here at the moment.'

'It's yourself that I've come to see Inspector,' replied May, with an uneasy smile. 'I think that I've found something important that you will want to see.'

'Then do come into my office, Miss Roper.'

Chard led the way and once they were settled, May produced the document that had been concealed in the lining of Davies's jacket.

'I think it's the reason for the break-in at the infirmary,' she suggested.

The inspector read the contents of the document with a furrowed brow, ignoring his visitor until at last he leant back in his chair and smiled.

'Miss Roper, you have done me a great favour. This may not be

the complete answer to all of my current troubles, but it is a great leap forward. I don't know how I can thank you.'

'You have already shown me a lot of kindness, Inspector. I know that you are aware of my medical problems and that you have shown great discretion. I would like to confess that in a moment of weakness, I attempted to open a drawer in Doctor Henderson's office some days ago. It contained laudanum and at the time I was desperate. A visitor to the infirmary observed my actions and attempted to bribe me. He wanted the document, though I hadn't discovered it at the time.'

'Who was he?'

'I don't know, but he said that he worked for the Taff Vale Railway. I should have told you about it sooner,' apologised May, with eyes downcast.

'Don't worry yourself. What you have done today has brought me closer to finding Mr Davies's killer. The noose is tightening on the poisoner and I intend giving it a good hard tug.'

***

It had taken just one phone call, a few words and a stunned silence at the end of the line. As a result, late that afternoon, Chard sat in the elegant boardroom of the Barry Railway Company accompanied by Constable Morgan.

Across the table from the policemen sat Thaddeus Cornwall, chairman of the Barry Railway Company. Also present, pacing up and down and refusing to be seated, was a highly agitated Benjamin Armstrong, chairman of the Taff Vale Railway.

'The agreement in this document makes it clear, Mr Armstrong. Despite the enmity between your two companies, the intention all along has been to plot a merger, or rather a takeover of the Taff Vale Railway by the Barry Railway Company. In return, you personally will receive payment for your shares far in excess of their worth. I assume that, for example, the decision to allow the BRC to run passenger services on your lines had nothing to do with parliamentary interference? It was just part of your scheming.'

'I am ruined! I am ruined!'

'Sit down, Benjamin. You will obviously be disgraced and forced

to leave the Taff Vale board, but they cannot take your shares from you. There will be sufficient funds to keep you solvent,' reasoned Cornwall. 'I don't suppose we can keep this quiet?' he asked, addressing the inspector.

'No, I don't suppose we can,' replied Chard sarcastically. 'After all, there have been break-ins at a hotel, Pontypridd Workhouse Infirmary and Porth Hospital with accompanying assaults. I assume that Cotter and Sykes work for you Mr Armstrong? That is no doubt why they broke into the hospital just after the cordon of Taff Vale men were conveniently removed from outside the hospital, on your orders.'

'Incorrect Inspector,' interrupted Cornwall with a frown. 'I may as well tell you that they work for me. The fools were not meant to harm anybody. I assume that no policemen were injured?'

'Fortunately not,' replied Chard.

'Good. In that case our solicitors will make sure that anyone else who might have suffered injury will receive compensation. We will settle out of court and ensure that it will not be in the financial interests of anyone to press charges.'

'That doesn't mean that we won't prosecute,' insisted the inspector. 'I am still not completely convinced that your men didn't poison Davies and Clark.'

'Why on earth would we have wanted to kill either of them? We didn't even know Clark. As for Davies, when our men arrived, they were aware that he might be carrying the document on his person. They could hardly manhandle him in a crowded town. Their first task was just to follow him, to make sure that he didn't hand on the document to someone else. If he did not, they were to tackle him at night when he was on his own,' explained Cornwall

'Which of course was thwarted when he was poisoned,' added Armstrong.

Chard frowned, realising that the explanation made sense. 'What I don't understand, Mr Armstrong, is why Davies was accepted by you when he left the Barry Railway Company?'

'It was part of our plan. I could only deliver my part of the deal if I remained as chairman. There was a long way to go. Gradually I would arrange for our more profitable trade contracts to be 'lost' and taken over by the Barry Railway Company until eventually I

could persuade the directors to accept a merger. However, I was under huge pressure from a troublemaker named Bowen.'

'I have met the man,' informed Chard.

'Then you will know what I was having to deal with,' continued Armstrong. 'He wasn't the only director trying to unseat me, but he was the most voluble. Bowen very nearly succeeded, so I had to make a pretence of fighting back against the Barry Railway. Thaddeus and I agreed that one way would be for me to bribe one of his best men over to our company. Davies was regarded as the most untrustworthy, so we put the plan into action. I didn't know that Thaddeus had put the document laying out our agreement in his safe, and neither of us expected Davies to break into it. Unfortunately, Davies decided to take the document as insurance against me reneging on my promises.'

'Which was the same reason that I had it in my safe,' added Cornwall. 'It was my guarantee that Benjamin would fulfil his bargain with me.'

'Someone went to the infirmary earlier this week in the hope that the document was still there with Davies's possessions. He said that he was from the Taff Vale Railway. Was that true, Mr Armstrong?' queried Chard.

'Yes. He is one of my men, the most loyal of my employees.'

Chard leant close to Armstrong and spoke quietly but firmly. 'If that man goes anywhere near the infirmary again, or speaks to anyone about the young clerk he terrified, I will hold you personally accountable. Do I make myself clear?'

'Yes, Inspector,' agreed Armstrong readily.

'Good. I am glad we understand each other. I will leave you both for now. No doubt you will be busy writing your resignation from the board of the Taff Vale Railway, Mr Armstrong. As for you, Mr Cornwall, you had better inform your solicitors that I am not ready to release Cotter and Sykes yet, even if those they assaulted don't press charges.'

'You realise, Mr Chard that it is now unlikely that our two companies will ever merge and a great financial opportunity has been lost,' remarked Cornwall as the inspector was leaving.

Chard turned. 'To be honest, I don't give a damn.

THIRTY

One of Dr Henderson's more disagreeable duties was the examination of new workhouse inmates. It wasn't so much that it was physically unpleasant, the doctor had dealt with many distressing injuries and illnesses in his time. What often made the examinations so difficult was the look of misery in the inmates' eyes. It was a soul-crushing experience to submit to the care of the workhouse; a damning admission of failure. Even though the institutions were more humane than in times past, the inmates wore drab workhouse uniforms and were forced to perform hard menial tasks to earn their keep. The system, harsh though it was, deterred all but the most desperate from asking to be taken in. It was the first time in a month that Doctor Henderson had been called out of the infirmary into the admittance hall of the main workhouse complex.

On seeing the new potential inmate, Doctor Henderson groaned. 'Not you again, Clever John. I am surprised you are still with us.'

'Hello Doctor,' replied the man with an inane grin. He looked gaunt and his withered body shook as he spoke. 'Nice to see you again.'

Clever John was a renowned alcoholic who every few months returned to the workhouse to 'dry out'. Eventually, he would be sober enough to be allowed to leave and being extremely literate would find a position to support himself. Unfortunately, he would return to his old ways, lose his job and end up scavenging in bins to eat.

'You know the procedure by now. I need to examine you to ensure you aren't bringing anything nasty into the infirmary. Apart from yourself that is,' added the doctor.

'That's very unkind, Doctor Henderson.'

'Let's have a look at you then,' said the doctor coming closer. '*Iesu Mawr!*' he suddenly exclaimed, stepping back. 'You stink!'

The two workhouse porters who had brought Clever John into the hall, stood nearby nodding in agreement.

'It's not my fault Doctor. I was poorly all last week and I haven't got a change of clothes. I've only been able to get up and about this last couple of days.'

'Really?' asked Doctor Henderson, his professional interest overcoming the repugnance of Clever John's odour. 'What's been wrong with you?'

'Shitting and puking everywhere,' explained the prospective inmate. Then I had a terrible time breathing. Couldn't get up and about. I just lay there. Never ate or drank a thing for a couple of days.'

'When did you first get the symptoms?'

'I get a bit confused with days, but about a fortnight ago. It was a market day and the town was busy,' answered Clever John shakily.

'Have you got any idea what might have caused the illness?'

'Well to be honest Doctor, I have my failings.'

'I think we all know that, otherwise you wouldn't be here.'

'I do have a tendency, when times get hard, to try my luck with whatever has been thrown away. You'd be surprised at what good stuff gets chucked in the bins or down by the river. I found a half bottle of brandy once,' said the man proudly.

'I dare say. Please continue,' encouraged the doctor.

'I will indeed. You see there wasn't much about. I had found a few drops in a beer bottle and some cough tincture but that was all. Then I spotted this funny shaped bottle. Small it was, and hardly anything in it, but I thought "let's give it a go". So, I did.'

'What happened next?'

'It was quite bitter so I threw the bottle away and headed off for home.'

'Home?' queried the doctor.

'I've been staying in this shed at the back of an empty house in Wood Street,' explained Clever John. 'When I got there, I fell asleep for a while. Sometime later I woke in pain, my guts emptied and couldn't breathe. It's a good job I hadn't drank any more of that stuff.'

'Quite!' agreed Doctor Henderson pensively.

'Well then. Can I have my workhouse clothes?'

Doctor Henderson beckoned to the porters and spoke abruptly.

'Strip him. Hose him down. Sort out some clothes and place him in a separate room away from everyone else until I return. I need to see Inspector Chard.'

***

Chard was reflecting on events as he sat at his desk. There was a mound of paperwork before him, including a folder that had come from the Superintendent, but he couldn't bring himself to touch any of it. The murder of Hughes had at last been solved, with the Rankin brothers in custody. On the other hand, it had been two weeks since the poisoning of Davies and he was no nearer to finding the killer. Then there was the murder of the prostitute at the Boot Inn. Could the culprit have been the same man that assaulted Maisy? It seemed likely. He considered once more whether it was too much to believe it might be Hector Bowen. Was it just wishful thinking because he was such a loathsome individual? It was a possibility that could be pursued. Chard had made discreet enquiries and found that Hector Bowen would be taking lunch at the New Inn, where he was currently staying. Perhaps if he turned up unexpectedly, it might be possible to catch Bowen off-guard.

The inspector's thoughts were interrupted by Constable Temple, who announced that Doctor Henderson had come to see him.

'Send him through, Constable,' responded Chard, puzzled by the unexpected visit.

'Good Morning, Doctor,' greeted Chard, getting to his feet and shaking Henderson's hand. 'What brings you to the station?'

The doctor sat down opposite the inspector and rested his arms across his ample stomach. 'I have something that might interest you. I have just examined a new inmate to the workhouse. An incurable alcoholic, but generally honest in what he says. Apparently, he was scavenging for any form of liquid that might contain alcohol, when he came across an almost empty bottle. After drinking the few drops from it, he subsequently experienced symptoms which seem similar to what afflicted Clark and Davies. Of course, I can't be certain, but I felt I should tell you right away.'

'Do you know where he found the bottle?' asked Chard, intrigued.

'I am sorry, I forgot to ask,' responded the doctor apologetically.

'Wait here a moment please, Doctor.'

Chard left the room and called Constables Temple and Morgan into the office.

'Accompany Doctor Henderson to the workhouse and interview the new inmate. He drank from a bottle which might have contained the poison that killed Davies. Find out where he found it and what he did with it. Then locate the bottle and bring it to me. Understood?'

Both constables nodded in response.

'Good. Let's hope this is the breakthrough we've been looking for. Thank you Doctor for telling us. I would come with you, but I have a luncheon appointment that I cannot miss.'

***

It was only a short walk through the crowded streets from the police station to the New Inn. As usual, shoppers had come from throughout the South Wales valleys to visit the Saturday market; and Chard was grateful that his distinctive uniform made people move to one side to let him pass.

At the hotel, the inspector headed straight for the restaurant. Chard had assumed that Hector Bowen would be taking his midday meal but he was nowhere in sight. Then, alerted by a loud guffaw coming from the lounge bar, the inspector walked in and found Bowen sat at a table. Opposite him, sipping a glass of wine was a smartly dressed man wearing a monocle. They had clearly been discussing something that amused Bowen, for he gave several guttural laughs that caused other customers to turn and stare.

As Chard approached, Bowen's companion looked up, whispered something; then got up and left, giving a polite nod to the inspector as he passed.

'I hope your friend didn't leave on my account, Mr Bowen,' said Chard sarcastically.

'Inspector Chard! What a nice surprise! Come and sit down. My business associate had other things to do. You are most welcome,' came the surprising response. Bowen gestured to a waiter and, without asking the inspector, ordered two brandies.

Chard took the seat recently vacated by the man with the monocle and sat opposite Bowen.

'You seem to be in good humour.'

'I am in capital humour, Inspector. The gentleman who just left is a fellow director of the Taff Vale Railway. Our chairman, Armstrong, has apparently resigned this very morning. This will be my last day in Pontypridd. I will be returning to Cardiff for an emergency general meeting. I don't know the full details yet, but with Armstrong out of the way I will finally be able to take over control of the company. *Ad astra per aspera* as they say,' laughed Bowen, fumbling in his pocket and pulling out a cigar.

'Exactly what adversity have you had, if I might ask?'

The director clipped the end of his cigar and frowned. 'Eh? What do you mean?'

'You used the Latin phrase, "through adversity to the stars",' replied Chard.

'Of course, there have been many obstacles in my way,' blustered Bowen.

'You mean like anyone connected with the Barry Railway Company for instance. I understand that your bid to take charge has been under the banner of fighting your business rivals, rather than establishing closer ties.'

'Well obviously,' answered Bowen, starting to lose his good humour.

'Perhaps Jeremiah Davies would have been one such obstacle? His acquisition from the Barry Railway Company must have been a coup for your chairman and, as it has transpired, Mr Armstrong was highly in favour of a merger.'

A waiter came across and placed two glasses of brandy on the table. Bowen indicated he needed a light for the cigar, and didn't reply to Chard until it had been lit.

'I had guessed that Armstrong wanted to feather his nest somehow by trying to make us merge with our rival, and I wasn't fooled by the Jeremiah Davies business. He was just trying to pretend he was fighting back to keep the support of the board of directors. I wanted to rip his balls off,' replied Bowen finally, blowing a great cloud of cigar smoke in Chard's direction.

The inspector waved the smoke away and despite being on duty, took a small sip of brandy, glad of the chance to pause and think. Clearly, the oafish braggart before him was cleverer than he appeared. He had seen through Armstrong's plans and grasped his intentions. Yet, apart from the obvious benefit of causing friction between the two railway companies, there was nothing concrete to link him with the murder of Davies. It was time to change the conversation to other matters.

'Where were you Tuesday night?' demanded Chard, keeping his eyes directly on those of his adversary.

'Eh? What? Why do you ask?'

The inspector noted a twitch and a momentary look of panic in Bowen's eyes.

'Just answer the question,' persisted Chard.

'I was in my room. I am a busy man and need my rest.'

'All evening?'

'Yes,' answered Bowen defensively.

'Can anyone else confirm that?'

'I was on my own. Why do you ask? What is this about?'

'A prostitute was killed at the Boot Inn,' answered Chard, convinced that Bowen had something to hide.

'Is that all, Inspector? Prostitutes get killed all the time. Why are you wasting your time on something so inconsequential?'

'She was a human being Mr Bowen,' snapped Chard.

'What has this got to do with me?' persisted Bowen.

The inspector ignored the question. 'Where were you the previous Thursday evening?'

Bowen waved his cigar around in annoyance causing ash to fall across his waistcoat. 'How should I know? It was over a week ago.'

'I have reason to believe that you met a young lady and went back to her room. Then you drugged and viciously assaulted her,' accused Chard.

'Dammit Inspector, that is slander!' responded Bowen loudly, causing the room to go quiet as the other customers in the room became aware of the drama taking place.

'Who has claimed such nonsense? Bring them before me. I demand that you tell me their name.'

'The witness has so far declined to give formal evidence,' admitted the inspector.

There was relief on Bowen's face as he realised from the look in the inspector's eyes, that Chard had been bluffing. He visibly calmed down and stared at the other customers in the room until they looked away and resumed their conversations. Then he turned back to the inspector and spoke quietly. 'You have nothing, Chard. Nothing. You had best depart, but finish your drink before you go.'

'I have suddenly taken a dislike to it. You can finish it for me,' came the inspector's terse reply as he got up to leave.

'You shouldn't make accusations when there is no way of backing them up,' declared Bowen loudly, with a smug expression.

'*Aut viam inveniam aut faciam,*' responded Chard as he left. 'I will either find a way or make one.'

THIRTY-ONE

Rather than return directly to the station, Chard called in at Hibbert's the jewellers to buy a gift for Alice. He chose a small silver locket that did not look too ostentatious, but which he knew she would appreciate as a token of their friendship. Deciding to drop it off at his house rather than take it into the station, he was surprised to see Doctor Matthews crossing the road in his direction.

'Ezekiel, how are you? I am pleased to say we might have a breakthrough on the poisoning case. Have you got time to discuss it?' greeted Chard, pleased to see his friend.

'I have neither the time nor inclination,' came the unexpected response.

Chard's smile faded from his face as he noted the furious expression on Doctor Matthews' face.

'Why, what is the matter?' asked the inspector, alarmed by his friend's demeanour.

'What is the matter? You might damn well ask! If I were a younger man I would strike you down,' answered the doctor angrily.

'Calm down Ezekiel! What have I done?'

'My name is Doctor Matthews and that is how you will address me henceforth. As to what you have done, you should damn well know!'

Chard realised that his friend must have somehow found out about his relationship with Alice. It had always been a risk, yet his reaction to it appeared far more extreme than anticipated.

'Is this about Mrs Murray?'

'Damn right it is. How dare you? My housekeeper! Seduced behind my back! Intolerable!'

'Hardly seduced, Ezekiel. She is a mature adult after all,' reasoned Chard.

Doctor Matthews spluttered with rage, his cheeks bright red. 'I have told you that we are no longer on first name terms. As for Mrs

Murray, she is a vulnerable widow and you have toyed with her affections.'

'I have done no such thing. My intentions are entirely honourable,' responded Chard, affronted by the accusation.

'How can you stand there and tell such bare-faced lies? Your dalliance with her was purely to further your investigations.'

Chard felt his own temper start to rise. 'Why would you say that? Who told you about us for that matter?'

'Mrs Murray herself. She came to me this morning in tears and confessed your relationship. What happened yesterday broke her heart and you didn't even have the courage to do it yourself.'

'I don't know what you are talking about. Talk sense Doctor,' demanded Chard.

'Mrs Murray informed me that she was interviewed yesterday by Superintendent Jones and a police sergeant. She was interrogated about the poisoning of Clark and Davies like a common criminal.'

'I know nothing of it, I swear!' objected the inspector.

Enraged, Doctor Matthews raised his cane as if to strike Chard, but suddenly stopped himself mid-swing. Slowly lowering the cane, Doctor Matthews struggled to regain his composure, before continuing to address his former friend. 'Superintendent Jones made it clear that the insinuations against her came from you. I am ashamed to have called you a friend when you are prepared to lie so brazenly. Mrs Murray asked me to give you this.'

The doctor handed Chard an envelope, which the inspector took and started to open. He took out a letter and looked up to find that the doctor had already walked away.

With a feeling of incredulity, Chard started to read Alice's words:

Dear Mr Chard,
I was foolish to believe and trust in you. You have been cruel and deceitful, leaving me broken-hearted.
Please make no attempt to contact me, for I hope to never see you again.
Your sincerely,
Mrs A Murray

Stunned by the contents of the letter and the exchange with Doctor Matthews, the inspector walked quickly to the police station. Once inside his office, he looked at the papers on his desk and picked up the folder that had come from Superintendent Jones.

Inside he found a note from the Superintendent informing him that the interview had been carried out in order to ease Chard's workload. The Superintendent had also written that he appreciated the extra time and effort that the inspector was putting into his investigations, and that Chard could rely on his full support and assistance.

The inspector let the note fall to the floor and picked up the transcript of the interview with Alice. He read the details feeling both wretched and embarrassed. Chard wanted to storm into the Superintendent's office shouting and screaming, but Superintendent Jones was not in the station and would not be back until Monday morning. There was nothing that could be done.

The inspector's despondency was interrupted by a knock on his office door. Without waiting for permission to enter, in came Constables Morgan and Temple, looking extremely pleased with themselves.

'We've done it sir. We've found the bottle,' announced Morgan, with a broad grin.

Glad to have something to take his mind off his troubles, Chard held out his hand and took the small glass bottle, which was an unusual shape.

'I might be wrong, but this looks familiar,' he exclaimed. 'Give me your full report.'

***

Chard stood in the cell facing the prisoners, with Constables Temple and Morgan positioned behind.

'Now then gentlemen, I know you are employed by Mr Cornwall. We had words yesterday.'

Sykes and Cotter looked at each other. Cotter raised an eyebrow and nodded towards Chard, but Sykes shook his head.

'I know you think I am lying, but let me convince you otherwise,' continued the inspector. 'Mr Cornwall clearly values your work, whatever that might be. I am sure that you may have done a number

of dubious acts on his behalf in the past. His intention is to pay off anyone that might have been injured in your clumsy efforts to obtain the missing document.'

Sykes and Cotter listened attentively with the latter giving a slight nod of confirmation.

'We're awaiting our solicitor and until he arrives, we've nothing to say,' commented Sykes with confidence.

'I would rethink that if I were you. Mr Cornwall has been informed in no uncertain terms that even if the injured parties decide not to press charges, then we shall. You are going nowhere,' added the inspector.

An expression of doubt started to form on Cotter's face and he looked at Sykes uncertainly.

'Unless,' continued Chard, 'you give me some assistance.'

'What sort of assistance?' queried Sykes.

'I understand that your instruction was to follow Davies and watch what he did, to the extent of seeing if he handed the missing document over to someone else.'

The prisoners shrugged, neither confirming or denying.

'In which case you must have been watching Davies very carefully indeed. Am I correct?'

Sykes and Cotter glanced at each other, then slowly nodded.

'Good. Then I'll explain what I am prepared to do. For my part, I will make a list of every person that needs to be compensated for your actions. If they agree not to press charges, which will require considerable sums of money, I will ensure that you go free and your employer's name stays out of the papers.'

'So, what do you want from us?' asked Cotter.

'All I need you to do, is to go through everything you observed on that day, step by step.'

Half an hour later, Chard left the cell with a satisfied smile on his face. The answer had been there all along, well at least in part. 'Thank goodness for the meeting with Hector Bowen,' he thought. Temporarily distracted from the problems of his private life, the inspector headed for the town centre. There was somewhere he needed to be.

***

Hector Bowen was glad to be back in Cardiff. It was a bigger town than Pontypridd, with more distractions of a carnal nature. Yet for a short while, those pleasures could wait. Queen Street was as busy as usual on a Saturday night, and the pavements were crowded with revellers, kept in order by the occasional patrolling constable.

Entering one of the many dining establishments, Bowen headed for the rear of the premises where Ernest Wilkinson sat, talking to a young gentleman. On seeing Bowen approach, the young man got up, tipped his hat politely and left hurriedly.

'Was that Jennings, the little turd?' demanded Bowen.

The immaculately dressed Wilkinson looked his colleague up and down, taking in the rumpled shirt, creased suit and unkempt hair, and adjusted his monocle.

'Indeed it was,' he replied.

'What was Armstrong's little pet doing here?'

'He's a resourceful fellow, and now that Armstrong is sunk, he seeks a new master. Jennings could be very useful to us, I mean you. I now have the whole story which you can enjoy whilst we dine on sirloin steak, washed down with a glass or two of claret.'

'After which we can talk about Monday's emergency general meeting,' suggested Bowen with a wide grin.

'Of course, Hector, of course. I would think that given the short notice, the directors will only agree to an interim chair initially. A full vote will have to go before all the shareholders.'

'Naturally, but you don't anticipate any problems?' asked Bowen, suddenly concerned.

'Not to your appointment as interim chair. You clearly have the backing of the members of the board. However, if word gets out that you were directly involved in arranging the disorder in Pontypridd, it might affect the wider vote,' cautioned Wilkinson. 'However, do not be concerned, my friend. I am confident that you will not have to worry about it.'

Bowen looked relieved. 'In that case, let's start the feasting!'

***

It was a happy Hector Bowen who left the restaurant after a fine five

course meal and two bottles of claret. His victory was assured. Power and wealth were there for the taking. Even better, the following Friday was one month to the day since he last visited the Torres woman, and she was a particular delight. He had ordered his chemist to alter the composition of his elixir after what happened at the Boot Inn. The stupid slut had choked on her vomit. Perhaps the mixture was a little strong? Still, no harm done. It would be just right for Mrs Torres and he had something special in mind. It would be a night for him to remember and for her to dread.

THIRTY-TWO

Chard had risen late on Sunday morning. It had been pointless going to the church service, for he doubted that Alice would be there. Even if his assumption was incorrect, Chard was put off by the likelihood that he would be snubbed, let alone the scene that Doctor Matthews would cause. He would have to let time heal things. After breakfast, Chard had a long discussion with his maid with a view to increasing her hours, before Constable Morgan knocked on the front door. As arranged, Morgan had arrived with the police van and they set off for their destination just before midday.

A bright sun shone out of a sky that was a beautiful pale blue and the air was fresh, which felt out of place considering the grim duty that Chard had to perform. The roads were almost empty, as was usual for a Sunday morning, and the two strong horses pulling the van made good time.

Chard knocked on the door and waited. It was eventually opened by Mrs Hughes. The young widow was wearing a white frilled blouse with a pale blue skirt and looked happier than their previous meeting.

'Inspector Chard, what a lovely surprise. Do come in. We are having tea in the kitchen.'

The inspector followed Mrs Hughes through the house and into the kitchen where Mrs Evans stood, cup and saucer in hand. The older woman had a solemn expression and initially looked away from Chard's gaze. Then, straightening her posture, she returned the inspector's stare and addressed him politely. 'Inspector Chard, may I offer you a drink of tea? It appears you are on your own today.'

'I have a constable outside, with the van,' he added pointedly. 'As for a drink, I think I will decline.'

'But I insist. You must try it. It is herbal, a nettle tea.'

Without waiting for a response, Mrs Evans took a cup and poured the herbal infusion from a teapot, before handing it to the inspector. 'Mrs Hughes prefers her own, but I fetched this to try, please taste it.'

Chard took a sip and found it not unpleasant.

'You don't seem surprised to see me here Inspector,' commented Mrs Evans.

'We passed Mrs Griffiths in the street and got into conversation. She said that you would be here in Mrs Hughes's house.'

'I can see from your face that you have some questions.'

'That is correct. I have most of the answers, but not all of them,' replied Chard.

'May I suggest that we speak alone?' asked Mrs Evans. 'I can assure you that we don't need Mrs Hughes present.'

Chard nodded his agreement.

Mrs Evans turned and spoke to her young friend, who had been standing nearby, silently sipping her tea. 'Be a dear and take your drink into the parlour. There are things I need to discuss privately with the inspector.'

Mrs Hughes gave a gentle smile and left the room, leaving Chard with her sorrowful friend. 'Let us take a seat, Inspector,' suggested Mrs Evans.

Chard gave a brief nod in agreement and they each took a chair at the small kitchen table.

'When did you find out?' she asked.

'Yesterday, when my constables found the bottle containing the fatal solution. Somebody had come across it amongst the bins at the back of the Butchers Arms, on the same day Mr Clark and Mr Davies were poisoned. There was a tiny drop of liquid left. He drank it, then threw it towards the river. Fortunately, it didn't reach the water and it was located in some bushes on the riverbank.'

'What happened to the person that drank from it?'

'There was only a tiny drop left, so he survived.'

'*Diolch i Dduw*! Thank God!' repeated the woman in English.

'It wasn't entirely clear to me, even when I was told where the bottle had originally been found. I had discounted the Butchers Arms involvement for a number of reasons. Mainly it was because

both Davies and Clark had been poisoned, and I had difficulty in finding a suspect who would have wanted to poison them both. To have put the solution in both their drinks would have been a deliberate act.'

'I cannot fault that reasoning,' agreed Mrs Evans.

'Then I recalled an incident earlier in the day. I had a meeting with a rather disagreeable gentleman who had ordered me a brandy. As I left, I told him that he could finish my drink as I didn't want it. I considered that perhaps something similar had happened with Mr Clark and Mr Davies. Yet why would one tell the other to finish off their drink? They hadn't fallen out with each other, so there must have been another reason.'

Mrs Evans nodded.

'There was another thing that caused me to ignore the Butchers Arms. The poisonous solution was most likely disguised in something sweet to hide the bitter taste. Given that our medical examiner was aware of a similar case that involved putting the aconitine in a piece of sweet cake, I suspected the tearoom. Then I realised what I should have considered much earlier.'

'Go ahead, Inspector. It is rather obvious.'

'You can hide a bitter substance by putting it in another bitter substance. I recently drank the new beer from the Captain's Brewery; and couldn't finish it due to the bitter taste. Given that possibility, I spoke to two men that are currently in custody. Unknown to Davies he was being followed by them with regard to his former employment. They confirmed that Clark was served a pint of beer which he found undrinkable after a few mouthfuls, but Davies offered to finish it off. Last night I went to the Butchers Arms and confirmed that they had a small barrel of the new 'Captain's Bitter' on trial sale when Clark and Davies were in there. Most customers found it too bitter, with only one or two finding it to their taste. Ironically, when I interviewed Clark at his bedside and I asked him if anything he had consumed tasted odd, he had given me the answer. He said "bitter" and I thought he was referring to a general taste. Of course, I now know that he was referring to the beer itself.'

'That still didn't give you the culprit,' pointed out Mrs Evans.

'That's right, it didn't. However, the bottle itself seemed familiar.

I knew I had seen it somewhere; it has a quite distinctive shape but I couldn't quite put my finger on it.'

Mrs Evans finished her tea and put the cup down as Chard continued.

'Then I remembered. It was the first time I came to this house; I recall looking around and seeing all those little glass bottles with the dried herbs in.'

Mrs Evans eyes followed to where the inspector was pointing at a shelf on the kitchen wall. 'There must be many people with those bottles. They are distinctive I grant you, but I am sure some can be found on Ponty market.'

'Very true, Mrs Evans. Very true indeed, but it did point the way. I was at least at the stage where I felt confident that the intended victim was Clark, and that the poisoning took place in the Butchers Arms. All I needed next was to find someone with the opportunity to poison the beer and who had a motive for killing Clark.'

'That could have been anyone in the bar,' suggested Mrs Evans.

'No, it couldn't,' responded Chard, taking another sip of tea. 'If the barrel had been tampered with, there would have been other victims. The poison must have been specifically put into Clark's glass. It had to be one of the serving staff.'

The inspector finished his tea and handed the cup and saucer to Mrs Evans who took it to the sink.

'When I went to the Butchers Arms last night, I wasn't just there to enquire about the beer they had on. I also asked for a look at their list of employees. We had of course had a look at it before, but we hadn't picked out anything in particular. Funnily enough there was a Mary Evans, which I understand is your full name. Yet it is a common name, there must be half a dozen in this town alone. There was also a Mrs Hughes, but a Sally Hughes. I did remember that I have a cousin Sarah who the family refer to as Sally, but then again it couldn't be your friend in the next room because she worked in the Tredegar Arms. So, as you can imagine, the whole matter perturbed me, as did something else.'

'What might that be?' asked Mrs Evans.

'It might be coincidence, but in the corner of my office I have a sack of remnants from the fire that killed Mr Hughes. Amongst the

debris are a few pieces of glass. I cannot be certain, but they seem similar to the type of glass used in the making of those glass bottles on the shelf. I cannot directly make anything of it, but it unsettles me.'

'Then I feel sorry for you,' answered Mrs Evans with a hint of sarcasm.

Suddenly, Chard's eyelids started to feel heavy and he found it difficult to stifle a yawn. Mrs Evans stared at him but as he returned the gaze, her facial features became hard to define. The inspector pinched himself on his wrist and shook his head.

'Pardon me, I have digressed. Where were we? Oh yes, I have a Mary Evans and a Sally Hughes working at the Butchers Arms; but you can't be the Mrs Evans in question because we know you were in the tearoom at the time. I saw you. Of course, the Sally Hughes in question can't be your friend, because she worked at the Tredegar Arms not the Butchers Arms.'

Drowsiness continued to afflict Chard, but once more he shook off the effects, then leaned towards Mrs Evans until the details of her face became clearer.

'Except of course, it was a lie,' he continued. She never worked at the Tredegar Arms and to our discredit, we never bothered to check. Not until this morning when I spoke with my maid, who does work there on the odd day; and who has never heard of a Sarah or a Sally Hughes. Now I know Mrs Hughes did it. What I don't know is whether or not it was you that concocted the fatal solution; and possibly schemed to poison her husband before the workshop was set on fire. It is time to take you both in. The van awaits outside.'

Mrs Evans remained unbowed. 'What you have said is purely circumstantial. Did Sally lie? Yes. Do you have a witness who saw her put anything into Clark's drink? No. Do you have any actual evidence that the poison was made by either of us? Again no. You are looking a little unwell, Inspector. Do you wish to lie down?'

Chard ignored the question and continued, though it was difficult to keep his head looking forward. 'The circumstances are strong enough to convict you. You have the means through your knowledge of plants and herbs to distil aconitine from monkshood. You have the motive of hating Clark due to his role in the Albion disaster inquiry and Mrs Hughes had the opportunity to commit the act.'

Suddenly Chard felt unable to keep his eyes open any longer. His lids closed and there was just blackness before he slipped into unconsciousness.

***

When he awoke, Chard found that he was in the same chair and Mrs Evans was still sitting facing him at the kitchen table.

'What did you do to me? How long have I been asleep?' he demanded through bleary eyes.

Mrs Evans face looked the picture of innocence. 'I am afraid that you had some kind of reaction to my nettle tea. That can happen you know.'

Mrs Evans glanced at a small clock on the windowsill, then turned and spoke calmly.

'You have been asleep less than thirty minutes, but I do I think we've been long enough, Inspector.'

'You drugged me to let your accomplice escape through the back door, haven't you?' accused Chard angrily.

Mrs Evans looked at him disparagingly. 'I have done nothing of the sort, Inspector. You are unharmed and the crockery has been washed. There is no evidence of you having been drugged, other than your body's reaction to a natural herbal tea that has disagreed with you. Please follow me.'

Puzzled and a little unsteady on his feet, Chard followed Mrs Evans out of the room and into the parlour. There, curled up on the sofa, clutching a little rag doll, lay Sally Hughes. She was deathly pale with a slight smile on her face.

'What have you done to her?' demanded Chard.

'It was necessary to keep you in the kitchen whilst the substance took full effect,' explained Mrs Evans. 'It had already been in her system before I arrived this morning. She had taken hemlock and there is no cure. I just needed to make sure that her last moments were not full of unpleasantness. The herbal tea I gave her arrested any vomiting but the inevitable respiratory failure was bound to happen soon.'

Chard stood in shock. 'There is nothing we can do?'

'She has already passed, Inspector. I have her written confession

in the other room, which I can now give to you. Let us return to the kitchen and I will tell you the whole story.'

Chard followed and they both sat down either side of the kitchen table, as Mrs Evans began to explain.

'Sally Williams, as she then was, lost her sweetheart in the Albion disaster. It left her distraught and she was never the same person. All of us who lost loved ones tried to come to terms with our grief. All our hopes focussed on the inquiry, where we were promised justice. Of course, that justice never came. Sally became unhinged, and as an outlet for the grief, her hate became focussed on the chairman of the inquiry, Theodore Clark. In fact, she took a knife out of the house one day, swearing to kill him. Her father raced after her and stopped her, but she became difficult to control. Things became worse after her parents died. Sally became withdrawn and morose, not wanting to eat. Then along came Will Hughes, much older than her, but a caring man. Someone with the patience to bring her out of herself and make her happy. Everything seemed fine until the disaster at Tylorstown earlier this year.'

'A dreadful event,' commented the inspector.

'It fetched it all back,' continued Mrs Evans, 'and Sally started to regress. Her anger returned and when Will started to have money problems they began to argue, though there was still love between them. The final straw happened when Clark started to go regularly to the Butchers Arms where Sally worked and she had to serve him.'

'I can see how that would have been difficult for her,' Chard empathised.

'I was aware of how she felt at that time, but I only found out what happened next when she told me this morning.'

'I assume she decided to take her revenge on Clark,' suggested the inspector.

'You are correct, but she made the mistake of telling her husband first. She thought he would understand. Instead, he forbade her to do anything. On the evening that she planned to do the deed, Sally went to the workshop and asked him once again not to stand in her way. He refused, so she put a harmless sleeping solution in his tea, then tied him up before going to work. There was no way Sally could have known that the workshop was going to be set on fire. She would

have come home and released him later that evening. He wouldn't have turned her over to the police, or so Sally believed. She has carried the guilt of her husband's death ever since.'

'Which is why I was convinced that her grief was genuine when I saw her previously,' asserted Chard.

'With her husband dead she was more determined than ever to kill Clark. There had to be some justification in her mind for her husband's death. I wasn't involved in distilling the poison, Sally always had a knack with plants and herbs. She learnt it from her mother. Then of course came the disappointment of her failure to kill Clark, and the accidental death of another innocent soul, when Davies took the poison. Sally told me this morning that she could no longer live with the guilt. She went to chapel this morning to ask forgiveness for what she had done, and for what she was going to do. As I said, she had already taken a fatal dose of hemlock before I arrived. Here is her letter, which confirms what I have just told you.'

Mrs Evans passed over a sheet of paper that had been lying folded on the windowsill, next to the clock. Chard read the contents and gave a sigh.

'I'll go and make the arrangements,' he said finally, putting the confession in his pocket.

Leaving Mrs Evans in the kitchen, Chard walked out of the room. He realised that the medical examination would lead to an uncomfortable meeting with Doctor Matthews, but quickly dismissed the thought as unimportant. Taking a final glance at the tragic figure of Sally Hughes in the parlour, he shook his head sadly, and walked out of the door.

EPILOGUE

There was a boisterous atmosphere in the back room of the Tredegar Arms. Although Sergeant Humphreys had wanted to keep it a secret, word had got out that he was retiring from the force, and the inevitable celebration had been arranged.

In anticipation that the sergeant's departure would not be allowed to happen quietly, Superintendent Jones had already booked and paid for the room, as well as a barrel of ale. The presentation of a silver pocket watch to mark the retirement had been emotional, with Humphreys clearly on the verge of shedding a tear, before Superintendent Jones saved his embarrassment by calling for three cheers.

Chard stood at the back of the room, his elbow resting on the top of a piano, holding a pint glass in the other hand. It was only five days since Sally Hughes had taken her own life and the memory still lingered. There were other things that played heavily on his mind. Doctor Matthews had refused to carry out the medical examination and departed for his home in Swansea, necessitating the appointment of a locum medical examiner at short notice. Possibly Alice had gone with him, for the house appeared to be empty and there had been no further word from her. There was nothing that he could do, other than hope that there might be a future reconciliation. Then he would confide to her about his past. The discussion with Superintendent Jones had been awkward. His superior had clearly been unaware of the relationship with Alice and felt embarrassed at his well-meant, but clumsy interference in Chard's investigation.

'You look a bit glum sir,' observed Constable Morgan, who had wandered across to interrupt Chard's contemplation. Drops of beer glistened in Morgan's muttonchop whiskers and he swayed slightly as he walked. 'Is it because of Mrs Murray?' he asked undiplomatically.

'It's impossible to keep anything quiet around here isn't it?' grunted the inspector.

'Well, you know how it is sir,' shrugged the constable. 'Are you going to pursue her?'

'Perhaps at a later date Constable. If I do, I will let you know,' Chard answered sarcastically.

Chard was relieved when everyone's attention was distracted by an unearthly sound coming from the other end of the room, as Constable Temple started to sing.

'Shut up you stupid Gog!' yelled Constable Jenkins, holding his hands over his ears.

'What did he call him?' Chard asked Morgan.

'He's from North Wales, if you remember sir. *Y Gogledd*, the North. So he's a Gog.'

The inspector paused half way through taking a swig of his beer, then groaned.

'What's the matter sir?' asked Morgan.

'I've just worked out the pun behind Temple's nickname,' explained Chard, grinning for the first time that evening.

In the background, Constable Davies's strong tenor had replaced Temple's caterwauling, to much acclaim.

'I think there is something I should tell you sir,' said Morgan, fidgeting slightly.

'Very well, and due to the occasion, you can stop calling me sir all the time,' answered the inspector downing his pint.

'It's about May. I've asked her to marry me.'

Chard gave a broad smile, then noticed that Morgan wasn't smiling in return.

'Did she turn you down?' he asked sympathetically.

'Not exactly. May explained the problems that she has been going through and that Doctor Henderson is helping. She wants me to ask her again when she is fully recovered.'

'That's probably wise,' emphasised Chard. 'Let's go and get some more beer and move away from the piano. I can see that Scudamore is cracking his knuckles and heading over to start playing it.'

Chard and Morgan walked over to the bar hatch where they ordered two more pints of ale before continuing their discussion.

'The superintendent seems to be in a good mood,' commented Morgan.

Chard looked across to where Superintendent Jones was indeed singing along with his men, having dropped his usual stern demeanour.

'He is probably trying to take his mind off the fact that we are back to just two sergeants,' answered the inspector, noting that the huge form of Sergeant Morris was standing well away from the unpopular Sergeant Jackson.

'He must be happy at our results though?'

'I suppose so. We've caught the Rankin brothers and they will get hard labour at the very least. The confession of Sally Hughes solves the poisoning of Clark and Davies. Clark is now out of hospital and back at home but will not be required as a magistrate in future. The local authority has appointed the town's first full-time stipendiary magistrate. There will be no unpleasant scandal around the conduct of the Barry Railway Company, because they have agreed to pay enormous compensation to everyone assaulted by Sykes and Cotter, in return for their freedom. There is something unsatisfactory though.'

'The murder of the girl at the Boot Inn?' queried Morgan.

'That's right. I know it was Hector Bowen, but I can't prove it. He seemed to like Latin phrases. I know a handful myself from my time at university. I wonder if Bowen has heard *Acta deos numquam mortalia fallunt?*'

'What does that mean?' asked Morgan.

'Mortal actions never deceive the gods,' answered Chard grimly.

***

Hector Bowen subconsciously fingered the phials in his coat pocket. It was dark, and he realised that the streetlamps had still not been repaired since his visit the previous month. At least it was milder, though many coal fires had still been lit in the terraced houses that he walked past. The anticipation of what lay ahead was almost too much to bear. Mrs Torres would be expecting him and quaking with fear. He bit his lower lip as the excitement drove his imagination on. Just one more street and he would come to the back alley. As Bowen

turned the corner he stopped suddenly, thinking that he had heard a clanking sound. He spun round suddenly, stared into the darkness and listened.

'Nothing there,' he convinced himself, before heading for the alley.

***

Opposite the alley, hidden behind a fence, a tall man in dark clothing reached for his wallet. Three large dark-skinned men stood around him. One carried a length of heavy chain, another a large sack and a third held a large spiked club.

'There's no need for payment. I am grateful, and my brothers are happy to help.'

'Yet you need to pay the boatman at the docks, and it is best to pay enough to ensure silence, Mr Torres. Take the money.'

Torres nodded his agreement and took the coins, gesturing to his companions to follow.

'Make sure he is dropped at least a mile out,' came the added command.

He watched the three men follow Bowen down the alley; then Ernest Wilkinson, future chairman of the Taff Vale Railway, turned and left.

AUTHOR'S NOTES

The Albion Colliery Disaster

When I wrote my first book, *Fortuna's Deadly Shadow*, I made a brief reference to the Albion Colliery disaster. The plot for that story had already been decided and mining was not going to play a part in it. Also, although I was aware that there had been a disaster around that time, I knew almost nothing about it. After the novel was finished, I decided that I should learn more, so I went back to contemporary newspaper reports of the disaster, the immediate aftermath and the inquiry. What I read profoundly shocked me, both in terms of the social impact on such a close-knit community; and also the failure to adequately punish the company for poor management leading to the deaths of so many miners. The details of the inquiry are too long to reproduce here, but having read contemporary accounts it was clear that the bench was very defensive on behalf of the company; and the prosecution was exceedingly frustrated. A key point arose when the prosecution fetched the managing director, Henry Lewis (who was also a local magistrate) into the box. He was asked if, when shift times had been altered, any consideration had been given to the timing of shot firing. The defence counsel objected. The prosecution stated that Lewis had admitted at the inquest that there had been no consideration given to shot firing. The chairman was reluctant to accept the point. Prosecuting counsel then intimated that he would subpoena the shorthand-taker from the inquest, in order to settle the matter beyond doubt.

Controversially, the chairman of the inquiry ruled that a member of a limited liability company cannot give evidence against his own company. He then dismissed all charges against the Albion Steam Coal Colliery Ltd. The hatred that the bereaved must have felt towards the inquiry chairman, must have been considerable.

In my personal opinion, in modern times the Albion Steam Coal Company would have been found guilty of corporate manslaughter, and the dependants of the victims heavily compensated. Yet that wasn't the case.

It wasn't the first mining disaster and it certainly wasn't the last. Tylorstown is mentioned in the narrative but more followed, most notably at Senghenydd.

This novel is of course fiction rather than a history book and I have made one major change to the story of the disaster. The chairman of the inquiry wasn't Theodore Clark and he certainly wasn't poisoned. The real chairman's name was Ignatius Williams. Whether he really was biased due to connections with the Albion's managing director, who was a fellow magistrate; or whether he was an upright member of society doing his best on a difficult case, I cannot say with absolute certainty.

Pontypridd museum has a list of all the victims of the tragedy, giving name, age, address and occupation. It makes sombre reading.

The Barry Railway Company and the Taff Vale Railway

The employees of these railway companies mentioned in this novel and their shenanigans are pure invention. However, the companies themselves were real and extremely profitable. They were indeed rivals and never merged, even though it would have probably made good business sense. The TVR was forced to let the BRC run passenger services on part of their network. Their passenger station on the Graig was opened in March 1896 as mentioned in the story.

Miscellanea
Aconitine.
Wolfsbane or Monkshood is a rather pretty plant when in flower and I used to have some in my garden (until my wife removed it). It is however not the only source of aconitine and minute amounts can be found in some culinary plants and herbs. Although chemical tests to determine the presence of aconitine were eventually developed, they had not been discovered at the time of this fictional story. It is the difficulty in detecting aconitine that made it such a popular poison in ancient times. The 'Old Bailey case' referred to in the story was real, as was the action needed by the medical experts to prove the case for the prosecution. In that instance the poison was indeed in the cake!

The 1896 Olympics
There were 43 events in the 1896 Olympics with the United Kingdom

getting two golds (tennis and weightlifting), three silvers and two bronze. The first marathon was a little under twenty-five miles.

Much Wenlock in Shropshire had been running its own Olympics for many years (it still does), and Baron de Coubertin was said to have got his idea for a modern Olympics from having visited the Shropshire town.

The Silver Teapot
The name sounds rather twee, but I didn't make it up. It really did exist, though my description of it is speculative.

Availability of drugs
Early in the book Constable Morgan tells Inspector Chard that he had offered May cocaine. This would not have been shocking. Drugs were readily available and were often ingredients in medicines and tonics, including those for young children. Those campaigning for legalising drugs should really research why they were banned in the first place.

It was only certain poisons that had restrictions and even then, they just had to be signed for.

The new school
The school on Tyfica Road was built in 1895 and opened in 1896 for boys and girls. In later years it became Pontypridd Boys Grammar School establishing a fine record of academic success. In the 1970s it became Coedylan Comprehensive School until its closure in 2003.

Taff Vale Park
This still exists, though largely for school sports, the stands having long gone. In its day it was regarded as a top venue and was at various times used for rugby, football, athletics and even speedway. I am indebted to the book *In Black and White (Pontypridd R.F.C. 1876-2003)* by Alun Granfield, for details of the Pontypridd team of the time; and for the little gem that there was a match between Pontypridd and Neath that was abandoned due to fighting in the crowd.

Pubs, corsets, smallpox, the Royal Clarence Theatre and Lady Llanover
Fortuna's Deadly Shadow involved me researching the pubs of the era. The

task was made difficult by the fact of them changing names every so often and I wanted to use the correct ones for 1895/1896. During the course of writing this book I have (with thanks to Samantha Rees and Andrew Harper) found a few more, of which the Boot Inn is one.

In the story, there is comment about May Roper having been found after the break-in at the infirmary without corsets. In the 1890s that really would have been scandalous. Even the female inmates of the workhouse were issued with corsets, for decency's sake.

There is a brief mention of an outbreak of smallpox in the Cardiff workhouse, which is historically accurate.

I do sometimes change dates of minor importance to suit the story, but I sometimes enjoy putting in real obscure facts. So, to that effect, *The Bells of Haslemere* was indeed performed at the Royal Clarence Theatre in 1896.

Lady Llanover who employed 'Dai Books' was a patron of Welsh culture who died in 1896.

Recommended Reading

I finally found the booklet of Valleys idioms called *Talk Tidy (The Art of Speaking Wenglish)* by John Edwards, which I had been looking for when writing *Fortuna's Deadly Shadow*. That said, I have still not overdone the local colloquialisms in case they look like grammatical errors.

Don Powell's book *Victorian Pontypridd* remains a superb reference work.

After writing my first draft, my friend Jim Edwards introduced me to *100 Lost Buildings and Structures of the Pontypridd Area* by Keith Jones, which from a personal perspective I have found to be an absolute delight. I now have my own copy which I purchased from Pontypridd Museum.

Thanks to my publishers

Finally, I would like to express my thanks to Mick Felton and the whole team at Seren for the support they've given in terms of editing, marketing and everything else that goes on behind the scenes.

I occasionally post photographs relating to my books on my Facebook page www.facebook.com/InspectorChard

The Author

Leslie Scase is a former civil servant, born and educated in south Wales but living now in Shropshire. His is a member of the Crime Cymru writers' collective, and of the Crime Writers Association. Through He has given talks on crime and punishment in the late Victorian period, and has appeared at literary festivals and has been interviewed on radio. This is is second Inspector Chard novel; the first was *Fortuna's Deadly Shadow.*

Other Books in Smart Skills Series

Meetings

Negotiation

Persuasion

Presentations

Working with Others

www.smartskillsbooks.com

www.legendpress.co.uk

www.twitter.com/legend_press